The Political
Foundations of
Development Policies

Oskar Kurer

University Press of America, Inc.
Lanham • New York • London

Library of Congress Cataloging-in-Publication Data

Kurer, Oskar.
The political foundations of development policies / Oskar Kurer.
p.   cm.
Includes bibliographical references and index.
l. Developing countries--Economic policy. 2. Economic
development--Political aspects--Developing countries. 3. Patronage,
Political--Developing countries. 4. Patron and client--Developing
countries. 5. Political corruption--Developing countries. I. Title.
HC59.7.K868 1996   338.9'009172'4--dc21   96-46349 CIP

ISBN 0-7618-0617-2 (cloth: alk. ppr.)

Contents

Preface

The genesis of this monograph lies in a journey from the University of Papua New Guinea to the center of Port Moresby. The occasion was this: my companion had just finished production of an election platform for a leading political party of which he was not a member, and which was adopted without further ado. This led to some obvious questions. Why was such a procedure adopted? What is the meaning of such a document? For those more versed in the ways of Papua New Guinean politics the answer was fairly obvious: it was meant for the consumption of the media and had hardly any importance for election outcomes which depend in the main on the distribution of material rewards to the followers of politicians. Indeed, Papua New Guinean system of politics exhibits the characteristics of clientelism to a remarkable degree.

The next stage was to explore the economic implications of this form of clientelism, and clientelism generally. It became clear that where clientelism dominates, it is often accompanied by corruption, factionalism, a high degree of politicization, and often by a low level of state autonomy. These factors in turn have a tendency to induce the failed inward-looking development policies pursued by a great many Third World countries after World War II, and tend to undermine security of property. It thus became clear to me that at least sometimes a certain set of policies was pursued because of the dominance of a particular political structure, in this case political clientelism.

Many of the examples which substantiate the thesis are drawn from

Africa. This is not accidental. On the African continent the political system exhibits most of the characteristics of the clientelism described in this book. Nor is it accidental that the political experience of that unhappy continent is generally one of unmitigated economic disaster: it originates, at least partly, from the nature of its political system.

I wish to thank all those who have contributed in various ways to the genesis of this monograph, especially my colleagues Roman Grynberg and Herb Thompson at the University of Papua New Guinea, Peter Carrol, Kerry Donohue, Tim Robinson and Christine Williams at the Queensland University of Technology, and Ted Kolsen of the University of Queensland.

1 Introduction

It is now widely accepted that major economic problems have resulted from the failed inward-looking development strategy followed in most parts of the Third World. Elements of the strategy include a process of import substitution, the expansion of the government sector and a comprehensive regulation of the private sector of the economy. Why was such a strategy widely adopted after World War II and why does it persist in many countries today despite its damaging economic consequences?

It is argued that a particular political structure, political clientelism, accounts for the adoption and the persistence of this strategy in a wide variety of circumstances. Such a political structure consists of an aggregation of patron-client networks bound together by the exchange of material benefits for political support. It can lead to factionalism, politicization, a high level of administrative corruption, a low degree of legitimacy, and a weak state that is exposed to increasing demands by political supporters for goods and services and for privileges. The inward-looking development strategy then results from attempts to satisfy these demands, a process that leads to the expansion of the government sector of the economy and a comprehensive regulation of the private sector which has the deleterious economic consequences widely prevalent in unsuccessful third world economies.

Since clientelism can be a feature of both democracies and autocracies, systematic policy failures can occur in both. Economic success, therefore, is not likely to be systematically related to such forms of government.

Moreover, the analysis suggests that a permanent transition to a superior development strategy hinges on changes in political processes such as the behavior of voters. Structural reforms in an unchanged political environment are therefore likely to be unsuccessful. In fact, their success will often be intimately related not only to economic but also to political change.

The first section of this introductory chapter outlines the central theme of the monograph. The second part defends the importance of political processes for economic development, describes the failures of the inward-looking development strategy, and reviews current explanations of these policy failures. It is argued that such explanations are severely deficient, but that an approach which locates the causes of inward-looking development strategy in the political system escapes these criticisms. The third section reviews the arguments why regime type - authoritarian or democratic - may affect the growth performance of economies. It is argued that there is no particular reason for the growth performance of different regimes to vary systematically, and that the empirical evidence supports this view.

1.1   Chapter Outline

The second chapter outlines a structure of political clientelism, comparing and contrasting it to the traditional landowner-peasant client relation, and to urban and rural political machines of the Third World. The ideal-type on which this analysis is based consists of informal relationships between patrons and clients, or politicians and their supporters, who exchange political support for material benefits. In this structure ideology does not affect political decisions. Clients belong to impermanent networks or factions where allegiance is due to a leader and not an institution, and these factions are engaged in constant conflict with other networks. The authority of the government is based exclusively on the transfer of resources to supporters. Its legitimacy, as well as that of the political institutions - evidently unable to generate legitimate rule - is likely to be low. Thus constitutional arrangements are viewed instrumentally, to be altered at convenience, and consequently tend to be impermanent. Factionalism and uncertainty as to the rules of the political game force rulers to build maximum winning coalitions, a process which creates an incentive to extend patron-client networks to every institution of potential political significance, such as the military or the bureaucracy. The state tends to be weak and unable to withstand societal demands for goods and services and rent by the competing unstable patron-client networks. In such an environment the scope for government action expands with the growth of patronage politics, and an inward-looking development strategy becomes dominant.

The third chapter explores some of the implications of this clientelist political structure, evaluates criticisms leveled against it, and compares it with different political structures. Clientelism may thrive in very different circumstances: regimes may be authoritarian or democratic, civilian or military, espousing socialist or capitalist ideologies. This is partly an outcome of the assumption that ideology does not influence action, and accordingly is useful only as a means to justify and to further self-interested action. Whereas clientelism is compatible with patrons constituting a class, however defined, clients do not consciously attempt to further their common interest. Indeed, clientelism obstructs the formation of class organizations. Specific assumptions about state-society interaction distinguish this approach from pluralism and corporatism. The tentacles of the clientelist networks of the political sphere that have penetrated every organization of society have reduced these organizations, including the bureaucracy and the military, to a mere shadow of a corporate existence. Organizations that traditionally were motivated to gain collective goods for a group as a whole have been replaced by clientelist networks attracting specific benefits for particular individual members through their influence on policy implementation. Conventional corporatist or pluralist analyses are therefore inapplicable in an environment where formal organizational aims and structures become increasingly meaningless as an indicator of how an organization operates in practice.

A discussion on the origins and the consequences of an inward-looking development strategy must consider the problem of endemic administrative corruption, one of the salient features of many Third World countries. Corruption is both generated by clientelism and simultaneously reinforces it. In order to make this point, the pertinence of the concept of administrative corruption is defended against those who believe that it is inappropriate, particularly in a Third World context. The chapter proceeds by outlining a cost-benefit analysis which investigates the factors that affect the level of corruption by influencing the costs and benefits of corrupt acts. Those explanations that attribute the causes of administrative corruption to the nature of punishment and the public administration are rejected. They are flawed firstly because they are exclusively concerned with material costs of formal punishment. Secondly, they overlook the fact that the nature of the public administration of the organizations policing corruption is influenced by wider issues, such as the political structure. Indeed, clientelism is a major factor in promoting administrative corruption. It generates incentives to disregard bureaucratic procedures in favor of providing private benefits to clients (such as jobs, preferential access to services, credit, and licences), and it encourages the expansion of government ownership and regulation and thus the scope for corruption. As corruption originates in the political sphere and is sanctioned at the highest level, there are few barriers to its spread, and thus it tends to permeate all spheres of public administration, including the law enforcement agencies and the judiciary. It is not only the body politic which promotes administrative corruption, but the behavior of the public as well: the willingness on the part of the voter to support politicians engaged in administrative and legislative corruption is one of the factors which may have generated clientelism initially. Clientelism and corruption may therefore be at least partially a reflection of the value orientations of the public. Their interaction becomes even more complex as administrative corruption reinforces clientelism. It further diminishes the already weak legitimacy of the government and the political institutions, partly because patronage politics necessarily conflicts with official morality.

The fifth chapter deals with the economic consequences of two salient features of clientelism: corruption and the expansion of state intervention. The chapter shows that a government that maintains power through clientelist exchange is likely to encounter the familiar problems associated with an inward-looking development strategy: the neglect of infrastructure, a misallocation of social overhead capital, an overstaffed and inefficient public administration, the expansion of an inefficient parastatal sector, and private sector regulations which reduce welfare. These factors in turn induce macroeconomic instability and low savings, and may lead ultimately to economic stagnation. Corruption in a clientelist setting appears to be less innocuous than some revisionists would like us to believe. The revisionist case is built on the implicit assumption that policy formulation is independent of corruption. However, if it is accepted that policy-makers take into account patronage gains when they formulate legislative measures, regulations will be systematically influenced by corruption. Moreover, the apologists' case that corruption increases the efficiency of the public administration is flawed. Nor will licences and contracts necessarily be allocated to the most efficient producers if it is allowed that politicians not only maximize bribe revenue, but take into account political support as well. Misallocation of resources, impaired productivity, lack of investment and a reduced rate of economic growth are therefore intimately connected to the prevalence of clientelism and corruption.

The absence of class formation among patrons is one of the main contributors to the pathological case of clientelism that prevails in Subsaharan Africa and has additional consequences for economic growth that are particularly destructive. In a clientelist environment profits of businesses are often a direct consequence of specific concessions received from the government, and of the willingness of corrupt officials to moderate extortion and bend the law. The continuation of the flow of profits thus can never be taken for granted, since any political change threatens a redistribution of property and quasi-property rights. Political change will engender large changes in property rights if the new incumbents at the head of different patron-client networks do not leave the gains of the former incumbents undisturbed, something which is likely to happen where patrons do not form a political class. The ensuing insecurity of property has the predictable consequence of slowing accumulation even further by reducing investment and encouraging capital flight.

So far, the examination of the causes of inward-looking development policies has been entirely in the tradition of political reductionism, where a particular policy stance and its economic consequences have been identified with a particular political structure. But what causes clientelism? An inquiry into the causes of clientelism is most interesting in a democracy, since it is not obvious why people support parties of the machine type if clientelism is not an attractive form of government for the populace at large. It may be, of course, that all competing parties are electoral machines and thus voters do not have a choice. Imperfect information may be another partial explanation of the puzzle. More importantly, however, it may be the rational course of action to support machine politicians because voters are caught in a dilemma: whereas the best outcome is a different type of politics, the worst one is not to be part of a clientele network. The incentives to support clientelism may be reduced by socioeconomic development. The reduction of poverty may diminish the importance of the benefits transferred through clientele networks, and improved education increases the level of information. The evolution of organizations pursuing collective interests may help to create a civic culture which might ease the voters' dilemma. On the other hand, there are strong forces pulling in the opposite direction: clientelism has a tendency to obstruct the evolution of independent organizations acting for collective aims, economic growth, and the efficient delivery of education. Where these conservative forces prevail and the type of clientelism which has been discussed dominates, then it is unlikely that the inward-looking strategy will be abandoned; by implication, structural reforms aimed at overcoming inward-looking development are liable to fail.

1.2   Economic Development and the State

1.2.1   Development Economics and Political Economy

There is a widespread resurgence of interest in political economy which attempts to establish systematic relationships between economic and political processes (Staniland 1985, 5). This revival may be illustrated by the positions taken by three leading practitioners. In 1965 W. Arthur Lewis was content with a distinct and self-contained field of economic development[1]: when it comes to explaining political issues, 'the economist must hand the development problem over to his colleagues in other social sciences' (1965, 15). Nearly three decades later the idea that economists can fruitfully operate independently of political science has been discarded:

> The second noneconomic factor that development economists cannot leave out of their calculations is the government's behavior .... [A]n economic analyst who tries to figure out the likely consequence of any economic event must assess how the government may react. We usually say that such situations require an interdisciplinary approach. Since in practice there is no interdisciplinary discipline, and since the economist's counsel is sought separately from that of political experts, the economist is forced *faute de mieux* to become his own political scientist. It then soon emerges that we need a sound political science a much as sound economic science (1984, 4).

Where Lewis focuses on the problem of policy advice, Hirschman sees the separation of economic development and political theory at the heart of the decline in the reputation of development economics. The 'failure of development economics to recover from the attacks it had been subjected to by its critics' was prompted by 'the series of political disasters that struck a number of Third World countries from the sixties on, disasters that were clearly *somehow* connected with the stresses and strains accompanying development and "modernization"' (1981, 20). The double frustration of practitioners, 'one over the appalling political events as such, and the other over their inability to comprehend them' (21) forces him to conclude that

> the challenge posed by dismal politics must be met rather than avoided or evaded. By now it has become quite clear that this cannot be done by economics alone. It is for this reason that the decline of development economics cannot be fully reversed: our sub-discipline had achieved its considerable luster and excitement through the implicit idea that it could slay the dragon of backwardness virtually by itself or, at least, that its contribution to this task was central. We now know that this is not so (23).[2]

Whereas Lewis and Hirschman are concerned with the interaction between political and economic processes and the disciplinary nature of the theory of economic development, Reynolds stresses the importance of political factors for economic development. He believes that the explanation why some countries have progressed much faster than others does not seem to lie mainly in the realm of factor endowments. 'My hypothesis is that the single most important explanatory variable is political organization and the administrative competence of government' (1983, 976).

That belief underlies this monograph: countries grew successfully where, for one reason or another, the political and social circumstances induced the government to introduce a set of policies conducive to economic development. But what were the circumstances which induced governments to implement a set of singularly unsuccessful economic policies, the inward-looking developing policies which were adopted by most Third World countries after World War II?

1.2.2 Policy Failures

It is generally agreed that an interventionist inward-looking development strategy, sometimes viewed as an attempt to control 'all large economic transactions' (Krueger 1992, 12) was a major obstacle to economic development. Indeed, it was pursued often in the face of mounting evidence that it reduced rather than advanced economic growth and welfare.

One of the conspicuous features of many Third World countries after independence was the growth of the public administration out of all proportion, until it absorbed a major part of the government budget.[3] The expansion was not generally accompanied by noticeable improvement in the services provided. Indeed, the opposite was often the case: sometimes bureaucracies 'widely lacking in knowledge, skill, experience and risk-taking ability' became 'almost autonomous corrupt and inefficient bodies' (Duignan 1986, 18).

The policies contained a pronounced emphasis on the operation of government-owned businesses in manufacturing and distribution activities (Krueger 1992, 17). These firms generally operated inefficiently, incurred financial losses, placed pressure on government budgets, and tended to absorb an inordinately large share of scarce savings and foreign exchange (28). Agricultural marketing boards which were supposed to end the exploitation of peasants by private traders often made farmers worse off as they offered low prices, graded dishonestly the quality of the produce, and failed to discharge their role properly as monopoly supplier of agricultural inputs (1992, 26; 1993, 96–98).[4]

The expansion of the public sector was accompanied by stringent private sector regulations. By its very nature, an inward-looking strategy involved the regulation of importation, which led to situations where access to import licences and foreign exchange 'virtually determined the level of output of individual firms', and 'government officials held the power of profit and loss over domestic import-substituting producers' (1992, 31). The regulation of imports was complemented by a system of licensing of most firms and by regulation of the labor market and the disbursement of credit. Difficulty with paperwork, erratic decision making and lengthy procedures significantly impaired the operations of firms. The pursuit of an import substitution strategy, with its accompanying neglect of exports, often combined with overvalued exchange rates, meant that foreign exchange was scarce. This situation was often exacerbated by the unavailability of import licences for inputs needed to produce exports. Moreover, the reluctance to adjust the exchange rate turned the terms of trade even further against agricultural commodity producers. All this contributed to a considerable decline in the developing countries' share in world trade.[5]

Not surprisingly, the 'typical' developing country that pursued such policies failed to enhance, or even to maintain its infrastructure facilities (17). Government roads were poorly maintained, public transport facilities deteriorated, the electricity supply became inadequate and unreliable. Port congestion and delays in paperwork and customs procedures added significantly to demurrage charges. Irrigation facilities operated only erratically, waiting lists of several years for telephone connection were common, and even when a telephone finally arrived, there was no guarantee that it would work (18). A number of factors contributed to these problems. For example, infrastructure facilities were typically underfunded because politicians were reluctant to raise bus fares, electricity and telephone charges, and the like. More fundamentally, the attention of those in government in a 'typical' developing country has been heavily focused on different activities: the 'operation of parastatal enterprises, and controlling private sector economic activity' (20). Delivery of 'social overhead' services such as education and health was not quite as unsatisfactory as delivery of infrastructure (21). But although literacy rates have risen, health and education have tended to be delivered to sectors where rates of return are relatively low: in expensive hospital facilities and higher education.

The budgetary problems of the governments then translated into macroeconomic instability. Inflation soared as public sector deficits stimulated by the inefficiencies of the public sector increased and were financed by printing money. Balance of payments crises became common as a consequence of the neglect of exports and of overvalued exchange rates, and in turn provided the rationale for foreign exchange rationing which aggravated regulatory inefficiencies.

What has been described is of course government failure on a large scale. The interest here, however, is not in the arid debate about the relative merits of markets and government action,[6] or of government versus market failures. The interest here is to explain why a particular government failure became increasingly common after World War II.

Why, then, were such policies pursued which led to such a massive government failure? Several kinds of explanation are possible. First, it is convenient to distinguish between 'ideal' and 'real' explanations: 'ideal' explanations look for an answer in the convictions of the policy-makers, whereas 'real' explanations attribute the choice of actions to structural factors such as the nature of the economy and the social and political system. Second, among those who attribute policy choice to 'real' phenomena or 'structure' we find both economic and political reductionists: economic reductionists attribute policy choice to economic events; political reductionists believe that it reflects political phenomena. In practice, of course, accounts are unlikely to comply with the purity of this distinction.

1.2.3 Explanations of Policy Failures

This section argues that interpretations which attribute the adoption of an inward-looking strategy to beliefs of politicians and their advisers are unsatisfactory because it is unclear why a particular set of beliefs has been selected over others. For their part, analyses where external causes are portrayed to be behind the implementation of such failed policies are unsatisfactory because such strategies have often been adopted in the absence of external pressure. Equally, attributing the departure from inward-looking strategies to economic crises fails to address the question of why these departures were sometimes permanent whereas in other cases the strategy re-emerged after short periods of structural reform. The explanation that policy cycles are a function of resource endowments is unconvincing. To impute policy changes to organized interest group pressure is equally unpersuasive in an environment where organized interest groups are concerned with private rather than collective benefits. Nor are predatory-state models much help in illuminating the process of strategy change since they abstract from the process whereby political power is gained and maintained, and reduce the art of politics to choosing the optimal level of taxation. A clientelist approach to explaining the policy failures escapes these criticisms.

Krueger gives an 'ideal' explanation of why such policies were espoused initially. She argues that 'the policies chosen were widely regarded to be those conducive to development' (1993, 38). The prevailing view, supported by the experience of the Great Depression, was that the market was malfunctioning (1993, 39).[7] In addition, the successes of the planned economy in the Soviet Union and of wartime planning seemed to point to a viable alternative to the market (1992, 153). Not the least important consideration was that 'there was an important underlying implicit political premise' that 'government was, or would behave as, a benevolent guardian in the Platonic tradition' (1992, 154). 'Thus, the current state of economic thinking was not inconsistent with government ownership, intervention, and controls' (1992, 154). The economic advisers, therefore, advised what their theory and experience had taught them, and not what was in their best interest.[8] Governments, on their part, accepted the advice because it increased welfare: 'A strong case can be made that in many countries immediately after independence the leaders had the well-being of their people at heart and wanted to be benevolent social guardians' (1993, 61).

Krueger's account of the adoption of the inward-looking development strategy suffers from the crucial weakness that it is unable to explain why governments preferred the interventionist inward-looking strategy to alternative policy prescriptions. Such alternatives did exist after all: for example, in the form of a liberal tradition[9] that was not given to nationalist rhetoric, was unconvinced of the benefits of Stalinism and wartime rationing, and remained unimpressed by market failure and guardian state arguments.

It is to this question that 'real' arguments suggest an answer: the policies were adopted because it was in the interest of the policy-makers to do so. This is not to say that the policy-makers believed the measures they advocated would take their countries down the road to rack and ruin; they may simply have chosen to believe, consciously or unconsciously, that those policies which happened to best serve their self-interest were beneficial to society.

In this vein, Ranis and Mahmood ask the question of why the permanent replacement of an inward-looking strategy by an outward-looking one occurred with much more ease in some countries than in others. Thus a typical Latin American country tends to oscillate between the two policy stances, whereas other countries like Taiwan and South Korea shifted relatively easily from one strategy to the other. The authors believe that the answer is to be found in the degree of abundance in the endowment of natural resources (1992, 6, 23, 215).

The shift from the inward-looking strategy in Ranis and Mahmood's scheme consists of moving from import substitution and covert 'under-the-table' income transfers and taxation to export-promotion and overt 'over-the-table' levies and transfers (5, 21). The main form of covert taxation is the inflation tax, where the increase in the supply of money reduces its purchasing power and thus taxes its holders. Negative interest rates, overvalued exchange rates, allocations of foreign exchange through licensing, protection and import quotas, and minimum wages lead to covert income transfers from one group to the other.

Ranis and Mahmood assume that the state acts in the interests of the domestic manufacturers who foist inward-looking development upon the nation because they gain from rents which are extracted from commodity producers through covert transfers and taxation. However, after the easy stages of import substitution have been exploited, diminished commodity production contributes to the exhaustion of foreign exchange reserves and the rapid accumulation of foreign debt. Inflation becomes rampant as a consequence of large money-financed government deficits. At this stage, the strategy is abandoned (vi). It may re-emerge during the next upswing, however.

At this stage of the argument resource endowments become important: manufacturers in a resource-poor country with fewer opportunities to extract rent have a smaller incentive to resurrect inward-looking strategy than those in resource-rich countries. The fact that in resource-poor countries the exploitation of primary commodity producers is relatively less remunerative makes it easier to abandon it permanently (53).[10] Hence it is mainly the resource-rich countries which tend to be caught in the typical Latin American stop-go cycle, whereas the resource-poor countries, such as Korea and Taiwan, escape it more easily.

The argument is obviously extremely simplified. But even if the simplification is accepted, the reasoning is flawed.[11] Why, for example, should domestic manufacturers ever want to give up protection?[12] Surely there are other strategies which allow both macroeconomic stability and import substitution. Those strategies correspond better to the interests of manufacturers who produce for the domestic market, and whose profits are threatened by an outward-looking orientation which involves the reduction of protection. The empirical evidence the authors muster is heavily dependent on the choice of countries: for example, both Malaysia's and Indonesia's resource endowment corresponds closely to that of the 'typical' Latin American country, but they do not exhibit the stop-go cycle supposedly characterizing these resource-rich nations. Differences in resource endowments thus are neither a sufficient explanation for the different policy choices nor probably a necessary one.

To be fair, the authors acknowledge that something is amiss. They introduce another variable, 'nationalism', which they claim 'has been commented upon but not fully integrated into our analysis to date' (223). This is somewhat of an overstatement, as there is only one reference to 'the importance of the strength of a pre-existing organic nationalism' in the text. This organic nationalism is in turn is 'itself undoubtedly related to the extent of the population's ethnic and/or cultural homogeneity' (55). Given that this constitutes the sum total of the analysis, the variable hardly sheds more light on the causes of policy cycles. And again, the empirical evidence is not all that favorable to the idea: both Indonesia and Malaysia are hardly examples where reasonably successful economic policies can be attributed to 'organic nationalism'.

Haggard produces a second attempt at explaining development policies. Again, at the heart of his explanation is the policy choice 'between countries that industrialized through expansion of manufactured exports and those which sought to build an integrated industrial structure behind protective walls' (1990, 3).

In general terms, Haggard's view of the choice of strategy revolves around a rational choice (4) type of approach which accounts for policy in terms of 'the preferences and organizational power of state elites' (43).[13]

These elites are engaged in the tactical give and take and coalition building that are characteristic of political life (3–4). What are the variables influencing this politics of give and take? There are four sources of policy changes: the international system, domestic coalitions, political institutions, and ideology (28, 3). These four variables, according to Haggard, vary greatly in importance. Indeed, there is one variable which is the driving force, so to speak: the international system. 'External shocks do provide a stimulus to reform, and social forces are broadly constraining' (28, 3).

Haggard's explanation implies that changes in policy 'are not well explained in terms of the expressed interests of societal groups' (42).[14] Rather, interest groups grow up as a consequence of a particular strategy choice and subsequently constrain changes to it.

Another social force that provides a major effective constraint on policy choice is the degree of state autonomy. The low degree of insulation of the state from society 'in liberal-democratic and clientelistic systems' means that economic policy 'is more likely to be explained by coalitional and rent-seeking pressures' (45). Haggard finds that:

> The cases examined ... suggest repeatedly that state-society linkages limiting the level of independent organization of interests were crucial in explaining several key transitions, including the move from the primary-product phase to ISI [import substitution industrialization], the move to "stabilizing development" in Mexico after 1954, the move to more market-oriented policies in Brazil after 1964, and above all the adoption by the East Asian NICs of the policies associated with export-led growth (45).

However, state autonomy explains only the capacity to formulate and execute an economic program. It fails to answer the nagging question of where state interests come from (46). At this stage ideology may step in and provide the missing link in the chain of reasoning (47).

In his empirical work, Haggard analyses the causes of policy change of the NICs in Latin America and East Asia: Brazil and Mexico, Korea, Taiwan, Hong Kong, and Singapore. In line with his theoretical arguments, he concludes that external factors provided the driving force behind introducing ISI: 'External constraints ... were the critical factors pushing Korea and Taiwan toward import-substituting policies immediately after World War II' (51, 97). In Korea, protection and exchange controls were not so much chosen as imposed by the virtual collapse of the economy after partitioning (54, 60). In Taiwan, strict import controls were introduced in response to a serious balance of payments crisis as a consequence of the political upheavals in the wake of the defeat of the Kuomintang on the mainland (85). In Latin America, the Great Depression and World War II proved to be the watershed in its economic history which led to the adoption of ISI (30, 165–171).

When it comes to the policy shift from import substitution to export promotion, the situation becomes more complicated. External shocks here are not equated to market and direct political pressures as Haggard's theoretical discussion would suggest (29, 32), but to any balance of payments crisis, independent of whether it was caused by changes in the conditions of international markets or by internal factors. Thus the external constraints that 'were crucial in providing incentives to reform' (98) in Korea and Taiwan were in fact balance of payments problems which had domestic causes. In the same way, the 'external shocks' which pushed policy away from ISI in Mexico and Brazil were largely a consequence of internal pressures. In Mexico, for example, reforms were prompted by the growing problems resulting from ISI: the neglect of agriculture and the decline of agricultural exports, increasing balance of payments difficulties, and a slowdown in the growth rates of leading import-substituting sectors (184).[15] Haggard's explanation of why inward-looking strategies have been abandoned, and that of Ranis and Mahmood, largely converge: they collapsed under their own weight as ballooning government budget deficits, balance of payments crises and runaway inflation became permanent features of the economy, a collapse helped along by the cycles in the international economy. However, such crises do not necessarily lead to a permanent departure from inward-looking development policies. These tend to be resurrected in many cases, as Ranis and Mahmood are well aware.

Haggard's stance that external factors were a crucial factor in deciding to adopt ISI has to be exposed to the counterfactual question: would ISI have been espoused in the absence of the events following World War II in Korea and Taiwan, and following the Great Depression and World War II in Latin America? If the answer is yes, then Haggard's stress on external shocks in explaining ISI is misplaced. The view taken here is that it might well have been: if some forms of clientelism are sufficient to account for an inward-looking developing strategy, then ISI might well have been embraced in Korea, for example, even in the absence of external shocks.

Whereas the counterfactual question must remain unresolved, inward-looking development strategies were in fact espoused in Africa and Asia after independence, in situations where neither international markets or direct political pressure from abroad worked in their favor. Moreover, similar events took place in earlier periods: in sixteenth-century England the 'Crown established policies simultaneously to discourage imports and encourage home industries, a policy known today as import substitution' (Peck 1990, 135). Simultaneously, these policies expanded the role of the state in regulation of society and the economy in other spheres through statutes and proclamations 'to control the use of land and capital, to support labor' (135).[16] Again, it is unlikely that external factors were responsible for an inward-looking strategy in sixteenth-century England. Thus *prima facie* evidence suggests that internal factors are sufficient to account for its emergence.[17]

A third explanation as to why dysfunctional policies are applied can be derived from Olson's theory of institutional sclerosis which is supposed to explain, among many other phenomena, 'stagflation' and declining growth rates observed mainly in developed countries (1982, ix).

His explanation revolves around special interest groups or distributional coalitions which attempt to capture a larger share of the national income (72). Such organizations, 'at least if they are small in relation to society, have little incentive to make their societies more productive, but they have powerful incentives to seek a larger share of the national income even when this greatly reduces social output' (75). Indeed, on balance their activities reduce both efficiency and the rate of economic growth (47, 72). The actions of distributional coalitions decrease efficiency by boosting regulatory complexity through additional regulation, the enlargement of the bureaucracy, and political intervention in markets (75, 72). Moreover, efficiency suffers as the incentive for engaging in rent-seeking behavior increases, and the incentive to produce diminishes (72). The rate of growth is adversely affected because special interest groups slow down the process of decision making (72, 75) and impair society's capacity to adopt new technologies and to reallocate resources in response to changing conditions (65).

The establishment of distributional coalitions, however, takes time. Hence even those groups that find themselves in situations where there is a potential for organization will usually be able to organize only if circumstances are favorable (75, 38). However, as time goes on, more groups will have enjoyed favorable circumstances and overcome the hurdles that stand in the way of collective action (75). Hence we find that stable societies[18] 'tend to accumulate more collusions and organizations for collective action over time' (41).

Olson concludes therefore that stable societies suffer from institutional sclerosis: 'countries that have had democratic freedom of organization without upheaval or invasion the longest will suffer the most from growth-repressing organizations and combinations' (77). The theory implies also that 'countries whose distributional coalitions have been emasculated or abolished by totalitarian government or foreign occupation should grow relatively quickly after a free and stable legal order is established' (75). The initial weakness of their distributional coalitions therefore lies behind the economic success of Germany, France and Japan, compared with Britain's relative failure, after World War II (75-79).

Olson's main argument applies to democratic industrialized countries. He does, however, deal with less developed or 'unstable' societies. What primarily hampers economic development in these countries is not excessive stability but excessive instability which diverts resources from productive long-term investments into forms of wealth that are more easily protected, or even into capital flight to more stable environments. Thus stable countries are more prosperous than unstable ones:[19] whereas political stability subverts growth in the long run, instability prevents economic development from taking off to begin with.

Instability in itself however fails to explain the nature of the policy choice.[20] In his attempt to account for it he immediately returns to his theory of distributional coalitions which 'predicts that the unstable society will have fewer and weaker mass organizations than stable societies, but that small groups that can collude more readily will often be able to further their common interests' (166). He goes on:

> The most basic implication of the theory for unstable societies, then, is that their governments are systematically influenced by the interests, pleas, and pressures of the small groups that are capable of organizing fairly quickly (167).[21]

In Olson's framework, therefore, dysfunctional policies, of which the inward-looking development strategy is an example, are the outcome of pressure that well organized small interest groups exert on Third World governments.

The world of clientelism is far removed from Olson's. Pluralists assume that there is a set of well organized interest groups who attempt to influence policy formulation in order to attain benefits for the group as a whole. Interest groups in a clientelist setting, on the other hand, are mainly interested in providing particularistic benefits for individual members, and thus focus not on policy formulation but on policy implementation. This becomes the natural strategy where corruption is endemic, and so policy formulation is only tenuously related to actual administrative decisions.

All-pervasive corruption is of course itself a consequence of patronage politics. Moreover, inward-looking policies were pursued in both authoritarian and democratic countries, and Olson's theory - which focuses on pluralist regimes - fails to account for their dominance in an authoritarian environment.

Whereas for Olson the culprit for both policy and economic failure is too much participation, for Deepak Lal[22] it is the lack of it. Lal perceives the state as a predator[23] 'which maximizes the profits of government' (1984, 1). Maximizing the net revenue of the government 'need not lead to the establishment of an efficient set of property rights' (3). Indeed, property rights which sustain an efficient market system, itself required for growth, call for curbing the inherent power of the state through various forms of representation (4).

Lal's political interpretation is based on an analogy to monopoly theory,[24] where a monopolist's markets are protected by barriers to entry. In an analogous way, rulers are being protected from 'political' competition by barriers to entry, barriers that may be external or internal. The barriers against external competitors consist of such factors as the geographical difficulties of a conquest (5) and what he calls 'amalgamation costs' (5), which are based on the loyalty to incumbent domestic rulers (6), such as feelings of ethnic solidarity which can be mobilized against an invader. The internal barriers include military technology, which may favor an incumbent to a greater or lesser degree, and the size of the territory and the natural geographical defensive barriers which influence the ease of takeovers (6).

The nature of property rights and ultimately economic growth, Lal holds, will depend partly on these barriers to entry because they influence 'the relative "bargaining strength" of the rulers and constituents' (7). The smaller the barriers to entry for domestic competitors, the greater the likelihood that the predatory state is held in check and efficient property rights are instituted. The effect of entry barriers against external rivals is more ambiguous (7): if these barriers are small, the bargaining power of the constituents is considerable; on the other hand, opposing the incumbent is risky, and hence constituents 'are less likely to press their case against an incumbent predator' (7). Property rights, then, are a function of barriers to entry because they govern the power of extortion by the predatory state *vis-à-vis* the populace.[25]

Lal is mainly concerned with policy failures of the modern Indian state which epitomizes such a predator and which, although it has recently garbed itself in representative clothes, 'has not changed its nature or essential purpose' (23). Indeed, with the ending of alien rule and the accompanying reduction of the danger of an internal nationalist revolt, the rent extracted by the government had once again risen to the higher levels prevailing before the colonial period (21). By implication, so too have the inefficiencies in the structure of property rights.

The problem with Lal's argument is that politics is reduced to the science of the optimal level of taxation.[26] Like the far-sighted monopolist, the predatory ruler will charge 'the annual equivalent of the discounted present value of the entry costs or barriers to entry facing new firms in the market' (5, 8). The

> sustainability on a dynastic basis of the newly established monopoly depended upon his heirs being farsighted enough not to extract more than the natural rent. If they did then there would be an incentive for internal competitors to arise and attempt to provide a competitive supply ... The ensuing breakdown of the Empire would be followed by another period of chaos until one or other of the feuding chiefs succeeded in establishing his hegemony but refrained from overcharging for the natural monopoly he had acquired (18).

Quite consistently, Lal drew a causal connection between the increased tax burden and the decline of the Moghuls.

By reducing politics to the choice of the optimal level of taxation, Lal is able to ignore the question how political power is gained and maintained. By contrast, the central thesis of this monograph is that political processes associated with the problem of how to remain in power are crucial in explaining policy failures. The need to transfer tangible private benefits to political supporters in order to sustain political power is at the heart of the policy failures described by Lal. Moreover, it is not the *degree* of participation that determines the inward-looking development strategy, but its *nature*, and in particular the extent to which supporters expect to be rewarded by material private benefits in return for their backing. An inward-looking strategy is perfectly compatible with both competitive elections and an authoritarian regime, a contention which, while hardly controversial, does suggest that degrees of participation may not be the crucial variable in explaining policy direction and economic growth.

Lal's analysis is an offshoot of North's New Institutionalism. North attempts to explain the nature of and the changes in institutional structure, the formal and informal rules designed to constrain the behavior of individuals. These rules in turn account for the performance of an economic system (1981, ix). A theory of institutional change must, according to North, focus on:

- a theory of property rights that describes the individual and group incentives in the system;
- a theory of the state, since it is the state that specifies and enforces property rights;
- a theory of ideology that explains how different perceptions of reality affect the reaction of individuals to the changing 'objective' situation (7–8, 17).

The state is assumed to structure the rules of the game, including property rights, in such a way as (1) to increase rents accruing to the rulers, (2) to reduce transaction costs to maximize output and (3) to avoid offending powerful constituents which threaten its power (24, 28). Inefficiencies in property rights are largely the effect of the conflict between these often conflicting aims.

The argument put forward here can be viewed in North's terms: that ideology (a set of attitudes towards politics) determines the nature of the state (the behavior of the government) and leads to a particular set of property rights (corruption and inward-looking development) which is economically deficient. However, the reason for the inefficiencies in property rights is not the conflict between the aims of the government and of its subjects, nor the effect of powerful interest groups, but the consequence of political actions by individual subjects. Their choice of a government that imposes inefficient property rights is at least partly a consequence of a dilemma: abandoning clientelist practices will increase everyone's welfare, but the worst case is not to belong to a clientelist network while clientelism persists. Finally, both analyses stress the importance of ideology, which in the clientelist case helps to overcome freerider problems of this kind; an individual's behavior may cease to be guided exclusively by a narrow calculation encompassing solely material gains benefiting the individual or a small group of relatives and friends.

To summarize: of the diverse approaches which shed light on the question of why an inward-looking development strategy was adopted and persisted for so long, the clientelist approach has significant advantages over competing explanations. By showing that it was in the interest of policy-makers to pursue such a strategy it escapes the problems of 'ideal' explanations, which are unable to explain why particular ideas prevailed. It does not attribute the strategy to external shocks, but, in line with empirical evidence, holds that internal factors are sufficient for its emergence. In contrast to predatory state models, the clientelist analysis takes account of political processes which indeed are at the heart of any explanation of the causes of policy choice. It deals squarely with the issue of corruption, one of the salient features of Third World countries, which is greatly promoted by patronage politics. It portrays a system of state-society interaction which is more in tune with an environment where corruption is rife than are conventional interest group or corporatist analyses. Finally, the sensible conclusion is reached that economic failure is not systematically related to the level of popular participation, but to its nature. Hence relative performance in terms of growth is not directly related to whether a system is democratic or authoritarian.

1.3   Democracy, Authoritarianism and Economic Growth

It is a major contention of this monograph that no generalizations can be made about any differential effect of authoritarianism or democracy on economic growth. Both authoritarian and democratic regimes are compatible with political clientelism and may therefore pursue the same type of policies, and if this is the case their resulting growth experience is likely to be similar. For this reason alone growth rates may not vary systematically between authoritarian and democratic regimes.

The traditional view, going back at least to the nineteenth century, holds that in the early stages of economic development democracy is incompatible with an optimal rate of economic growth. Robert Heilbroner, among others, argues that 'only political leadership of the most forceful kind can ... carry the Great Ascent along' (1963, 132, 135, 138), and DeSchweinitz thinks that if less developed countries 'are to grow economically, they must limit democratic participation in political affairs' (1964, 277).[27] Others have questioned the notion that democracy is a luxury in early stages of development (Pye 1966, 72).[28] On the contrary, they say that 'at present in most situations rapid economic growth is more likely to be stimulated by a reduction in authoritarian practices and an increase in popular participation' (73). If our hypothesis is correct, such generalizations are much too sweeping.

1.3.1   Savings and Investment

Compared with democratic regimes authoritarianism is beneficial for growth, it is argued, because it is conducive to savings and investments and to a more efficient allocation of resources. Thus demonstration effects engender 'rising and often competing demands' which 'impinge upon the political system while the developing country's economic system is not advanced enough to satisfy the demands' (Bollen 1979, 573). These demands may prevent democratic governments from levying the necessary taxes to finance development expenditure, and may create a bias in favor of government consumption expenditures such as welfare payments rather than investment spending. It is also thought that the forces of public opinion would ensure an income redistribution favoring low-income groups with a small propensity to save.[29] A democratic government, for example, might be more prone to legislate high minimum wages for urban workers. The political problem is thought to be particularly acute because 'growth at the early critical stage of the take-off is a discriminatory process which favors the few who are able to take the steps necessary to raise the rate of net investment' (DeSchweinitz 1964, 56). Moreover, the allocation of resources might be less efficient in a democracy that is more exposed to interest group pressure, and thus more prone to introduce special interest group legislation. This type of reasoning underlies Bhagwati's conclusion (1966, 203–204) that democratic regimes are at a disadvantage compared with totalitarian socialist regimes which are able to disregard opposition and can focus single-mindedly on development, or DeSchweinitz's more dramatic opinion that democratic participation and economic growth are incompatible (1964, 277).[30]

The question is complicated by the optimal rate of growth argument. In principle, an authoritarian government might be able to extract the whole output produced by a country that is not needed for subsistence of the populace, and invest it efficiently. This Stalinist-type method will lead to a rapid rate of growth, but fewer investments, less growth, and a higher level of current consumption might well be socially optimal. Proponents of the view that authoritarianism is good for economic development who are aware of the problem therefore usually introduce the notion that a democratic regime tends to reduce savings and investment, and thus growth, below some optimum rate.

The culprits behind this alleged bias in public preferences are ignorance and the willingness to shift the burden of development to future generations. The latter position was taken John Stuart Mill when he stated that voters might advocate measures which 'would be for the selfish interest of the whole existing generation' (1861, 443), for example by increasing government consumption at the cost of investment expenditure. The former position, that voters' ignorance is responsible for sub-optimal growth, can also be traced to Mill, who had said that voters 'cannot be expected to be, and, as experience shows, hardly ever are, accessible to any views of their own ultimate interest which rest upon a train of reasoning' (1835, 32).

DeSchweinitz argues along Mill's lines: the political leaders of under-developed countries 'can conceive of prospects and objectives' which the average individual is unable to imagine and therefore 'may have only the vaguest connection with the preferences and conduct of individuals' (1964, 274). In addition, people's ignorance is supposed to relate to their time preference because they do not value future states sufficiently. In both these cases, people 'might have to be taken in hand and led forward *in their own interests'* (275).

Other arguments, however, support the position that democracy can lead to a superior growth performance. Pye thinks that democracy would satisfy to a greater degree the need for identity of a large number of people and foster integration and adjustment to change (1966, 73). These factors, according to Pye, have positive economic consequences. In addition, democracy is able to 'mobilize greater involvement in the tasks of economic development than is possible with autocratic, but unpopular leaders' (74). Pye's belief about the mobilized populace has a peculiar outdated ring to it; hardly anyone, either before or since, has thought that economic development could be greatly influenced by a mobilized populace acting altruistically and laboring for the common good.[31] But more importantly, a traditional Western-style democratic system with independent press and judiciary[32] may limit some of the worst excesses of authoritarian rule.[33] Whereas authoritarianism might open the possibility of faster growth than in a democracy, it also allows for the worst performance, because it lacks the inbuilt mechanism to avoid the worst excesses (Cohen 1985, 124).[34]

Moreover, even if it is accepted that, in principle, authoritarian regimes are able to extract resources from the populace and use them optimally, they might not do so in practice. True, there are 'strong' authoritarian governments, fairly well insulated from societal pressures, which conceivably might engage in successful growth strategies; but there are also 'weak' authoritarian governments whose hold on power is precarious and which may have to pursue similar policies to those of weak democratic ones.[35] A postulate that authoritarian regimes have generally a great degree of autonomy and are therefore able to override interest group demands is far from self-evident (Nelson 1989, 15–16, Haggard and Webb 1993, 145–146). Moreover, even if it is accepted that 'strong' authoritarian governments might adopt unpopular growth strategies, there is no particular reason to assume that they will. An institutional argument that focuses attention on the capacity to formulate and implement policy must be complemented by an argument about why politicians have an incentive to promote economic efficiency (Haggard 1990, 263).[36] A new causation about how democracy and autocracy could affect economic growth was added by the 'basic needs' approach to development (Streeten 1977), where the satisfaction of basic needs is 'not primarily a welfare concept; improved education and health can make a major contribution to increased productivity' (1981, 3).[37] If democratic regimes are more likely to satisfy basic needs,[38] and that leads to higher rates of growth, we have another mechanism by which political structure may affect growth.

1.3.2 Stability and Economic Growth

So far democracy affected economic development through the effect of popular pressure on savings, investment, and the efficiency of the resource allocation. There is another strand of thought which argues that democracy is incompatible with stability, and therefore with economic growth.

The idea was traditionally associated with the Latin American stop-go cycle: a weak democratic government's stabilization policy fails as it proves unable to keep wages, prices, and government expenditures in check. As a result, inflation mounts again after initial successes, and the next foreign exchange crisis is in the making.[39] Empirical evidence as to the relative performance of democratic regimes with regard to stabilization policy is mixed, as one would expect (Haggard and Webb 1993, 146). Indeed, some have claimed that democracies have done particularly well. In her 1986 study of Latin American countries Remmer, for example, comes to the conclusion that 'democratic regimes have been no less likely to introduce stabilization programs than authoritarian ones, no more likely to break down in response to their political costs, and no less rigorous in their implementation of austerity measures. If anything, the evidence suggested that the edge with respect to program implementation was with the democracies' (1990, 318, 1986).[40]

1.3.3 Empirical Evidence and Evaluation

For some two decades, a battery of tests have been applied to shed some light on whether authoritarian or democratic regimes grew faster. In their review of these empirical studies, Sirowy and Inkeles conclude that 'only few basic insights appear to have been gained' (1990, 151). Among those is that 'the evidence would seem to suggest that political democracy does not widely and directly facilitate more rapid growth, net of other factors' (150). Hence the 'compatibility perspective' according to which democracy promotes economic growth finds little support (150). However, 'these studies present a very mixed and confusing picture' (137), such that almost 'twenty years of research efforts on the issues of economic growth and socio-economic equality have produced few if any robust conclusions' (150). Przeworski and Limongi conclude their review even more bluntly: '... we do not know whether democracy fosters or hinders economic growth' (1993, 64).

These scant results are hardly surprising, even if only the practical problems of testing are considered. To begin with, 'democracy' is hard to define. Then there is the notoriously unstable political situation in many Third World countries: if regime type does affect growth but with a lag, it becomes increasingly difficult to determine which periods are supposed to be correlated. Next, the data on growth, however defined, are often unreliable. Moreover, simply looking for a correlation between growth and democracy in different countries may lead to spurious results if tests leave out variables that do explain differences growth rates.[41] Unfortunately, the theory of economic development is vague about which variables should be included, and the statistical procedures may lead simply to the *ad hoc* introduction of control variables and to entirely spurious correlations.[42]

However, even if these practical problems could be overcome, and if it were established beyond doubt that the average performance of authoritarian or of democratic regimes is relatively superior,[43] little might be gained. As long as the correlation is not perfect - in other words, if authoritarian regimes do sometimes better and sometimes worse in any given set of circumstances - the finding has few policy implications, if any. It obviously does not follow in a particular case that a change of regime type would necessarily accelerate growth.

Not only do these studies have few practical consequences, they come close to testing without theory, or what Schumpeter called the 'Ricardian vice', 'the habit of establishing simple relations between aggregates that then acquire a spurious halo of causal importance, whereas all the really important (and, unfortunately, complicated) things are being bundled away in or behind these aggregates' (1954, 668).

One of the things 'bundled away' in the aggregates is the nature of the democracy and of the authoritarian regime. These are obviously not homogeneous entities, and if the wide variety of institutional arrangements observed among both democratic and authoritarian regimes is taken into account, one would expect both democracies and autocracies to pursue a variety of policies and thus differ in their growth performances. On the other hand, both regime types may sometimes exhibit structural similarities which lead to similar development experiences. Thus clientelism occurs in both democratic and autocratic settings and will be shown to have determinate consequences for policy making. Indeed, economic failure is often better explained by how close a political system approximates clientelism than by its democratic or autocratic features.

1.4 Conclusion

The aim of the monograph, then, is to establish the thesis that in many countries one reason for the adoption and persistence of welfare-reducing inward-looking strategies was a particular political structure, political clientelism. Some caveats need to be made, however. Clientelism is obviously neither a necessary nor a sufficient condition for the emergence of a doomed inward-looking development strategy and thus of economic failure. In particular, clientelistic political behavior may not lead to the institutional characteristics - such as factionalism, endemic corruption, politicization, and lack of government legitimacy and state autonomy - which are seen to induce policy failures. As in the case of a potentially damaging virus in a human body, the presence of clientelism may never lead to the pernicious full blown symptoms.

Nor does this analysis imply that import substitution strategies necessarily fail. The monograph attempts to explain a particular historical phenomenon: why, in the wake of World War II, many countries adopted and pursued manifestly welfare-reducing policies of the inward-looking type. It demonstrates that in many cases clientelism bears a responsibility. However, this leaves open the question of whether import substitution might promise success in a different political environment.

The thesis does suggest that, in a clientelist environment, structural reform involving a shift towards an outward-looking strategy and less intervention is unequivocally superior to inward-looking development. But it does not imply that an outward-looking strategy and non-intervention is the most successful strategy in the pursuit of economic growth in all circumstances.

Nor should the argument be construed as condemning government intervention generally. Inward-looking development is closely associated with a substantial degree of government intervention and it will be shown that, in a clientelist setting, this stifles growth. That does not preclude the success of intervention in different circumstances. For example, the proposition that 'governing the market' has spurred economic development in a number of East Asian economies looks increasingly convincing (Wade 1990, World Bank 1993).

Notes:

1. Economic development here is defined as an increase in output per head of the population. This 'old' view of development has been questioned, party because it neglects distributional issues. Nevertheless, it remains trivially true that before something can be distributed it has to be produced, and, at least in the long run, the poor tend to be better off in countries where output per head is high than where it is low.

2. Hirschman was concerned with political issues in his early work. However, he was still operating in the tradition of assuming a benevolent government which was swayed off course by public pressure. Hirschman's advice to the practitioner therefore is that 'to understand some of these real problems under which policy makers of underdeveloped countries labor will help in making our technical assistance more constructive' (1957, 368).

3. 'African bureaucracies have grown enormously in the past twenty-five years; they have consumed too much of the gross domestic product by employing too many people and paying senior officials salaries too high for the resources of the state' (Duignan 1986, 17). For example, 'Kenya went from a civil service of 45,000 in 1955 to 170,000 in 1984. Senegal employed 10,000 in 1960 and over 70,000 in 1984' (19).

4. 'One author, after a meticulous examination of fraudulent practices, claimed to have established a provisional total of 142 distinct variants of graft in the state marketing institutions' in the Senegal (Cruise O'Brien 1975, 129).

5. From 32 percent in 1950 to 16.5 percent in 1975 (Krueger 1992, 35).

6. Which must end inconclusive because the question involved is, as Krueger has pointed out, 'inherently unanswerable' (1990, 11), at least if the institutional context is not considered.

7. Also Killick (1978, 1–2).

8. Their advice might well have been related to self-interest, such as the availability of consultancy money and travel allowances for those participating in the process of central planning, and the sheer excitement associated with such assignments. Toye unintentionally reinforces such a jaundiced view. He says that development economists 'knew that they were largely ineffective and felt morally uncomfortable', but that there was a 'diplomatic imperative' which required 'tact and tongue biting'

(1991, 113).

9. Represented by the Austrian tradition, especially Von Mises, or in the field of development economics proper by Bauer and Yamey (e.g. 1957).

10. In addition, the greater the level of natural resource endowment, the more the system is exposed to 'exogenous shocks or fluctuations in the terms of trade. The amplitude and periodicity of these exogenous fluctuations moreover affect the rate of secular organizational/institutional change' (Ranis and Mahmood 1992, 223–24).

11. Their explanation becomes increasing *ad hoc*. For example, it purports to account for the difference in economic policy between Thailand and the Philippines, where it can be 'traced in part to the different composition and distribution of their natural resource endowments, i.e., more equally distributed rice land in Thailand versus more concentrated traditional crops in the Philippines' (Ranis and Mahmood 1992, 187).

12. There is little evidence to support the contention that manufacturing industry dominated policy change. 'In Korea or Taiwan there is no evidence that local industry was the driving force behind export-oriented policies ... In Singapore local manufacturing was actually marginalized by a strategy based on multinationals. In Hong Kong ... the large commercial and financial establishment acted as a force for laissez-faire *against* the interests of manufacturing' (Haggard 1990, 39).

13. Mainly top political leaders in the executive branch (Haggard 1990, 43).

14. E.g. in Korea and Taiwan (Haggard 1990, 98).

15. Singapore's adoption of export orientation follows the 'external shock' explanation in the conventional sense: It was adopted after the dissolution of the federation with Malaysia (Haggard 1990, 107). Hong Kong, of course, never adopted ISI.

16. Peck has little to say on the emergence of these policies. She seems to take at face value the official policy aims which were 'to maintain order, to strengthen the Crown, to avoid scarcity and famine, to create a prosperous people, to finance the state through duties and rents, and to cement ties of the localities to the center' (1990, 135). A clientelist approach would search for changes in the patronage structure to explain the phenomenon.

17. This is of course not to say that there are other reasons, including external ones, for adopting ISI. Tariff protection was adopted as a revenue measure by many countries, including India under the Raj (Lal 1988, 182–203, 219).

18. Stable in terms of 'unchanged jurisdictional boundaries' (Olson 1982, 128).

19. Other things being equal, the most rapid growth will occur in societies that have lately experienced upheaval but are expected nonetheless to be stable for the foreseeable future (Olson 1982, 165).

20. Or what Olson calls the 'systematic element in economic policies' (1982, 167).

21.   This opens the following problem. Olson seems to suggest that in a society where there are only small distributional coalitions their influence is the same as those of large groups in a society where large groups are abundant. This seems to be implied by the statement that 'small groups that can collude more readily will often be able to further their common interests. The groups may be at any level, but usually those which can gain from either lobbying or cartelising at a national level are small groups of substantial firms or wealthy and powerful individuals' (1982, 166). Since it is accepted that small groups are easier to organize, then there is no reason for sclerosis at all. Government policy will be driven by special interest group interest from the beginning; only the *type* of interest groups changes.

22.   1984, 1988 (especially 294–306).

23.   Drawing heavily on North (1981).

24.   Particularly contestability theory.

25.   Apart from barriers to entry, the set of property rights is affected by 'the relative importance of internal versus external trade', which in turn 'is likely to depend upon natural resource endowments' (Lal 1984, 8). This is important because the self-interest of the predators induces them to expand the tax base of an economy through external trade. That should give an incentive to set up reasonably efficient property rights to underpin a mercantile economy (8). This aspect plays a secondary role in Lal, and is neglected in the monograph.

26.   The same kind of criticism applies to other neo-classical 'predatory state' models. In Findlay's models the sovereign maximizes income, and if labor can be employed either in the state or the private sector, the optimal distribution of labor among the two sectors is where their marginal product is equal. All the sovereign does is choose a tax rate, or alternatively an amount of state employment (Findlay and Wilson, 1987, Wellisz and Findlay, 1988).

27.   These views were shared by such writers as Bhagwati (1966, 203–204), Adelman and Morris (1967), Marsh (1979), Sorensen (1991, 10), Heilbroner (1963, 132, 135, 138) and Kitching (1983, Ch. 2).

28.   LaPalombara and Weiner thought that 'there is little convincing evidence that the best or only road to economic modernity is that of an authoritarian or totalitarian regime dominated by a single party' (1966, 6).

29.   Kitching (1983, 48), Cohen (1985, 123-136), Marsh (1979, 217, 244). McCord (1965, 15) quotes Aneurin Bevan: 'It is highly doubtful whether the achievements of the Industrial Revolution would have been permitted if the franchise had been universal. It is very doubtful because a great deal of the capital aggregations that we are at present enjoying are the results of the wages that our fathers went without.'

30. Says Chirot: in order to grow and 'to escape their problems semi-peripheral societies need to be closed, hard, and *frozen*. That is, internal politics must be controlled by a small, tight elite that freezes debate and imposes its will on the majority' (1977, 224, 207–8). For some of the antecedents of these positions see Marsh (1979), Weede (1983), Sirowy and Inkeles (1990) and Sorensen (1991).
31. Except perhaps in the short term (e.g. Remmer 1986, 3).
32. And sometimes independent auditors.
33. This is probably what McCord had in mind when he suggested that an authoritarian regime 'as in China, may possibly aid in stimulating economic advance; it may, as in Indonesia [under Sukarno], cause a potentially irrevocable depression. A democratic policy may make economic mistakes, but they seldom have the permanent effects of errors committed by a dictatorship' (1965, 242). It might be argued therefore that the variation of rates of growth is less in democratic than authoritarian countries.
34. Others have argued that political pluralism is important for the survival and vitality of economic pluralism which in turn is essential for economic growth (Goodell and Powelson 1982). Events in Latin America and Asia clearly refute such a broad generalization.
35. For an example see Haggard (1990b).
36. Weede's more suggestive findings point in the direction that what matters most is not democracy as such, but the size of the state. Hence in 'nations where the state controls much of the economy, whether more of less developed, political democracy is a major barrier to economic growth' (1983, 36). When looking only at countries with a relatively large government sector, he found that 'political democracy looks like a major barrier to economic growth in those countries where the state strongly interferes in the economy' (32). This approach throws the argument back to the question why some countries have larger government sectors than others.
37. Newman and Thomson tested the hypothesis that social development is a cause of subsequent economic growth (1989, 464) and found indications that 'the level of basic needs satisfaction ... also significantly contributes to subsequent economic growth'. Even the authors, however, suggest that caution 'is warranted in the interpretation of the findings' (467).
38. A hypothesis supported by King (1981), who found that rural material inequality is greater in bureaucratic-authoritarian states than in democratic ones. However, a higher level of political democracy tends not to be widely associated with lower levels of income inequality (Sirowy and Inkeles 1990, 151).
39. And often the military then seizes power. 'This pattern is visible in the so-called bureaucratic-authoritarian regimes in Latin America' and in Indonesia in 1966 and Turkey in 1971 (Haggard and Webb 1993, 145).

40.   Remmer might wish to reconsider after the recent events Brazil, Venezuela and Peru.

41.   These issues are discussed in Sirowy and Inkeles (1990).

42.   For example, if difficult economic conditions result in autocratic regimes becoming democracies, but not the other way round, a bias is introduced against democracies (Przeworski and Limongi 1993, 62–64).

43.   Even assuming that more growth is unambiguously better than less.

2   Political Clientelism

This chapter develops an ideal-type of political clientelism from which it will be possible to derive a set of policies which are likely to be pursued in this particular environment and which affect economic development. The first section sets out the common behavioral and structural assumptions of political clientelism and gives a few historical examples of clientelist systems. The second section describes some salient institutional features which are the probable consequence of political clientelism and encourage inward-looking development. The third section explores some repercussions of political clientelism for the nature of the institutional framework and for policy making.

2.1   The Structure of Political Clientelism

Clientelism describes an exchange relationship between a client and a patron.[1] The exchanges may relate to economic well-being, political power or social status. Since status is of little relevance in this context, it is convenient to think of two kinds of exchange: purely economic, where patrons and clients exchange goods and services; and political, where economic benefits are traded for political support. In practice, these two types of exchange are often inextricably interwoven.

What is exchanged, the terms of trade of the exchange, who are the clients and who the patrons will depend on the institutional setting in which the exchange takes place. However, there are several characteristics common to all forms of clientelism.

First, clientelism suggests the existence of a hierarchical structure, an organizational 'tree' where some clients are connected to a patron, forming a *patron-client cluster*.[2] Moreover, the lower level patrons of political clientelism may themselves be clients of a higher level patron, and we get a pyramiding of patron-client ties or a *patron-client network*. Such networks may, as in Italy or Venezuela, 'provide quite lengthy chains of linkages - from the peasant to the President or Prime Minister' (Powell 1970, 418).

Second, in a patron-client network each client is individually connected to the patron by a personal or 'face-to-face' relationship. Ideally, there are no horizontal ties among clients: the cluster is held together exclusively through each individual member's connection to the leader, which precludes horizontal ties among clients and therefore collective or group action on their part. The assumption is too drastic to be useful. Still, even if horizontal ties exist, the cohesion of a client group depends on the existence of the leader, without whom the group disintegrates or changes significantly. Hence even horizontal ties are a function of the vertical ties to the leader.[3] In practice, collective actions of clients at the bottom rung of the ladder are related to purely local or narrowly focused issues.

Third, the exchange relationship is entirely *informal*, going beyond the relationship which may exist by virtue of officially sanctioned social roles. The mutual obligations at the heart of the clientele arrangement are not enforceable, since they are neither based on formal and explicit contracts nor rest on governmental or religious law (Landé 1977a, xviii).

Fourth, the exchange is entered into *voluntarily*. Coercion, authority, manipulation and so forth may play a role in the exchange, but if they come to be dominant the tie is no longer a patron-client relationship (Powell 1970, 412). Thus while clients are hardly on an equal footing with their patrons, neither are they entirely a pawn in a one-way relationship (Scott 1977a, 22).

To be able to specify the nature of patron and client and their exchange it is convenient to distinguish between economic and political clientelism.

2.1.1 Economic Clientelism

Economic clientelism is a form of clientelism where the patron-client exchange is 'grafted' onto a formal and enforceable economic exchange. In classical traditional clientelism the roles of patron and client coincides with the roles of the owners of the means of production and those who provide labor.[4] More specifically, the prototype of patron-client ties is that between landlords and their tenants or sharecroppers in a traditional agrarian economy (Scott 1977b, 125). Hence granting access to land for cultivation is the central core of the classical patron-client bond (1977a, 23). The patron then is first and foremost the provider of the means of production, and the client his economic dependent. However, a landowner-tenant relationship as such does not establish a patron-client tie because the mutual obligations are part of the institution of tenant farming as it has developed in a particular locality, thus are contractual and may be enforced by the state (Landé 1977a, xxi). Clientelism transcends this formal and enforceable exchange of labor for pay, or of land for rent, by its inclusion of additional economic, social and political exchanges.

The additional economic services provided by clients which go beyond the formal landowner-peasant relationships may include, for example, supplementary labor services, the client's wife helping out occasionally with housework, offering some choice produce from the farm, or a client refraining from cheating his or her landlord. In terms of social exchange, clients show respect and deference towards their patrons, speak well of them in public and profess devotion to them. Moreover, in all likelihood clients will be voting for the candidate of the patron at election time, and they may actively support the patron's election campaign, or perhaps find out what the local rivals are up to (Scott 1977a, 24; 1977b, 126; Wolf 1977, 175; Silverman 1977, 296).

In return the client receives, in the main, economic benefits. The clientele tie increases security of tenure, or provides subsistence insurance against crop failure or other calamities. In addition, a client receives help to extract benefits from the state or obtains protection against it. For example, the patron may intervene on the client's behalf with the authorities in case of problems with the law, or to obtain a scholarship (Scott 1977a, 23). The experience of Signora M., 'whose husband was killed during World War I, tried in vain for months to collect a government pension for war widows, and only after the patron spoke of her case to the appropriate officials did she succeed in getting it' (Silverman 1977 298), speaks the language of a widespread predicament of the poor. Furthermore, patrons may use their influence to secure a loan for a client, or occasional help may be forthcoming in the form of loans or transportation in cases of emergency.[5] Beyond these purely individual benefits the patrons may advance the *community's* interests through contributions from their own resources to communal activities or by securing works and services, administrative favors, community loans or agricultural assistance from the government which benefit the village as a whole (Scott and Kerkvliet 1977, 444).[6]

The patron-client relationship in this setting is by its very nature multiplex and diffuse, involving a plethora of social, economic and political obligations on both sides. Moreover, it involves deferred exchanges, thus establishing claims for the future. A case in point is 'subsistence insurance', where small gifts to the landowner can be viewed as insurance contributions to cover future emergencies. In addition, the web of mutual obligations often creates trust and affection between the partners, resulting in what has been called 'instrumental' or 'lop-sided friendship' (Pitt-Rivers 1954, 140).[7] In general, only the presence of a minimum amount of affection can establish the trust which underwrites the promise of future mutual support (Wolf 1977, 174). The connection is sometimes strengthened by additional religious or social ties, for example if the patron acts as a godfather for a client's child, which creates, at least in Latin American cultures, a formal bond between the parents and godparents which is of some social significance (Mintz and Wolf 1977, 1–15).[8]

If we take the landowner-tenant clientelism to be the prototype of economic clientelism, then it follows that the structure of the exchange involves not only the criteria which were outlined previously - an informal voluntary face-to-face exchange between patrons and clients. In addition clients are necessarily the patrons' inferior in status, wealth, and influence (Powell 1970, 412); moreover, the exchange is multiplex, and the ties often involve some degree of mutual trust and sympathy.

What has been called the 'political exchange', trading political support for economic benefits, presupposes that the client is unable to obtain access to some crucial government resources and therefore requires the intermediation of the patron. There may be many reasons for this blocked access, ranging from the client's illiteracy, or physical remoteness from government offices, to the practice of allocating services only to those who have 'connections', as in the case of Signora M. In this context, then, the landlord is seen as a mediator, a link between the local life of a peasant community and the state, or, more generally between a local and a national social system (Silverman 1977, 293).[9]

What is the link between the landowner and the government? One possible mechanism connecting the two is the neo-traditional political machine, where the landowner is able to induce clients to support a particular political party, which in turn gives patrons the necessary political influence to attract government resources to themselves and their peasant-clients.

The neo-traditional machine is prominent in Third World countries where, particularly around the time of independence, political parties without sufficient organizational backing and political support in the countryside allied themselves with local big-men who delivered the votes. Voters had to be mobilized quickly, and to draw upon traditional authority was often the most efficient way to do so. In this manner machines captured traditional groups and used them as vote-banks (Bailey 1963, 113). The party apparatus then sits, usually uneasily, on existing hierarchical social structures: representative politics operates in the mold of traditional society as solidarities of a traditional type are incorporated into a broader institutional framework (Lemarchand 1981, 21; Bailey 1963, 113).

Neo-traditional machines, of course, may not be based exclusively on landowner-peasant clientelism, or even on economic clientelism for that matter. Any traditional authority may be used to mobilize political support. The great marabouts, the traditional leaders of Muslim religious sects in Senegal, occupy a crucial position as mobilizers of votes. At some stage, the Grand Khalifa of a large brotherhood, for instance, was able to mobilize at least 400,000 assured votes in a country with a total population of 3,200,000 (Foltz 1977, 246). The neo-traditional machines in northern Nigeria provide another example, 'where the dependency that derived from the vast network of clientage relationships inherent in the traditional society were transferred to the party'. Loyalty to it 'became a way of defraying traditional political obligations' (Whitaker 1965, 375).[10] The Turkish case from the early part of this century conforms more to the pattern of conventional landowner-peasant clientelism: the ruling party organized its units by recruiting notables in the provinces into its ranks through systematic use of patronage and economic regulation (Sayari 1977, 106).

2.1.2 Political Clientelism

Political clientelism is distinct from economic clientelism in that patrons do not have to be owners of means of production and therefore the capitalist-worker or landowner-peasant relationship is not an essential part of the patron-client tie. This, of course, does not mean that the patrons as a class may not own the means of production, only that an individual client is not, as a rule, employed by a patron, nor does he rent the patron's land.

Whereas in economic clientelism the power base of the patron is founded on the control of means of production *and* political power - political power being indeed often a consequence of the ownership of the means of production - the power of the patron in political clientelism is in the main derived from the ability to obtain access to resources of the state and to transmit them to his followers. Lower level patrons become brokers, intermediary between their clients and higher level patrons who control the government and the bureaucracy.

Two examples of different structures of political clientelism are outlined here, the urban *cacique* and the orthodox political machine.

2.1.2.1 Urban Cacique

A peculiarly fertile breeding ground for the urban *cacique*, a Latin American version of a patron, are that region's squatter settlements (Cornelius 1975, 161). In the main, three layers of actors are involved: the government and party officials, the *cacique*, and the squatters. What do the different parties expect from the exchange?

First to the squatters, who, in the early life of the settlements they inhabit, do not possess legal title to the land on which their houses are built, and therefore suffer from insecure land tenure. They also often experience extreme service deprivation, since settlements start off without even the most basic physical amenities such as water, sewerage, roads, schools or hospitals (161).

The rule of *caciques* flourishes because they may be able to remedy such deficiencies. Indeed, 'the cacique's effectiveness as a leader is measured primarily by his success in maintaining a constant flow of material benefits both to the community as a whole and to individual residents' (150). Among the collective benefits the *caciques* provide, the most important are security of titles and amenities, but in addition they supply the kinds of individual benefits supplied by patrons everywhere, from recommendations to prospective employers, or help in procuring business permits or licenses, to getting children enrolled in already overcrowded local schools, securing medical treatment and so forth (1975, 150; 1977, 343).

Cornelius believes that the *cacique's* 'primary aim is to increase his personal wealth' (1975, 143). In all three squatter settlements in Mexico City which he studied the *caciques* were deeply involved in a variety of illicit moneymaking schemes (143). Often the most important source of income for *caciques* was illicit land deals, but exploiting local mineral resources, charging fees for access to basic urban services such as electricity, and the 'frequent collection of "donations" from the residents may have been equally lucrative' (1975, 143). This exploitative behavior will be tolerated as long as 'it appears that the individual and collective interests of community residents are being advanced as a result of the *cacique*'s leadership' (1977, 343).

Caciques stand in a symbiotic relationship to low level government functionaries, both relying on each other's help. The functionaries tend to have a sympathetic view of the *caciques'* role in the political system, since they are expected by their superiors to maintain social and political control within their jurisdictions, as well as to secure high turnouts for the ruling party at rallies and the polls. *Caciques* are able to provide both control and political support. Thus they have found it easy to gain and hold power in small communities, both rural and urban, because they make it so much easier for an ambitious lower-echelon official to do his job (1975, 164).

In order to be successful, the *caciques* have to be recognized both by the residents of the community in which they operate and by the supra-local authorities as being the most powerful persons in the local arena. Only if they are able to make decisions that are binding on the community under their control will public officials invariably deal with them in all matters affecting the community. Hence they become 'a sort of government within a government, controlled by a single dominant individual who is not *formally* accountable to those residing in the community under his control or to external authorities' (141).

The *cacique*, as much as the landowner in the previous example, monopolizes the crucial link between client and the supra-local government authorities and other suppliers of services such as lawyers, doctors, architects and engineers (1977, 340). Indeed these contacts enable - or are viewed by the clients as enabling - the *cacique* 'to deal effectively with external actors and secure benefits for the community which would be beyond the reach of someone lacking regularized channels of access to higher levels of authority' (341). The power of the urban *cacique* of the Latin American slum is based therefore on the ability to shape and to monopolize crucial connections to the outside world, which then allow him to act as a mediator between a locality and its often hostile environment.

The connection between squatter and *cacique* is a purely utilitarian one. Because of the lack of 'affective underpinnings', the *cacique*'s position 'can be quickly undermined by particularly flagrant financial indiscretions and abuses of authority, or by his failure to meet certain standards of performance over an extended period of time' (1975, 143). However, open opposition may be difficult, as the *cacique* generally controls the actions of the police within the community and makes effective use of them to intimidate dissidents and potential rivals (146). Other means of coercion are economic, including threats to reallocate plots of land: the mere suggestion 'that one's plot of land might be reallocated to some other resident, or even to an outsider, was usually all that was needed to compel obedience' (147).

2.1.2.2 Orthodox Machine Politics

In orthodox machine politics the party machine is the arena for clientelist exchanges and patrons higher up the party hierarchy provide particularistic benefits to their clients in exchange political support. The party structure is little more than an assemblage of competing client-networks, 'a multi-tiered pyramid of personal followings, one heaped upon the other. Each link in the chain of vertical dyads is based upon personal assurances of support and conditional upon downward flow of patronage and spoils' (Landé 1977b, 86).[11]

The difference between the neo-traditional and the orthodox machine is to be found in the micro-level clientelistic structures. Whereas the authority of the neo-traditional patron rests at least partly on foundations unrelated to the party machine, such as the ownership of the means of production or religious sanction, the micro-level patron of the orthodox machine is entirely its creation. Thus where in neo-traditional clientelism deference, tradition or economic power influences allegiance, the orthodox machine is held together chiefly by the flow of concrete, short-run benefits *derived from the government*.

The political machines of American cities in the late nineteenth and early twentieth century are the classical examples of orthodox machines. The Italian Christian Democratic Party was a more modern and more sophisticated case: it dominated national as well as local politics and its clienteles were much more diverse, ranging from the entrepreneurial middle classes to the public employees and the urban poor (Lemarchand 1981, 22). African machines developed around the same time. Zolberg was perhaps the first to draw attention to the close parallel between the American and African machines such as the ruling party of the Ivory Coast, which since 1951 'has controlled for practical purposes a rather large budget and has been able to determine where schools or roads will be built, who will get government loans, and who will be appointed to a variety of public boards, much as in an American city' (1966, 19).[12]

The difference between the orthodox and neo-traditional machine should not be overstressed. In both cases clients expect to receive particularistic benefits from the government through the intermediation of the patron, and benefits will be allocated to political supporters who expect particularistic benefits, such as the Turkish peasants who

> have come to Ankara in search of assistance from their deputies. The help which they seek usually involves particularistic favors: extension of the deadline for the repayment of the loan borrowed from the State Agricultural Bank, a permit to go to Europe as a worker, or a hospital bed in Ankara for a relative who is critically ill. Deputies spend a good deal of their time trying to secure preferential treatment from various bureaucratic agencies on behalf of their constituents (Sayari 1977, 105).

In both cases the party structure is permeated by personal clientele networks. Hence the party does not have a single coordinated and unified machine. At elections, at least on a national level, it must rely on a considerable number of machines, of different sizes, each attached to a person in or in temporary and uncertain alliance with the party (Bailey 1963, 153). This leads, as in the Philippines, to campaign techniques where candidates for elective office

> find it necessary to build what are essentially personal campaign organizations. In this they seek the help of lower level political leaders who have personal followings whose votes they can deliver, and of candidates for even higher offices who are willing to help finance the candidate's campaign in exchange for aid in their own search for votes (Landé 1977b, 86).

As we moved from economic clientelism to political clientelism, from the landowner-peasant type to the orthodox machine type, we find that exchanges become less multiplex and more short term, and that ties which were affective become increasingly instrumental. The association is likely to become less long term as the patrons cease to own the resources which underpin it, and therefore have to rely on their ability to monopolize resources and transfer them to clients at more favorable terms than someone else. The implicit contractual arrangement becomes less multiplex, as the economic element in the exchange is missing. Increasingly, rationally calculated benefits and costs determine the exchange, and it becomes less and less meaningful to talk about lop-sided friendship: in fact, we are more likely to talk about the party boss than the patron (Scott

1977b, 127).[13] In the end, we have arrived at a situation which closely resembles a conventional market in so far as individuals exchange goods and services without regard to the welfare of the other parties to the transaction. And as in any other market, the nature of the exchange relationship will depend on initial endowments and the market structure. Moreover, the hierarchical structure changes. Whereas economic clientelism implies that the patron is higher up the social hierarchy, this becomes less clear with political clientelism. We may well encounter a situation where a businessman ranks higher in terms of both wealth and status than his patron operating in the political sphere.

2.2   A Framework of Political Clientelism

After having discussed particular cases, this section develops an ideal-type of clientelism that abstracts from these and other types of clientelism. It provides a foundation for the discussion of the reasons why particular policies are likely to result from this political structure, and what their economic implications are. The outline presented here provides an overview and leaves the discussion of the main contentious issues to the following chapter.

2.2.1 Basic Structural Assumptions

The actors in the framework that will be employed here consist of patrons, brokers, clients, and non-clients. The patrons are the politicians in power at the national level, the brokers local politicians connected to these patrons, and the clients[14] correspond to the supporters of these local politicians. The non-clients are those individuals who are unconnected to a politician in power at a particular moment in time.[15]

An extremely simplified political structure is assumed. There is a set of high level politicians who control the government. Middle level brokers are assumed to act as agents of clients and patrons, as a neutral link. There is no local or regional government.[16]

The relationship between a patron and a client is exclusively a political one in which material benefits are traded for political support. This 'dyadic contract' is still to some degree undefined, involving vaguely specified obligations, where there is a general expectation of some future return whose 'exact nature is not stipulated in advance' (Blau 1964, 93).[17]

All actors maximize their expected net income and assume that everybody else does the same. Banfield's amoral familism may serve as an the archetype: individuals maximize the advantage of the nuclear family and assume that all others do likewise (1958, 83). Hence people will not concern themselves with public affairs or with furthering the interest of a group or community except in so far as it contributes to their private advantage. As officeholders they do not identify themselves with the purposes of the organization for whom they work and will exploit it for private advantage if they can get away with it. The public assumes that whatever group is in power is self-serving and corrupt, appeals to public interest and ideology are regarded as hypocritical, and the law will be disregarded when there is no reason to fear punishment (85–101).

All income flowing into the system originates from the government. It may take two forms: government expenditure, or what will be called 'privileges'. Government expenditure corresponds to the tax revenue derived from clients and non-clients plus government borrowing.[18] The aggregate net income to patrons from this source is the government expenditure minus what is transferred to clients and non-clients.

Individual clients attempt to attract as much government spending as they can, and to pay the smallest possible amount of taxes. Patrons determine the level and the nature of taxation, and at any level of government revenue, they will attempt to keep as much as possible for themselves.[19] Only that amount of government revenue just sufficient to keep them in power will therefore be transferred to clients and non-clients. One would expect a patron to leave politics if the amount spent on clients exceeds the amount of government revenue received.

Resources have to be transferred to non-clients to avoid total disaffection and possibly open revolt. In the case of Spain at the turn of the century, for example, the fact that the law was twisted by the *cacique* does not mean that it was always infringed to the disadvantage of the poor. Patrons 'often feared disturbances far more than the wrath of the local rich, and often bought social peace through the imposition upon the latter of decisions favoring the former' (Romero-Maura 1977, 61).

The second source of income is material benefits which do not involve government spending: what have been called 'privileges'. Privileges are property rights granted by the government which allow the owner to earn economic rent. Examples are the transfer of assets to individuals below market value, or the granting of income-earning opportunities such as licenses which generate incomes above opportunity cost for their owners.

The total amount of benefits can be divided into individual (or private) and general (or collective) benefits. Private benefits are specific inducements that can be offered to one person while being withheld from others (Banfield and Wilson 1963, 102, 115); collective benefits are general inducements that 'can be given only to all members of a given group; if one gets it, all must get it by nature of the case' (103).

This categorization takes Olson's distinction between collective and private goods as a starting point. Unfortunately, Olson equated collective goods with the public goods of economic theory (1965, 13–15). However, collective goods as defined here[20] are a much broader category, of which public goods are a subset. Public goods have two characteristics: their *physical* nature is such that if they are provided for one person everyone else can consume them too at no additional cost (non-rivalness); and people cannot be excluded from consuming them (non-excludability). Typical examples of goods close to pure public goods are defense expenditure and radio waves.

Collective goods are defined not by their physical characteristics but by the nature of their provision. As long as everybody who fulfils certain criteria receives them they are considered collective goods. The category therefore includes not only public goods, but also all goods distributed according to bureaucratic criteria. In the latter case, individuals who fulfil the criteria cannot be excluded from consuming a particular good, not because it is physically impossible but because it infringes laws and regulations. On the part of the individual consuming it, the good has all the characteristics of non-rivalness, as everybody who fulfils the bureaucratic criteria will have access to it.

There are two implications. The first is that some collective goods can be turned into private goods. Goods which are collective goods by virtue of their bureaucratic allocation process can become private goods if this process is abandoned, and allocation according to patronage principles takes over. For example, the provision of health facilities to everybody who needs them is a collective good, but if special connections are needed to access it, it becomes a private good. Similarly, the existence of government employment in a locality constitutes a collective good if jobs are allocated according to specific rules; the collective benefit turns into a private benefit, however, if patrons allocate these jobs to their supporters according to their own discretion.[21]

The second implication is that patrons have an incentive to favor private over collective goods. The latter are an inefficient means of remunerating clients for their political support, as each member of the class benefits, clients and non-clients alike. This has obvious implications for the allocation of resources: one would expect that collective goods would be underprovided, and that patrons would soften bureaucratic allocation, thereby converting collective into private goods, an issue we will discuss at greater length in a later chapter.

A clientelist political system may be competitive or non-competitive.[22] If the system is competitive, and regular elections are held, patrons compete for the vote of their constituents. The vote is taken to be the political support expected from the client, for which a tangible return is expected. Given our assumptions, clients will vote for the patron who provides the greatest net-benefits. As soon as the patron fails to perform, his followers drift away and attach themselves to a different patron.[23] Like Scott's machine, clientelism bases its authority largely on its distributive activity.

For a client, the task of choosing a patron is not an easy one. He has to assess the probability that a patron will retain or gain power, and the amount of resources coming his way in consequence. If competitive elections are held, the task may become daunting: the client has to estimate first the probability that the patron will win the election; second, the probability of his belonging to the ruling faction if he does win; and third, what amount of resources he will be able to attract and how much will be transferred to his client.

2.2.2 Terms of Trade

The terms of trade are defined as the proportion of material benefits - goods and services in the main - the collectivity of clients manage to extract from the patrons. An improvement in the clients' terms of trade means that they collectively receive a larger proportion of benefits relative to the patrons. The terms of trade will depend in the main on the how vital the patrons' services are, to what degree they are able to monopolize these benefits, and their need for clients (Scott 1977b, 131).

The more vital the benefits to the clients, or in other words the greater the utility of the goods and services which the patron can offer, the less income the patron has to part with in order to gain the necessary political support to retain power. A client who relies on a patron for both protection of life and property and of subsistence insurance has little negotiating power. A decrease in banditry, therefore, is likely to improve the bargaining position of the client and his terms of trade.

The terms of trade for clients improve if there are alternative sources for the services the patron provides. An increase in the client's income may open up the possibility of crop insurance or improved access to credit facilities, thereby reducing the need for subsistence insurance offered by the patron. Better access to government services, perhaps as a result of increased literacy, better transport, or a better geographic distribution of government facilities, reduces the client's dependence on the patron. Scott takes the example of improved access to these resources in Southeast Asia, where patrons who once dominated 'now faced competitors who might be local administrators of state welfare and loan programs, teachers in new secular schools, a local trader or businessman, or the resident manager of a foreign-owned plantation' (1977b, 138).[24]

Scott's conclusion that the independence of the clients increases with the number of alternative sources of supply, and therefore with competition among suppliers, is of course true only if everything else remains the same. The client may have more options to choose particular patrons for getting particular things, but on the other hand he may need more things. Cypriot villagers now require licenses and permits if they want to import vehicles, run taxis and buses, sink boreholes, plant certain crops or transfer land. They need support in legal proceedings, in applications for scholarships or for exemptions from military service. Hence it 'would only be helpful to say that he now had more choice if what he once needed and now needs were the same', whereas now he needs new things, 'has other *new* things demanded of him, so his area of dependency on external decisions has increased, in some senses' (Loizos 1977, 131).

Political competition will affect the terms of trade: unable to depend on outright coercion, and faced with competition, the electoral patron knows he must generally offer his clients better terms than his rivals if he hopes to maintain his hold over local power (Scott 1977b, 140). In a perfectly competitive system politicians would have to spend all resources they attract from the government on their clients if they were to avoid being outbid by a competitor. On the other hand, if the political system is non-competitive, there is little or no incentive to redistribute public resources below the 'charmed circle of intimates who happen to be on the receiving end of the line' (Lemarchand 1981, 25). As the political arena shrinks, clientelist networks atrophy, and social exchange frequently takes the form of unrestrained corruption and extortion (25).[25]

The terms of trade are likely to depend on political stability and the predictability of elections. The point may be illustrated by the case of a member of parliament who deliberates the trade-off between present and future income. The current income derived from government sources may be allocated either to private use or to supporters in order to win the next elections. The greater the probability of losing the next election, the greater is the incentive to keep all income to himself. This is obviously the optimal course of action if the probability of losing the next election approaches certainty. In a politically unstable environment there will be a relatively large number of politicians with a small probability of being returned, whose optimal course of action is to enrich themselves. Ironically, this may mean that increased political competition may lead to a worsening in the terms of trade of clients, if this increase is associated with a greater fragmentation of political parties and more uncertainty about the prospect of re-election. In a highly competitive but politically fragmented system such as in Papua New Guinea, where politicians win elections frequently with the support of only a very small proportion of the electorate and often with a very small margin of votes, the incentive to provide benefits to clients with a view to winning the next election is likely to be lower than in a less competitive and less fragmented system.

It has been said that the benefits from the exchange in subjective terms are larger for the client than for the patron. 'A client, in this sense, is someone who has entered an unequal exchange relation in which he is unable to reciprocate fully. A debt of obligation binds him to the patron' (Scott 1977b, 125). The reason is that 'the patron often is in a position to supply unilaterally goods and services which the potential client and his family need for their survival and well-being. A locally dominant landlord, for example, is frequently the major source of protection, of security, of employment, of access to arable land or to education, and of food in bad times' (1977b, 125).

The argument falters in its exclusive focus on the direct exchange between patron and client, without taking account of indirect effects. In fact the patron benefits not only from the services of the clients but also from the revenue derived from the government by virtue of being a patron. But - perhaps most importantly - political influence derived from the support of clients may well secure the patron's economic survival. A particular landowner, for example, may be a landowner only because of the political system which perpetuates that class. Patrons are undoubtedly the main beneficiaries of the system.

The terms of trade, therefore, will be more favorable to the client the less vital the goods and services the patron has to offer, the better the alternative access to these services, the greater the competition among patrons, and the smaller the uncertainty surrounding political processes. In the ordinary course of events patrons will be able to direct a significant amount of the flow of benefits generated by the government into their own pockets, and so will be the main beneficiaries of the system.

2.2.3 Beliefs and Ideology

The approach taken here follows the New Political Economy tradition, where the individual is the unit of analysis and individuals rationally pursue their material self-interest (Grindle 1991, 45). Political action then becomes entirely a function of the flow of material resources. This view conflicts with Krueger's contention discussed in the previous chapter, that political action by governments is caused by their desire to improve welfare and their beliefs about the means to achieve such an end. Krueger's ideal account of policy choice, as we have also seen, fails to account for why a particular set of ideas is chosen over competing ideas.

This does not mean that there is no role for beliefs in a clientelist account of policy determination. Very few people will be found who state that 'I am a greedy person and want all the money I can extract from the government'. Such demands are not only bad politics, but conflict with most people's sense of dignity or self-respect. 'In political life, economic claims are seldom presented as simple demands for more; they are usually couched in terms of "economic justice"' (Fukuyama 1992, 173). However, people have a great capacity to find reasons why it is just that they obtain or ought to obtain certain rewards. Like the businesspeople at the helm of large private Western enterprises who come to believe that their remuneration of millions of dollars is nothing more than their due, patrons and clients alike begin to think that they are striving after just rewards, and that therefore they are engaged in a meritorious pursuit. Political behavior, therefore, may still be seen as simply a function of power and wealth, and demands for justice as a derivative of it, without independent status, degenerating often into an only thinly veiled justification of selfish pursuits.

2.3   Institutional Repercussions

What kind of political institutions are likely to emerge, given the structural assumptions of clientelism? There will be a tendency for political life to be dominated by factionalism, a low level of legitimacy, and weak institutionalization, all of which contribute to the adoption of an inward-looking development strategy.

2.3.1 *Patron-Client Networks and Factionalism*

A faction is usually defined as a 'loosely ordered group in conflict with a similar group over a particular issue' (Boissevin 1977, 280), whose members are recruited by a leader without a clear single principle of recruitment except allegiance to the leader, and, partly as a consequence, lack the permanence of corporate groups (Nicholas 1977, 58). Are clientele networks factions?

The basis of recruitment of networks corresponds to that of factions, and the nature of the membership is one of the causes of the impermanence of networks. Because recruitment is not based on any similarities in background such as sex, age, religion, occupation or social class, cohesive attitudes are unlikely to prevail among networks. Moreover, networks are unstable because they are predicated on personal relationship which has to be continually reinforced, and may well be severed if there is discontent. In addition, shifting dispositions and magnetisms of ambitious men in a region may induce fluctuations in factions, and the death of an important patron 'can become a regional political trauma: the death undermines the personally cemented faction, the group dissolves in whole or in part, and people re-group finally around rising pivotal big-men' (Sahlins 1977, 223).

Factions imply factionalism, as conflict is the '*raison d'être* of factional membership' (Nicholas 1977, 58) and the concept of a single faction is a contradiction in terms. In principle, of course, one could imagine an all-encompassing patron-client network which dominates politics where factionalism is absent. However, the necessary discipline may be difficult to impose. Hence although 'Senegalese politics is dominated by one political party' which, on paper, 'looks like a hierarchical, disciplined, and ideologically-oriented political party', 'little central control is possible, discipline is nearly non-existent, and ideology consists of catch words that have little demonstrable effect on action' (Foltz 1977, 244). All this leads to rampant factionalism: rare is the electoral district which does not have two or more competing, and often bitterly rival, clientelistic leaders with their followings attaching themselves to various national politicians (244). In a multi-party state factionalism is hardly avoidable, as in the Philippines, where 'political leaders wander in and out of parties with their personal followers in tow, feeling no strong obligation, and being under no real pressure, to support their party mates' (Landé 1977b, 87). Accordingly a clientelist political system, at least in the ordinary course of events, will comprise numerous competing clientele networks.[26]

A patron-client network therefore is a faction, a loosely ordered group of a leader's personal following organized to compete with other factions.

2.3.2 Legitimacy and Institutionalization

Clientelism, as opposed to Weberian patrimonialism,[27] is a type of regime which lacks legitimacy because authority is based exclusively on the amount of material resources transferred to clients and non-clients and thus has no other sources from which to draw legitimacy, such as tradition or a widely shared ideology.

As Weber pointed out in the case of the relationship between an authoritarian ruler and his staff, '*Purely* material interests and calculations of advantages as the basis of solidarity between the chief and his administrative staff result, in this as in other connexions, in a relatively unstable situation' (1968, 213). Weber's case can easily be extended to rulers and their subjects generally. Moreover, the existence of widespread corruption is likely to undermine legitimacy even further.[28] A modern clientelist regime operates in an environment where rules and regulation are at least nominally in force. The neo-patrimonial ruler may habitually disregard these rules and regulations, but he is unable to dismiss this 'modern' tradition itself and revert to patrimonialism.

> Patronage may not always and necessarily be illegal or corrupt, and it does have its own pride and morality; but though it may despise the official morality as hypocritical, fraudulent, or effeminate, it nevertheless knows that it is not itself *the* official morality (Gellner 1977, 3).

A government, by disregarding constitutional and bureaucratic rules and turning public offices into prebends, becomes illegitimate government.

The lack of legitimacy and the high level of factionalism are two of the causes which undermine the stability of institutional arrangements. A political system unable to generate legitimate rule is likely to be viewed as weak and impermanent.[29] Thus basic institutions are constantly under review, both government and opposition perpetually discuss experiments with new structures. This highly politicized state may be contrasted with a situation where 'depoliticization, or institutionalization, has closed off certain areas from political contention, through a structure of power so overwhelming that it precludes fundamental questioning for long periods of time, or through agreement or apathy so profound that the questions are never raised' (Chalmers 1977, 41–42).

The lack of permanence of political institutions means that there are no permanent rules of the political game. In an institutionalized state there is a final decision-making process which is routinized and to the extent possible freed from the possibilities or reordering, and the actors concentrate on the mechanical application of some device (such as vote counting). In the politicized state, however, such a mechanism, 'if it exists, is in effect only one of the instruments shaping the outcome' (1977, 26). Thus in such a politicized process 'at every crisis, and to some extent for every decision, the actors are called on to determine the way in which the system will operate' (25).

2.3.3 Expansion of the Networks and State Autonomy

Two outcomes are likely if the future institutional arrangements are continually in doubt and factional competition rampant: an unrelenting pressure to expand clientele networks into civil society, and a low level of 'state autonomy'.

The volatility of the rules of the political game makes building majorities difficult, since the definition of what constitutes a majority is in constant flux. If the political class wants to be certain of the minimum necessary support to maintain power it has to build 'maximum winning coalitions'.

> Political leaders are driven to build their political support in ways which ensure the largest possible base ... (not a "minimum winning coalition"). In the politicized state the chief executive must constantly build and rebuild his political support to meet the threat of attempts to overthrow him. His support must be exceptionally broad and flexible (Chalmers 1977, 31).

Integrating social groups into the coalition means, in a clientelist world, integrating into the patron-client networks those individuals who head major social institutions from which political threats might emanate. These institutions usually include the armed forces, the bureaucracy, trade unions, tribal unions, cooperative societies and so forth (31-32; Sandbrook 1972a). Thus the lack of institutionalization provides a rationale for the colonization by patron-client networks of politically important social institutions.

Politicization and factionalism, reflecting a fragmented political system, are likely to affect the degree of state autonomy, or the extent to which states 'as organizations controlling territories and people may formulate and pursue goals that are not simply reflective of the demands or interests of social groups, classes, or society' (Skocpol 1982, 4). The degree of state autonomy in a clientelist system is likely to be low. In a democratic regime elections, coupled with factional competition, are sufficient to ensure that the government pursues goals reflecting the interests of clients to a significant degree. In an authoritarian regime, the assumption of factionalism and institutional uncertainty has a similar effect; the high degree of politicization forces the incumbents continually to respond to pressure from different competing factions and to secure their power by continually building and rebuilding alliances with potential competitors. Hence on closer acquaintance what looks like a highly autonomous authoritarian state, for example Senegal, may in fact reveal itself to be an amalgam of competing factions organized along clientelist lines, and highly responsive to the demands of major sectors of society.[30]

2.3.4 Inward-looking Development Strategy

We set out to explain the emergence and persistence of a failed inward-looking development strategy: the regulation of the private and the expansion of the public sector. Clientelism, when accompanied by full blown factionalism, a low level of legitimacy and institutionalization and a low level of state autonomy, generates intense pressures to provide revenue to patrons and clients and is likely to foster the growth of the government administration itself. One of the most coveted benefits has proved to be positions in the public administration. Overstaffing, then, becomes a consequence of the insistence by individual clients on finding employment in public service,[31] and of politicians' need to accommodate their demands to shore up political support.

The relentless pressure to increase the amount of rent available for distribution to patrons and clients provides a rationale for the widely observed transfer of productive capacity from the private to the public sector and the setting up of new government business ventures. The gains to patrons and clients from integrating government enterprises into their networks are considerable. The resources of the nationalized firms are now available to increase their income and their political support: board of directors' positions become open to politicians and their followers and less important clients can be appointed further down the hierarchy;[32] suppliers can be chosen not only for the quality of their wares but also for their political sympathies or their personal connections; and the price of output can be manipulated to suit political ends.

The overregulation of the private sector is another probable consequence of the relentless search for particularistic benefits. A system of licensing and quotas that protects firms from domestic and foreign competition and provides selected access to foreign exchange adds to the rent-earning opportunities of patrons and clients. Import-substituting industrialization becomes a particular case of the general tendency towards rent-generating regulations. Indeed it is seldom observed in isolation, but in conjunction with a system of licensing that excludes the entry of domestic competitors and thus assures the perpetuation of the rent accruing to the monopolist.

2.4 Conclusion

The chapter has located a number of forces that are able to generate failed inward-looking development policies in the structure of politics, or in a particular kind of political clientelism, at least where it is accompanied by factionalism, endemic corruption, politicization, and a low degree of legitimacy of government and of state autonomy.

The argument does not preclude that different kinds of clientelism may result in export promotion. Thus it is not applicable to cases of oligarchic rule based on land ownership (as in Latin America at some stages of its history). There, clientelism has indeed been associated with outward-orientation (Mouzelis 1994). Nor does the thesis imply that all inward-looking development policies, or even all the failed inward-looking development policies of the kind described in the previous chapter, are a consequence of political clientelism.

In order to establish a relationship between political structure and development policy the method was adopted to examine the behavior of politicians in a particular hypothetical environment. This does not mean that a clientelist analysis reduces politics 'to the interplay of patron-client networks' (Moore 1977, 258). Political clientelism as constructed here is an ideal-type, and political reality is never accurately described by such concepts as clientelism, corporatism, or pluralism. Nevertheless, it is useful to ask what kind of economic decisions are likely to eventuate in an environment where the ideal-type prevails in its pure form.

But even where the behavioral assumptions that were employed do not generally apply and institutional arrangements are not accurately depicted by the ideal-type, they may contain an approximation to reality to some degree. It is then likely that the implications that were developed apply to some degree too: that corruption is partly a political phenomenon, that economic policies of authoritarian and democratic regimes are unlikely to differ, that policy failures are related to the nature of the political system, or, more specifically, that politicians adopt an inward-looking development strategy and persist in pursuing it to the detriment of the society because it is in their interest to do so.[33]

Thus a clientelist analysis cannot be dismissed simply because neither in Tunisia nor Egypt 'are political decisions reducible to an interplay between the presidential patron and his clients, together with their personal following' (Moore 1977, 260). What is true is that the account is more applicable in some contexts - notably Sub-saharan Africa and some East Asian countries[34] - and less in others. But it is believed that clientelism and its institutional accompaniments are sufficiently widespread and have some relevance in explaining policy-making in a large proportion of Third World countries.

Notes:

1.   Patrons and clients may be entire households. In Silverman's study of a Central Italian community, the landlord became patron not to an individual but to an entire household ... On the other hand, the wife of the landlord became *la padrona*, and she was expected to adopt the role of patroness, especially toward of the peasant family' (Silverman 1977, 297).
2.   Patron-client clusters are not groups in the conventional sense. They lack common characteristics separating them from other groups, thus do not have common interests in the conventional sense, and clients may not interact with each other.
3.   Networks constitute 'quasi-groups' in Mayer's sense (1977, 43).
4.   Another classical example is that between a moneylender and his debtor, where the moneylender transforms the economic leverage into political power. Loizos speculates that in the 1930s in Cyprus the economic leverage available was used in this way (Loizos 1977, 117; see also Attalides, 1977).
5.   This description is based on Schmidt (1977, 305) and Silverman (1977, 296).
6.   An even more 'traditional' form of patron-client exchange existed before the agricultural communities were integrated into the nation state. In that situation, the client relied on the landlord often for physical protection,

but on the other hand the role of mediator to the wider community was absent. For example: 'It was only after the community became incorporated into a complex nation [i.e. Italy], a nation which made demands upon and offered opportunities to individuals and which required extensive contact between the local and the national system, that the dominant features of "traditional" ... patronage emerged' (Silverman 1977, 299).

7. 'One Colleverdese women explained her economically advantageous relationship with he patroness with the statement, "We are old friends, so we always ask each other for favors"' (Silverman 1977, 298).

8. Known as *compadrazgo*.

9. Wolf, in his famous definition (1956, 1075) referred to the 'brokers' as persons who stand guard over the critical junctures or synapses of relationships which connect the local system to the larger whole.

10. Quoted from Lemarchand (1977, 109).

11. As Malloy wrote of the ruling party in Bolivia in the 1950s: 'Behind the formal institutional facade, the de facto structural reality was a proliferation of patron-client networks that radiated outward from the party leadership factions into sectoral and regional groupings' (1977, 470).

12. See also Bienen (1971); Tamarkin (1978); Campbell (1978, 86).

13. A Chicago party boss disagrees with this, however. 'I never take leaflets or mention issues or conduct rallies in my precinct. After all, this is a question of personal friendship between me and my neighbors' (quoted by Banfield and Wilson 1963, 117).

14. Depending on the social situation, it is more convenient to think of clients as households instead of individuals. The ideal-type excludes, however, the possibility that clients are corporate groups, such as the one described by Wolf where, 'among corporately organized Indians in Middle America, the individual can approach a patron - hacienda owner or political power figure - only as a member of the group, and the patron then acts as power broker relating the entire group to the institutional framework outside' (Wolf 1977, 175).

15. They are called non-clients even if they are part of a patron-client network not connected to people in power.

16. For a study of locally generated patronage opportunities in Greece see Campbell (1977).

17. It can be equally well described as an 'implicit contract' of economic theory, where mutual obligations are not stipulated explicitly and remain to some degree undefined.

18. This assumes that patrons do not pay any taxes.

19. Brian Barry has criticized the implications that politicians are a 'collection of rogues', suggesting that at national level politicians in democratic countries are motivated 'either by policy concerns or service of a personal kind to their constituents' (1985, 301). Even if Barry's

argument is perfectly true, it may still be the case that in practice the requirement to retain power, and pressure from relatives and friends, override altruistic concerns. It is for this reason that corrupt politicians frequently complain about the system which forces them to act against the public interest.

20. In the sense Olson uses it in his practical reasoning.

21. Romero-Maura describes Spain at the turn of the century where 'centralization, in the context of the liberal, Napoleonic State, had created goods of which there was a cheap and inexhaustible supply, and which were often vital to the citizen: decisions by the administration, constitutive, sanctioning, or whatever. These had to be distributed, and their distribution could be controlled. Authorization, certificates, court and police sentences, exemptions, and the like, were as important to the cacique, if not more so, than jobs and other resources allocated to clients and non-clients' (1977, 56).

22. For a study of authoritarian clientelism see Waterbury (1970).

23. This is one distinction from traditional clientelism, where political support is based on traditional patterns of deference and is not exclusively a function of concrete economic benefits. The difference should not be overstated. For example, even the traditional ties between the Senegalese religious leaders and their followers cannot prevent that those 'clients who have been rewarded soon lose their sense of gratitude' (Cruise O'Brien 1975, 165). Similarly, if the patron consistently fails to deliver, followers 'may (and do) change their allegiance to a more favorably placed local leader: no saint can afford a record of failure in his intrigues with the national or local government authorities' (177).

24. See Weingrod (1968) for the example of Sardinia.

25. Hence in those rare instances in Africa 'where electoral pressures and party competition are still in existence, the scope of patronage politics is relatively extensive, as in Senegal and Zimbabwe; on the other hand, where electoral competition is nonexistent or elections resemble plebiscites, as in Zaïre, patronage hardly goes beyond the confines of the presidential clique' (Lemarchand 1988, 155).

26. President Banda of Malawi, however, succeeded in virtually eliminating all factionalism and totally subordinating all would-be leaders (Jackson and Rosberg 1982, 49).

27. For a detailed discussion see the following chapter.

28. Partly because it affects the voting process. Joseph concludes that 'since the operation of Nigerian elections is susceptible to manipulation, victory will go to those best able to outperform their opponents in skulduggery' (Joseph 1987, 156).

29. A scenario described by Chalmers in the Latin American context (1977, 25).

30. Grindle distinguishes between 'society-centred models' where policy is 'driven by societal interests', and the state is a more or less neutral arena (1991, 52), and 'state-centred' models where policies reflect the preferences of politicians. The model which has been developed here is society-centred.

31. This presupposes, of course, that the employment conditions in the public sector contain an element of rent. This does of course not mean that the actual wage has to be above the market wage. Rather the total of the benefits associated with employment, such as access to credit, perquisites, and income from extortion and bribes, relative to the work performed are above the remuneration elsewhere.

32. In Sicily in 1973, of the 414 executive positions all but a handful were political appointees. 'These positions have been widely used by political figures to engage in rampant patronage hiring as well as favoritism and corruption in buying and marketing practices' (Chubb 1982, 118).

33. Thus no precise causal weight can be attributed to clientelism as a determinant of actual policy choice, which must depend on the historical circumstances of the particular case at hand. In reality not only may clientelist structures have other consequences than those which lead to inward-looking development, but in addition no political system is exclusively clientelist and thus other forces are operating at the same time.

34. E.g. the Philippines and Papua New Guinea.

3   Clientelism Compared

The chapter explores some of the implications of the clientelist model, evaluates some of the criticisms leveled against it, and compares it with different political structures. It argues that clientelism may thrive in very different circumstances: regimes may be authoritarian or democratic, civilian or military, espousing socialist or capitalist ideologies. Clientelism has a number of features which distinguish it from other analytical constructs commonly employed. In particular, class analysis is only partly compatible with clientelism, the state-society interaction of clientelism is distinct from that of pluralism and corporatism, clientelism's lack of legitimacy contrasts with patrimonialism, and it goes beyond the concept of personal rule by not being tied to authoritarian rule, but compatible with both autocracy and democracy.

3.1   Clientelism and Ideology

Clientelism, as has been shown, shares Mill's dictum that 'men will, in the majority of cases, prefer their own interest to that of others, when the two are placed in competition'. 'Whoever denies this', Mill continues, 'denies the principle on which, it is most certain, he himself habitually acts, when the interest at stake happens to be his own' (1835, 19). That individuals' political actions are governed by self interest, and more specifically, material incentives, has been under attack since time immemorial, an attack which recently took the form of explaining political behavior in terms of core beliefs.[1] Whether the self-interest assumption is widely misleading and ought therefore to be abandoned is ultimately an empirical matter. Nevertheless, some of the claims about the weakness of the self-interest assumption are clearly beside the point.

The fact, for example, that individuals claim that their political actions are motivated by injustice or self-defense or are a reaction to repression does not refute the self-interest assumption, because such concerns may directly reflect material self-interest.[2] In particular, 'injustice' might simply indicate personal dissatisfaction with one's position in the distributive scale. Thus the existence of such concerns does not to show that to restrict 'our attention to economic motivation is to receive a partial and distorted picture' (Anderson 1990, 107).[3]

Alternatively, two sets of political actions are specified, one which a social scientist thinks is in the interest of a category of people, and one which is thought to contradict their interests. If individuals prefer the latter, the self-interest axiom is deemed to be refuted.[4] This, however, is by no means the case. The self-interest axiom states that people maximize *expected* benefits, an assessment which is inherently subjective, and may not conform to that of the social scientist. The issue matters a great deal if account is taken of the long term, when it becomes exceedingly difficult to determine what is and what is not in one's self-interest.[5] The self-interest assumption is only misplaced if individuals consciously, deliberately and actively[6] support political actions which they perceive as opposing their self-interest, or, in the more narrow materialistic version,[7] are unambiguously perceived to reduce the material welfare of themselves and that of their children.

Self-interested rational agents take account of expected future benefits; past benefits influence behavior only in so far as they provide a guide for assessing the nature of future benefits. The self-interest axiom establishes no presumption that 'those workers who have benefited materially under the existing regime should be more likely to extend political support to the established political institutions than the less fortunate' (Davis and Speer 1991, 325). The statement errs not only because it confuses current with future benefits, but in addition because subjective satisfaction with a particular development may be quite unrelated to actual changes in income.

The self-interest axiom is supported by a large body of evidence to the effect that ideas are relatively unimportant in at least some contexts. For example, Powell observes that in Italy both the Communists and the Christian Democrats were frustrated by the manner in which the clientelist mentality of the peasantry thwarted their policy and doctrinal preferences (1970, 422). To take another example, a member of legislative assembly in India is not seen mainly as the representative of a party with a policy which commends itself to the voters, 'not even a representative who will watch over their interests when policies are being framed, but rather a man who will intervene in the implementation of policy, and in the ordinary day-to-day administration. He is there to divert the benefits in the direction of his constituents, to help individuals to get what they want out of the Administration, and to give them a hand when they get into trouble with officials. This is the meaning which the ordinary villager ... attach[es] to the phrase "serving the people"' (Bailey 1963, 25).

Ideology is generally believed to have been foreign to those engaged in traditional machine politics. The machine depends crucially upon the optimal mix of inducements that are both specific and material. The machine, therefore, is apolitical, interested only in income and distributing it to those who run the machine and work for it. 'Political principle is foreign to it' (Banfield and Wilson 1963, 115–116). Similar observations have been made in Africa: thus ideology is thought to have played a quite subordinate role in Nigerian party politics (Joseph 1987, 36).[8]

There is little doubt that the choice of ideology was often guided by highly opportunistic considerations. It is true that Nyerere of Tanzania is usually referred to as a prime example of a person whose actions are influenced by core beliefs, but he seems to be the exception rather than the rule, at least among African rulers. Perhaps at the other extreme we find Ngouabi of Congo-Brazzaville, who 'not only mastered the jargon but also the Byzantine intricacies of developing a radical dialectic while holding centrist positions and purging the true militants in the political system' (Decalo 1976, 164).

Indirect evidence of an instrumental use of beliefs is provided if members of government acquire their creed only shortly before or after coming to power, if the ideology which has been espoused is *ad hoc* and does not follow received lines of doctrine, or if the policies which are actually implemented have weak ideological foundations. On these grounds, one must assume that false consciousness was a major factor in many African socialist regimes, because throughout the 1970s African military juntas declared themselves socialist after they came to power[9] and the leading figures of the new regimes generally had no previous record of Marxist convictions.[10] Unsurprisingly, their commitment to socialism was often doubtful,[11] their programs eclectic,[12] and the results of the actions of the regime hardly in accordance with the publicly espoused aims.[13] Opportunistic use of ideology, therefore, does seem to be widespread among politicians, at least on the African continent.[14] Still, even in this rigid framework ideology has some uses. It might serve, for example, as a signal indicating the distributive bent of the government. People may believe they will benefit, individually or as a group, from the implementation of the policies they associate with a particular ideological outlook. For example, socialism provided Ratsiraka of Madagascar with the answer to the question as to 'how to revive a demoralized and fearful peasantry, a worn-out economy lacking in inspiring perspective, and a morose and discouraged political class' (Young 1982a, 58). Ideology, then, by containing implicit or explicit promises, may be used to bolster political support. Moreover, the choice of ideology might be designed to attract economic and military aid (Jowitt 1979, 134).

If the rigid framework is relaxed somewhat, conventional uses for ideology come to the fore. Ideology may be limited purely to manipulating symbols in a general way, for example by affecting the self-perception of a community through increasing the self-respect of its members. Typically politicians promote real or mythological interpretations of history which glorify the past, or proclaim the renaissance of a real or imagined national culture. Attempts at such cultural redefinition range from Senghor's negritude to Mobutu's authenticity. The effect of these attempts to increase political support through the manipulation of symbols is likely to be limited. The example of Zaïre is typical: if authenticity in Zaïre initially had genuine resonance, the reality of clientelism in due course undermined its effects (Young and Turner 1985, 220). Alternatively, an ideology may serve as a means of internal differentiation, offering a new elite a means of justifying its authority and power (Jowitt 1979, 141).

It is unlikely, however, that the use of ideology will be limited to the manipulation of symbols without narrow political purpose. In particular, one would expect those credos to be promoted which justify clientelist exchange relationships and denigrate practices which inhibit the working and expansion of clientelism. One of the practices which inhibits the flourishing of clientelist exchanges is bureaucratic allocation, and clientelist politicians therefore have an incentive to denigrate 'bureaucracies' and 'bureaucrats' by contrasting those alien 'anonymous' procedures to the 'personal' traditional practices of a mythical 'African' or 'Melanesian' way.

In the economic sphere a crude kind of economic nationalism prevalent after independence, the reverberations of which can still be felt today, was another way to feed clientelist exchanges. The widespread agreement after independence that nominal political independence had to be supplemented by economic independence (Young and Turner 1985, 209) served admirably to justify the increase in the power of patronage and the acquisition of wealth through the takeover of expatriate and foreign-owned firms, their nationalization, and the expansion of state regulation of the economy.

As ideology is purely instrumental, clientelism is indifferent to socialism and capitalism which may both serve as a structure in which it can flourish. The main instrument for maintaining political support is patronage, and the vast expanse of the state sector of a socialist regime provides a fertile breeding ground for clientelist relations. The ruling elite may even anchor its economic dominance through socialistic policies: upon attainment of independence, the first task of the newly-installed bureaucratic class in Mali 'was to create an extensive public sector so as to economically anchor its politically dominant position, basing its power on collective, rather than private ownership of the means of production' (Martin 1976, 44). Alternatively, in a capitalist regime a policy of indigenization may serve the same purpose, having the added advantage of turning patrons and the important clients into owners of businesses. Additional patronage in a nominally capitalist environment may be created by intensified regulation of the economy and the creation of parastatals. Even more dramatic is the example of Mobutu, who, when faced with the manifest failure of a disastrous Africanization campaign, chose to force the pace by announcing that the larger businesses were to be placed in the hands of the state. On this occasion, the political class entered the scene as 'delegates-general' to manage the newly nationalized firms (Young 1982a, 249).

If it is indeed true that ideology is unimportant, one would expect that labels such as capitalism and socialism would be of little importance in a clientelist environment. Thus where socialism prevailed, from Sukarno's Indonesia to the Ba'ath regime in Iraq and the African socialist regimes,[15] its main and sometimes only distinctive characteristics were the forcible acquisition of the larger private enterprises and the enlargement of the state sector in other ways. However, the extension of government control over the economy was not limited to socialist regimes, as is shown, for example, by the 'strong statist thrust of Ivorian policy' (192). If policies are unlikely to be much affected by ideology beyond perhaps a greater degree of state ownership in socialist countries, it is hardly surprising that their performances are not significantly different in terms of state capacity, the level of equality they engender and economic growth. Thus Young fails to discern an extensive overlap of patterns of state capacity and ideology (323). Even in terms of egalitarianism, the performance of socialist regimes is ambiguous (307). Rural income does not seem to have have benefited from socialism if taxation is taken into account (304–5), and as to education, 'what stands out from available statistical information is the absence of [a] correlation between ideology and performance' (305). Finally, ideological complexion does not seem to have been strongly related to economic growth. True, economic growth has eluded the Afro-Marxist states, but they nonetheless often performed better than their sundry predecessors (300), and relative successes and conspicuous failures can be found both in the populist socialist camp[16] and among those who favored market economies (301).[17] The absence of a connection between ideology and economic growth conforms to our main thesis that clientelism as a political system affects growth independent of the ideology of patrons and clients. Hence the nature and degree of clientelism may be a better indicator for the growth performance of a country than the regime's official ideology.[18]

In summary: the assumption that political action is determined by material incentives, does seem to be defensible as a first approximation, at least in some contexts. Ideology then becomes purely instrumental, perhaps providing a conscious or unconscious justification of the actions of politicians and their clients, or a method to shore up political support. The absence of a relationship between growth performance and ideology gives at least some credence to the view that ideology is not an independent factor determining growth.

3.2   Clientelism, Corporatism and Pluralism

It will be argued that clientelism assumes a very different organizational structure and process of interactions from corporatism and pluralism. An analysis based on corporatism or pluralism assumes a process of bargaining among interest groups and the state over collective benefits for the generality of the members of the group, whereas in a clientelist environment interest groups are concerned with not collective but individual benefits. Moreover, as organizations become permeated by clientele networks dominated by politicians, they lose their independence.

Corporatism assumes that corporations and the state are permanently linked by a process of negotiated exchange, and that the state typically invests the corporation with the right to represent exclusively a particular group in society. The members of the group may acquire certain privileges which convey economic rent, such as the monopoly right to pursue an occupation. This rent increases the benefit which a member derives from belonging to the corporation, and the fear of losing it provides the leadership of the corporation with the leverage to control and discipline its members. The government in turn may rely on the corporation for information, administrative support in implementing policies, abstention from criticism or outright political support. Corporations are supposed to be interested in extracting from the state collective benefits for the group as a whole, such as monopoly rent or additional privileges which the government confers to the members at large.

According to this clientelist view, not only has the state become an arena for clientelist exchanges, but corporations have as well. Corporations, or more precisely their leaders, are connected with individuals in the government through patron-client ties. In this way, the corporation has become an integral part of the political structure of the country and *de facto* lost its status as an autonomous body. Moreover, its leaders have themselves established clientele networks which pervade the corporation. Thus the cohesion of the membership of collective organizations in Southern Italy, for example, 'in many cases is due less to the ideology or programmatic goals of the organization than to a series of parallel individual ties to the leader, who carries this personal following with him even if he changes party or union organization' (Chubb 1981, 81).

When a corporation has been successfully integrated into the clientele networks, its formal aims are increasingly divorced from its actual pursuits. The major problem for the leaders of the corporation is no longer to supply collective goods to members at large, but to channel private benefits to their supporters. Whereas in traditional interest group politics the primary aims of the contending parties are to transform their orientations and interests into general policy, in a clientelist structure business organizations, trade unions and ethnic groups will be interested mainly in personal benefits for *particular* members rather than in general legislative measures. Where corporatism perceives corporations as a kind of interest aggregation machine where the 'general will' of a group is somehow articulated, clientelism looks at corporations as aggregations of clientelist networks engaged in attracting particularistic benefits for particular individual members (Landé 1977a, viii). The central behavioral feature that distinguishes corporatism from clientelism is that the former provides collective, the latter individual benefits.

Again, the proviso has to be added that by dismissing formal rules and norms as facades to provide legitimacy for clientelist activities an extreme case has been built up. Perhaps one might think in terms of a continuum, with organizations which are genuinely concerned with collective goods towards one end, and other organizations where that commitment is purely ritualistic towards the other. Equally, one would expect societies to differ in the proportion of corporations which are located towards one or the other end of the continuum.

Sandbrook describes the trade union umbrella organization in Kenya shortly before and after independence, illustrating the clientelist end of the spectrum. Prominent politicians 'sought to control the national trade union federation by acting as patrons of its foremost office-holders or contenders for these posts' (1972b, 3).[19] The political leaders gained from the process of cooptation the funds available from international labor organizations, as well as additional power of patronage through the ability to allocate the jobs within the movement, and, perhaps most importantly, 'the trade union movement provided a ready-made, poly-ethnic, territory-wide, organizational network for any politician who wished to establish his own political machine' (5).

What are the benefits for the trade union leaders operating at the level of the national federation, for the heads of single unions, or for a trade union organizer at the bottom of the scale? The prime services that the heads of individual unions can offer to contenders for power in the trade union federation are their unions' votes at the federation's elections. In exchange, the patrons at the federation level provide their clients primarily with the funds required to capture or maintain control of 'their' unions. Moreover, patrons undertake to protect their followers against any unfavorable government actions or decisions on the part of the Registrar of Trade Unions who is responsible for supervising the administration of trade unions and deciding who are their legally recognized office-holders (4). For the individual trade union organizer, the incentive to enter into a clientele relationship is the increased employment and promotion prospects associated with it, and in addition there is the hope of being able to use the union as the 'ladder' to political office, to which accrue the highest rewards (5).

The fundamentally different nature of corporatism and clientelism is often overlooked. A case in point is Callaghy, who follows the conventional line that 'corporatism is state structuring of group rather than individual or class interests' (1984, 16, 69). Next, he postulates the existence of corporatism in Africa generally and Zaïre specifically: the urban sector in Africa tends to be controlled by using corporatist structures (36), and in Zaïre the government party has become a corporatist structure for controlling the 'relatively modern' urban sector 'by consolidating and incorporating unions, producer cooperative associations, the press, and business, youth, sociocultural, and even occasionally, religious groups within the party structure. The party usually grants them monopolistic representational rights while closely controlling their leadership and representational functions' (43).

Africa is dominated not only by corporatism, but also by clientelism. Callaghy proposes that foremost among the similarities between Latin American and African regimes is the predominance of patrimonial rulership. This, according to him, often takes the form of a president or a small group where the leader grants 'power, privilege, and material goods ("benefices") to clients or subjects in return for acknowledged authority, support, loyalty, deference, and obedience. This pattern is replicated downward through a complex and often shifting patron-client system' (26).

In principle, of course, Callaghy's implicit scenario is possible: that there is indeed a political structure dominated by clientelist exchanges, and that at the same time the major corporations are not integrated into the clientelist networks and negotiate for collective benefits with the state. Indeed, that may be a reasonable view of the interaction between the Catholic Church and the Zairian state.[20] But for the rest of the corporations, the unions for example, which 'were forced to merge into a state-controlled union federation' (175, 316), and are controlled by the leading politicians, this is hardly an apt description of reality. It is surely inadmissible to argue that politics is clientelist, and then simply to assume that this fact has no bearing on how corporations operate.[21]

So far the discussion has dealt exclusively with the relationship between clientelism and corporatism. But the features that distinguish clientelism from corporatism also set it apart from any other conceptual framework that is based on interest group theory. All these theories are united in assuming that interest groups have some degree of independence from the state and represent the broad aims of the membership. These organizational and behavioral assumptions may well be inadequate, as in the Philippines, where much of the effort of a leader of voluntary organizations is devoted to interceding with public officials on behalf of specific individuals and firms. Indeed, 'many such associations are widely thought to be the personal instruments of their leaders whose private interests receive first attention. Ordinary members of the category for which an association professes to speak usually have little to gain through membership unless they have personal ties with the leaders sufficiently close to justify the hope that special efforts at intervention will be made in their behalf' (Landé 1977b, 87). For these reasons, then, a pluralist model, like the one put forward by Olson which was discussed in the introduction, is based on particular institutional arrangements which are significantly different from those discussed here.

Kaufman criticized the distinction between organizations providing private benefits and groups aiming for collective ones on the grounds that interest groups have always tended to deliver some sort of narrow, selective benefits or sanctions (1974, 301). His argument is based on Olson's proposition that 'common goals' are rarely, if ever, the basis for sustaining membership (301): when only collective goods are provided which are available to both members and non-members, an individual has little incentive to incur the costs associated with joining the corporation (Olson 1982, 21). This argument is beside the point, because Olson accepts not only that corporations do deliver collective goods in addition to private goods, but that the provision of private goods is a means to improve the ability to provide collective goods. This, quite clearly, is a long way from the clientelist assumption of a corporation exclusively concerned with individual benefits.

There is both a push and a pull factor which induces interest groups to join networks and thus change their character. The state may attempt to coopt existing corporations,[22] both to neutralize potential threats through autonomous mobilization and to increase political support by extending the scope of patronage.[23] Methods to win over or to coerce trade association leaders or individual industrialists include graft, and, particularly in the case of business organizations, special favors or threats to credit allocation and the imposition of quantity regulations to the leadership (Leff 1968, 115–117).

The push factor lies in the decline of the importance of collective benefits in a clientelist environment. As we have seen, clientelism conflicts head-on with bureaucratic allocation since it is inextricably wound up with corruption. Corruption, as Scott has pointed out, can be seen as a way of influencing government decisions on the enforcement instead of the policy formulation or 'input' stage of government decision making (1972, 21–23). But in an environment where corruption is endemic, policy decisions are only tenuously related to the actual administrative decisions at the implementation or enforcement stage. Hence the need to influence policy decisions decreases, and the focus of pressure group activity is likely to shift to the implementation stage. In other words, the main concern of such groups becomes to influence particular administrative decisions affecting individual members of the group.

3.3   Clientelism and the Bureaucracy

Let us visualize the state as a set of rules and offices, and, following Mosca, call the incumbents of these offices the 'political class'. The purpose of the political game is to control the offices and the power to determine all or some of the rules, and, through this, control access to the revenue of the state. How does the bureaucracy fit into this picture?

The traditional Weberian view would suggest that politicians formulate policies and administrators implement them according to bureaucratic procedures. Bureaucratic allocation, then, is commonly seen as a constraint upon governments which clientelist politicians have an incentive to abrogate. One would therefore expect them to engage in attempts to gain influence over policy implementation, and thus to deflect the bureaucrats from their traditional mission.

In order to further this quest to soften the bureaucracy, politicians integrate the bureaucrats into patron-client networks. Positions within the administration are allocated to political supporters and the administration becomes penetrated by clientele networks originating in the political world (Legg 1969, 99). The bureaucracy becomes 'party-politicized' and will make its resources available for political contests on a party-political basis (Etzioni-Halevi 1989, 298). Public administrators cease to be bureaucrats, beholden to abstract rules and regulations; instead their actions become determined by the need for an ubiquitous mutual exchange of favors.

This may lead to the depressing situation reported from Africa, where the bureaucratic positions increasingly became prebends leaving, for example, the Nigerian state 'prebendalized and then squeezed of its resources to satisfy the unceasing struggle among massed communities and their (self-serving) patrons for access to the public till' (Joseph 1984, 34).[24] Or there is the complete disintegration of the bureaucracy of Mobutu's Zaïre, where the Zairian absolutist state has created its own political aristocracy, whose power is exclusively derived from its connection to Mobutu, either directly or through the intermediation of a patron. Among this political aristocracy Callaghy counts the ministers, some key advisers and the upper echelons of the administrative and military staff (1983, 66–67), most of whom either head their own patron-client network or are part of one (67). Bureaucratic rules, in this situation, have become increasingly meaningless, and bureaucrats a collection of a leader's personal retainers (Scott 1972, 77).[25]

Moore questions the notion that the Egyptian bureaucracy was permeated by client networks and in the process touches on some more general notions.[26] He accepts that rapid promotion of an administrator requires some support by an individual in the political hierarchy. But he argues that because of security of tenure officials only need 'one-shot' boosts, and that after they have received their shot, so to speak, there are few reasons for them to remain clients of their benefactor. Such an official remains 'his own man, dependent not on any one patron but only the system' (1977, 263).

Moore supports his theory of 'one-shot' boosts by pointing out that bureaucrats were supported by different politicians at different stages in their career. This does not, however, prove the absence of an ongoing patron-client relationship. It is clearly possible for a client to have more than one relationship successively over time.

Moreover, the benefits flowing to the bureaucrat-client go well beyond 'one-shot assistance' in a single promotion procedure. The client will usually expect help not only in future promotion, but in appointing his relatives and supporters, in attaining security of tenure of a lucrative position, or in being able to enjoy the fruits of a prebend without molestation. The relationship, therefore, is a continuing one.[27] Indeed Moore nicely illustrates the point with the history of a career of a civil servant acting in the interests of his patron: first latching on to Ali Sabry's bandwagon and helping him reform the universities, and then 'Sabry sent his loyal "client" to the Arab Socialist Union, which he had been attempting to build up as a power base' (Moore 1977, 262).

The argument does not rule out that administrators may use their administrative positions to build up a power base for themselves. They may even become the dominant elite, a process Meillassoux describes in Mali where after independence the bureaucracy, 'originally the instrument of the colonial bourgeoisie and administration' (1970, 105), 'overcame the traditionally dominant class and came into power' (108), acquired control of the economic infrastructure, especially the parastatal sector and acts in 'the position of a managerial board of a kind of State corporation' (106). The position of pre-eminence was achieved because the members of the bureaucracy branched out into politics and became the governing elite. Nor does the argument exclude the possibility that a patron at the center may use the clientele-bureaucrats as a major instrument to control the political party nominally in power. It is said, for example, that 'Kenyatta ruled Kenya mainly through the provincial administration which he had inherited intact from the colonial government' (Tamarkin 1978, 306); in these conditions, civil servants not only wielded administrative power but manipulated local party branches, thereby providing the backbone of the regime (307).

Thus clientelism assigns a secondary role to the bureaucracy *qua* bureaucracy in terms of both policy formulation and implementation because of the dependence of the individual bureaucrats on their political patrons. This structure implies that the bureaucracy does not act as a corporate group. Indeed, as Waterbury finds in his study of coalitions in a number of Third World countries[28] that their bureaucracies are too sprawling and internally stratified to act corporately (1989, 41). Clientelism therefore excludes the possibility that the bureaucracy might dominate policy-making by virtue of its superior expertise, experience, and access to information.[29] This rules out both the villain and the hero role of the bureaucracy in development: that the 'dead hand of bureaucracy' undermines initiatives from the top (Leys 1976, 44), and that the endeavors of a progressive bureaucracy are sabotaged by politicians or other reactionary forces in society.[30]

3.4 Clientelism and the Military

There has been a tendency to attribute to military hierarchies certain characteristics like 'professionalism, nationalism, cohesion, and austerity that impel them to move into the political arena and to rescue the state from the grip of corrupt and self-seeking elites' (Decalo 1976, 11–12,

23–37). At least in the African context, little of this professionalism and cohesion was observed: African armies have rarely been cohesive, nontribal, Westernized, or even complex organizational structures. On the contrary they resembled 'a coterie of distinct armed camps owing primary clientelist allegiance to a handful of mutually competitive officers of different ranks seething with a variety of corporate, ethnic and personal grievances' (14–15). Not surprisingly, seldom have soldiers ruled as a corporate entity (Jackson and Rosberg 1982, 35). Similarly, Latin American military rarely act politically as a unit, except in moments of crisis (Chalmers1977, 33).[31] The military, therefore, followed the pattern of behavior that one would expect of faction-ridden clientelist formations rather than conventional corporatist organizations.

The replacement of a civilian by a military administration therefore may simply mean the replacement of one clientelist network by another, different only in so far as more of the beneficiaries of government largesse now reside in the military hierarchy. A successful military ruler, however, is unlikely to restrict his clientelist networks to the military, but will 'develop a clientelist political base among civilian leaders and interest groups'. It is this which President Mobutu Sese Seko has succeeded doing in Zaïre, and its absence explains General Acheampong's failure in Ghana (Cammack 1988, 126).

Given the way in which power is maintained one would expect that the rescue operation of the state from the corrupt and self-seeking civilian elite by the military would not be particularly successful. Indeed, despite their promise to provide honest and efficient administration (Decalo 1976, 24), their performance record is mixed, and there are the usual disasters: the later Acheampong years in Ghana (1975–78) were marked by massive corruption, and in military-ruled Nigeria 'the name of state governor had, by 1975, become a by-word for corruption' (Cammack 1988, 124). On the whole, there is little evidence for the argument that the military provides the order to spur economic development (146; Decalo 1976, 233).

In terms of the argument put forward here, there is no reason to distinguish between civilian and military regimes. What matters for the character of the institutional arrangements for policy choice, and for economic growth is the nature of behavior of the actors in the political realm, and there is no *a priori* reason to expect it to be different among civilians than the military. It does not come as a surprise, therefore, that 'in the character of their rule, soldiers and civilians differ very little' (Jackson and Rosberg 1982, 32), and that 'empirical studies have failed to establish any strong relationship between regime type and public policy' (Remmer 1978, 50).

3.5 Clientelism and Ethnicity

It is hardly surprising that individuals seek out their kinfolk for patronage and support (Joseph 1984, 30), and that therefore kinship and ethnic affinity are the most frequent bases for clientelistic network formation (Young and Turner 1985, 158). In Africa, this tendency towards an ethnic foundation of clientelism is reinforced by 'normative expectations, shared by bourgeois, *petit bourgeois,* and plebeians alike, that the struggle for a share of public goods will be conducted and assessed along ethnic and other sectional lines' (Joseph 1984, 29). In turn, clientelistic relations have reinforced and even promoted ethnic clustering because of the transmission of resources from patrons downwards to clients through this channel (29). Joseph introduced the term 'ethno-clientelism' which aptly describes a society segmented along ethnic lines: where the village and provincial or state capitals link those at the center to the people in the periphery through a pyramiding of ethno-clientelistic networks (29).

Ethno-clientelism introduces an additional consideration into the system: an individual will not, as a rule, become a client of someone of a different ethnic hue. This may mean that someone will prefer to support a politician of the same ethnicity even if another politician of a different group offers a higher benefit; the assumptions about client behavior, therefore, have to be amended accordingly. Alternatively, it may mean that an individual generally believes that a politician of a different ethnic group is unlikely to provide more benefits than a person of one's own group.

Joseph suggests that these ethnic clientele clusters operate as corporate groups when he talks about 'the capacity of ethnic groups to serve as functional or interest groups in their own right' (1984, 27). His position seems to be supported by the fact that 'competition for access to resources in Nigeria has taken place predominantly between ethnically defined constituencies' (31), or that ethno-regional claims are put forward for such goods as 'representation, healthcare facilities, educational opportunities and investments, transportation and communication, and targeted development funds' (Rothchild and Foley 1988, 258), and consideration of ethnical balance plays an important role in their allocation. However, this does not prove that networks generally operate as corporate groups.

That they do not constitute corporate groups is indicated first by the intensive factional strive within the ethnic networks. Indeed, as Sandbrook has pointed out, tribal conflict is 'to some extent explicable in terms of patron-client politics' (1972a, 106). Often in intra-tribal politics competing patrons seek clients within the same clan or lineage (106), and tribal politics is replaced by clan politics as clientelism dilutes tribal solidarity and weaken the tribe as a relevant political factor: 'In the context of the rural constituency the tribe is irrelevant, the clan being the main mobilizing agency' (Tamarkin 1978, 314).

Moreover, if it is accepted that the exchanges which take place follow the clientelist pattern, the nature of the benefits which are generated will follow the clientelist pattern also: benefits tend to be particularistic and divisible so that they can be doled out to individual supporters. In this respect, ethno-clientelism will have economic consequences similar to those of networks organized along different lines.

3.6   Clientelism and Class Analysis

It has been accepted, at least among some Marxist scholars, that patron-client ties are 'among the most conspicuous features of the societies' in the Third World, 'so that any attempt to understand their political dynamics ... must come to terms with clientelism and incorporate it in more adequate explanations of the political process' (Flynn 1974, 145). Furthermore, there seems to be agreement that some features of politics cannot be fully accounted for by horizontal class ties, or that 'some elements are best understood in class terms, others not' (141). The disagreements begin with the assertion that clientelism is a 'mechanism of class control' (134, 150).[32]

To establish this point, Flynn essentially argues that clientelism tends to benefit those at the top of patron-client networks. In Italy, for example, there is no question 'of the irrelevance of class analysis as the whole system is ... working in the interests of a small narrow ruling class manipulating the clientelistic machinery for their purposes' (148). It is undoubtedly true that clientelism benefits disproportionately those at the top of the patron-client hierarchies. But that in itself does not signify class control, except as a tautology where patrons are *defined* as a class, which is at the heart of Flynn's argument. If the tautology is to be avoided, then it needs to be established that patrons either are a class, constitute a subset of a class, or at least act in the interest of a class.[33]

Clientelism supposes that there are a group of people who dominate the government by virtue of dominating the patron-client networks. This common interest is likely to generate similarities in their behavior. It is trivially true that if we make this common interest the mark of a class, patrons constitute a class. They may remain, however, a class in this limited sense, a class *in itself*[34] where the class members may not be aware of their collective class interests, and even if they are conscious of their common interests might not engage in organized class action but be absorbed by intra-class competition. There is no need for patrons to constitute a class or part of a class *for itself*,[35] imbued with class consciousness, deliberately shaping decisions in favor of the class, and devising boundaries between themselves and other groups. Nor is it clear that patrons stand in a particularly well defined relation to the means of production, which is after all the central ingredient of Marxist class analysis. It therefore seems to be premature to talk of class control when it is unclear in what relation patrons stand to the means of production, and whether they constitute a class *for itself* even if we abandon the narrow Marxist definition.

Clientelism has traditionally been seen as retarding the development of class formation among clients by undermining class consciousness and collective action. When clientelism integrates people in the social and political systems, 'it does so in a (dyadic) way which prevents the restructuring of society along associational lines' (Graziano 1973, 5). Hence patron-client clusters 'are based on individual ties to a leader rather than on shared characteristics or horizontal ties among followers' (Scott 1977b, 128). For example, patron-client networks of the Senegalese ruling party 'may be aligned on the basis of lineage, ethnic group, religion, or other independent criterion, but most often simply reflect the diffuse clientele of a popular and successful individual' (Foltz 1977, 245).

Moreover, organizational efforts and class consciousness are undermined through the conferral of divisible benefits. As Bates has observed in the context of rural Africa, these benefits

> make it in the interests of individual rural dwellers to seek limited objectives. Political energies, rather than focusing on the collective standing of the peasantry focus instead on the securing of particular

improvements ... The politics of the pork barrel supplant the politics of class action (1981, 117–118).

The supply of individual benefits and the successful attempts to coopt and clientelise corporations, to recast them into a corporatist shell with a clientelist substance, severely weakens the potential for the development of class consciousness and class action. For interest group activity to re-emerge, therefore, 'particularistic ties of personal-concrete dependence must cease to be predominant' (Graziano 1973, 6). 'Genuine associational ties are possible only when the governmental concerns of individuals and firms are not likely to be solved through personal connections' (Legg 1969, 99).

Clientelism, then, may well be consistent with traditional class analysis if the patrons can be shown to belong to a class *for itself*, particularly if its members own the means of production. However, this is not always so, as will be shown later on in the African case.[36] Moreover, clientelism severely impairs the development of class consciousness and class action on the part of the clients.

3.7   Neo-Patrimonialism

In 1968 Roth resurrected Weber's concept of patrimonialism which greatly influenced the analysis of politics in Third World countries. One consequence of Roth's analysis was that not unfrequently 'patrimonialism was linked with or treated as synonymous with patron-client relations' (Theobald 1982, 548). But are the two concepts really identical?

3.7.1 Patrimonialism

Weber as concerned with legitimate domination: specific commands are obeyed in great part because they are considered to be legitimate (Weber 1968, 212). One type of legitimate domination is traditional in character, where the claim to legitimacy rests on 'an established belief in the sanctity of immemorial traditions and the legitimacy of those exercising authority under them' (215). Patrimonialism is a form of domination of this kind (232) where 'the political patrimonial ruler is linked with the ruled through a consensual community which also exists apart from his independent military force and which is rooted in the belief that the ruler's powers are legitimate in so far as they are *traditional'* (1020).

Weber's patrimonialism is autocratic where the ruler's use of power is limited only by tradition, which may lay down the content of commands or the sphere where power can be rightfully exercised (227). Depending on the scope of discretion, Weber distinguishes between patrimonialism and sultanism: where authority is patrimonial, domination is primarily based on tradition, and sultanism applies where it primarily operates on the basis of discretion (232). However, the distinction is a matter of degree; sultanism too is backed up by tradition: even if it sometimes appears that its authority 'is completely unrestrained by tradition', 'this is never in fact the case' (232).[37]

What had Weber to say on clientelist exchanges? Ironically, the case where authority hinges on sufficient provision of material benefits is a mark of charismatic rule, not patrimonialism. The charismatic hero 'gains and retains it solely by proving his power in practice ... Most of all, his divine mission must prove itself by *bringing well-being* to his faithful followers; if they do not fare well, he obviously is not the god-sent master' (1114). This is opposed to patrimonialism, where custom is seen as the main foundation of authority.[38] That, of course, is not to say that those surrounding the patrimonial ruler do not materially benefit, nor that they will not desert him if he fails on that count, only that tradition is a main independent factor which legitimizes his rule.

Weber credits patrimonial regimes with originating bureaucratic structures (229, 232), albeit of a distinct patrimonial kind. To begin with, 'the position of the patrimonial official derives from his purely personal submission to the ruler, and his position vis-à-vis the subjects is merely an external aspect of his relation' (1030). Moreover, jurisdiction of the office is delimited not by rules and regulations, but by the ruler's personal discretion, with the exception of traditionally stereotyped functions (1029, 1094). Last, the patrimonial office lacks above all the bureaucratic separation of the 'private' and the 'official' sphere (1029). This is true for the ruler for whom political administration is treated as a purely personal affair and 'political power is considered part of his personal property, which can be exploited by means of contributions and fees' (1029). But it is also true for his administrative staff:

> Wherever traditional or stereotyped prescription does not impose strict limitations, patrimonialism gives free rein to the enrichment of the ruler himself, the court officials, favorites, governors, mandarins, tax collectors, influence peddlers, and the great merchants and financiers

who function as tax-farmers, purveyors and creditors. The ruler's favor and disfavor, grants and confiscations, continuously create new wealth and destroy it again (1099).

Patrimonialism then is authoritarian rule legitimized by tradition, unencumbered by constitutional or legal restrictions. The bureaucracy are appointed and derive their authority by virtue of their personal links to the ruler, and that authority is prescribed by the ruler and by tradition, where offices are prebends to be exploited for personal benefits within the limits derived from these personal links.

3.7.2 Patrimonialism and Clientelism

Roth, in his famous article of 1968, argued that 'in some of the new states patrimonial features ... are more important than bureaucratic and charismatic ones' (1968, 199). That article provided a timely reminder that the prevailing tendency of treating 'almost all political leaders in the new states as "charismatic"' (200) was hardly apt. In the process Roth significantly reinterpreted patrimonialism.

To begin with, apart from exceptions such as Ethiopia, traditional legitimacy had disintegrated (194). Roth suggested therefore the existence of a second type of patrimonialism, 'personal rulership on the basis of loyalties that do not require any belief in the ruler's unique personal qualification, but are inextricably linked to material incentives and rewards' (196). In other words, patrimonialism now stands for political clientelism.

The stress on patron-client relations in Roth's definitions then leads to the implication that patrimonial regimes need not be authoritarian after all. Patrimonialism 'belongs to a typology of beliefs *and* organizational practices that can be found at any point' on a 'continuum stretching from pluralist democracy to totalitarianism' (197). In this view, traditional American machine politics and Nikita Krushchev's personal apparatus both become expressions of patrimonial rule, as both function primarily 'on the basis of personal loyalty ... and material reward' (198).

The only notion common to the Weberian concept of patrimonialism which remains in the end is 'personal rulership', as opposed to 'legal-rational legislation and administration in the new states' (203).

Ironically, Weber's concern with legitimacy, that tradition provided legitimacy as the foundation of both dominance and obedience, was largely buried in the process of reformulation. Roth's patrimonial rulership is based on loyalties linked to material incentives and rewards, and, as we have seen, Weber did not think that purely material interests and calculations of material advantages can provide legitimacy (213). Roth therefore describes a kind of rulership which *lacks* legitimacy. Clientelism and patrimonialism then are widely differing concepts. Patrimonialism describes authoritarian rule where obedience and loyalty are partly based on legitimacy derived from tradition, and where the distinction between an official and a private sphere of the ruler's action is absent. Clientelism on the other hand is characterized by the lack of legitimacy such as tradition; obedience is based on material incentives and force. As a consequence, clientelism is compatible with both authoritarian or democratic rule.

3.8 Personal Rule

During he 1980s there has been a proliferation of analyses of African countries based on neo-patrimonialism, personalism or personal rule, which involved some modifications of Roth's concepts. The focus of attention again reverted to authoritarian regimes.[39] This, no doubt, was partly a result of the fact that the analyses happened to deal with authoritarian states where traditional authority had disappeared. What remained was Roth's focus on patron-client relations as a means of shoring up loyalty and support.[40]

Jackson and Rosberg's account, with their stress on patron-client networks (1982, 19, 29), patronage (42, 43), and weak institutions (10), resembles most closely the exposition pursued here.[41] They call their 'distinctive type of political system' (4) one of 'personal rule' which 'plays a very important role in the political life of the new states of Black Africa' (2).

One significant difference emerges when Jackson and Rosberg introduce loyalty into their system of clientelism: 'Opportunism and expediency are important elements in the behavior of followers, but they do not account in full for the durability of some of Africa's personal rulers and the stability of their regimes' (1982, 39). Loyalty seems to be a necessary condition to maintain 'organizations and relationships during times of trouble' and to overrule 'the temptation to desert or "exit"' (41, 40, 75).

It is unclear why opportunism would not lead to some degree of stability: it may well be the optimal course of action to stick to one's patron in times of troubles, even if only expected future benefits are taken into account. Jackson and Rosberg accept that in practice loyalty and benefit maximization or patronage are 'undoubtedly interwoven and indistinguishable' (1982, 42). They furthermore find that personal rule is characterized by 'clientelism and patronage, factionalism, coups, purges, plots, succession crises, and similar characteristics and dynamics of institutionless government' (6) which throws some doubt on the importance of loyalty.

The idea that a client 'has a strong sense of loyalty' (Wolf 1977, 174) plays a large role in the Maussian tradition where a system of exchange creates 'debts of gratitude' (e.g. Wolters 1984, 56).[42] This scenario fits the traditional rural patron-client ties, and is unlikely to hold in the modern setting where political exchange is divorced from or only weakly related to other social ties. For example Sorauf finds that, judging by registration and voting records of American patronage appointees, these 'job-holders would appear something less than loyal, vocal partisans' (1956, 1046). Even of those who 'felt they "owed"' something to the Republican party' fewer than half 'also reported voting a straight ticket' (1053). In a different context, even 'the pure type of strictly defined or old-fashioned, *genuine* client' changed his allegiance after he was offered 'a secure salary, easy hours, light work, and some social status' (Loizos 1977, 125).

Overtly expressed feelings of loyalty which point to an affective tie not easily disrupted may not be of great significance. The individuals concerned may not be entirely honest, or the feelings themselves may be waxing and waning with the expected future net benefits derived from a clientele relationship. Moreover, breaking patronage ties is made easier by a number of time-worn strategies to avoid a sense of guilt and recrimination, such as 'the discovery or invention of a grievance, such as an affront to one's ... self-esteem, of such weight that when thrown into the balance of reciprocity, it cancels out an outstanding debt' (Landé 1977a, xvii). Hence even if one allows for personal allegiance, a client is unlikely to support a politician who is manifestly inferior in providing benefits. Loyalty, at best, will offset loss of material benefits only temporarily.[43]

A second major difference between clientelism and personal rule is that the latter is inherently authoritarian; at the apex of all personal regimes 'is a ruler, a paramount leader who enjoys a position of uncontested supremacy as long as he succeeds in retaining power' (Jackson and Rosberg 1982, 22). Thus personalist rule is arbitrary and usually 'uses law and the coercive instruments of the state to expedite its own purposes of monopolizing power and denies the political rights and opportunities of all other groups to compete for that power' (23).[44]

As opposed to personal rule, clientelism encompasses both authoritarian and democratic regimes. This is important for three reasons: First, the economic consequences of clientelism are likely to be similar in both democracies and autocracies. Second, clientelist structures may help to explain the widespread emergence of authoritarian regimes. There is little doubt that the economic failures of liberal democracy contributed to the emergence of authoritarian regimes. Most of the political crises in formerly French West Africa 'had at least this much in common: a military response was made possible in most cases because the first civilian regimes simply failed in conflict management, resource mobilization, and economic development' (LeVine 1986, 102). Similarly, in Somalia the military intervened in 1969 only after the civilian institutions collapsed under the weight of their own talks (Laitin 1979, 175; Clapham 1986, 276). The large scale failures of democratic experience just before and after independence may well have been the consequence of clientelism. Third, if we limit clientelism to authoritarian regimes we exclude the question of why voters support candidates who stand for patronage politics, a question addressed in a later chapter.

3.9 Conclusion

We have developed an outline of a political structure where political action is purely a function of material benefits, where the tentacles of clientelist networks have penetrated every organization of society and ultimately relegated these organizations, including the bureaucracy and the military, to a mere shadow of a corporatist existence. Ideology is irrelevant as an explanatory factor of political behavior. Clientelism precludes the existence of classes *for themselves* on the client level and undermines their formation. Patrons may well constitute such a class, but there is no presumption that they are the owners of the means of production. Clientelism can occur in both a democratic and an autocratic environment. The failure of the political system to convey legitimacy accounts for the purely mercenary behavior of individuals when they engage in political action. This in turn causes the regime characteristics that have been described in previous chapters, such as the low degree of institutionalization, the constant changes in the political system, and therefore the high degree of uncertainty. The high degree of uncertainty about the rules of the political game then puts pressure on politicians to build up clienteles in every organization of society and at the same time to generate resources to service these clienteles. In other words, state autonomy is low.

Notes:

1. By schools of thought that believe 'symbolic' politics is important, that people hold 'expressive' orientations which are not easily shed (Sears and Funk 1990).
2. Answers may also reflect the gap between civic norms and civic behaviour (Almond and Verba 1963, 133).
3. Similarly, party-identification is sometimes taken as an expression of 'symbolic' politics. It might equally well be read as an expression of self-interest.
4. See, for example, Sears and Funk (1990).
5. Empirical tests of the self-interest axiom tend to focus on the short term (Sears and Funk 1990, 148; Davis and Speer 1991, 321). The defence that 'one would expect short-term self-interest to have a stronger political impact' because, among other things, it is 'more emotionally evocative, and easier to calculate' (Sears and Funk 1990, 167) imposes the observer's valuation on the subject whose behaviour the observer is supposed to explain.
6. It is not enough to hold beliefs that one ought to support some political action.
7. And to escape the danger of tautology.
8. Similarly, the political system in Africa 'is more a game in which individuals and factions struggle for power and place rather than an arena in which groups or parties compete for policies' (Jackson and Rosberg 1982, 19).
9. Indeed, the political structures they created were sometimes entirely incompatible with the ideology they espoused. For example, the Ethiopian *Derg* 'itself was the antithesis of the vanguard Leninist party: entirely military, secret, and inaccessible' (Young 1982a, 78).
10. Examples are Ngouabi in Congo-Brazzaville, Kerekou in Benin, and Ratsiraka in Madagascar (Young 1982a, 22, 36, 50); a similar leftward shift took place in Ethiopia after the military coup in 1974 (78).

11. It was doubted by 'both by non-socialist foreign observers and the doctrinally pure scientific socialist intellectuals at home' (Young 1982a, 50).

12. Usually colonialism rather than class struggle remained the defining referent (Young 1982a, 31, 64).

13. In Dahomey, for example, 'despite the superficially sharp divergence of Kerekou's policies from the previous leaders, civilian and military, the concrete domestic reality is systematically similar' (Decalo 1976, 83). Alternatively, although the Congo 'was henceforth a socialist state based on Marxist-Leninist principles' that ideology 'was not accompanied by social and economic policy shifts' (140); rather, 'much of the revolutionary zeal in Congo camouflaged personalist ambitions, while the factional 'ideological' clashes and purges often covered up interethnic competitions and the settling of old accounts' (145). Last, while the Malian leaders were 'loudly proclaiming their faith in the virtues of socialism' they allowed the condition of the peasantry to gradually deteriorate (Martin 1976, 46).

14. Diamond attempts to introduce ideology to explain the bitterness of the conflict which racked Yoruban politics in 1962–63 (1988, 114). Undoubtedly, official pronouncements are riddled with ideological statements, but that does not mean that they are of great importance. Hence in order to inflate the role of ideology Diamond has to emphasize Awolowo's socialist leanings, although he admits that 'the program of "democratic socialism" adopted by the party in 1960 was surprisingly lean on specifics' (114). Moreover, he has to play down the importance of ethnic conflict between the Ijebu Yorubas, generally aligned behind Awolowo, and the Oyo Yorubas supporting Akintola (113). Next, he has to overlook Awolowo's propensity for attracting political support by patronage and his involvement in corruption. Even Diamond, who is particularly partial to the Chief, accepts that he built up his position by means of patronage and that there 'was probably little doubt that Awolowo was at the hub of an intricate financial network that diverted vast sums of public money to his party' (104). All this does not suggest a committed socialist. The bitterness of the conflicts is easily accounted for when we take into account that the loser is going to be dislodged from the positions which convey both power and wealth. Diamond admits this last point: even if Awolowo's Action Group 'had not pitched its opposition on class-based themes, the mere possibility of its winning the next election was profoundly threatening to the existing power groups' (123). His conclusion that among the causes of the crisis, 'the growing polarization at the level of class and ideology was most fundamental' (124) is therefore hardly warranted.

15. Young (1982a, 59, 65, 102).

16.   The experiments in Algeria, Egypt, and Tanzania 'could claim reasonable growth success, Ghana, Guinea, and Mali had mediocre results' (300).

17.   Whereas the Ivory Coast and Kenya had done well, others such as Liberia and Zaïre had fared badly.

18.   This is of course not a final proof that ideology does not matter. Socialism might have failed because of external dependence or organisational constraints such as the lack of coercive capacity (Callaghy 1979; Jowitt 1979, 134, 136).

19.   In practice, the neat 'distinction between "politician" and "leaders of the trade union federation" is somewhat artificial; the latter have usually been palpably politically ambitious and, indeed, have often held political office themselves' (Sandbrook 1972b, 3).

20.   Similarly, it has been argued that the organisations representing the white-dominated economic sectors of commercial agriculture, manufacturing, mining and commerce operate along conventional interest group lines (Skalnes 1993).

21.   Young and Turner reason in the same way. They accept that patron-client networks 'ramify through all levels of Zaïrian society' (1985, 157). Nevertheless, they continue to talk about the 'corporatist role' of the ruling party, needing 'to impose its grid upon those recognizable groupings which were actually or potentially corporate entities. This was done by forcing all such groups to organize into single national bodies, which could then be incorporated within the party structure as ancillary organizations' (194) such as trade unions (199).

22.   And to found new ones.

23.   In the Sudan, for example, officials encouraged business associations, but 'their overarching aim was ... to facilitate state domination of the private sector' (Tignor 1987, 211).

24.   Crook believes that the successful outcome of economic policies in the Ivory Coast may well be due to the containment of patrimonial elements in the political system which have 'not been allowed to override the commitment set from the top to legal-rational forms of control, effective performance and the implementation of an economic program' (1989, 225).

25.   To take a less extreme example: 'Like a seventeenth-century office holder in England, a Thai administrator tends to view many of his subordinates as personal retainers who owe him a personal loyalty beyond mere bureaucratic norms' (Scott 1972, 65). This, for example, finds expression in the fact 'that a superior will tolerate many violations (often corrupt) of administrative regulations among his subordinates, whereas he will strike with dispatch against any junior official who shows personal disloyalty to him' (65).

26. The first reason why Moore rejects the argument that patron-client networks dominate the Egyptian bureaucracy is that the *shilla*, 'which is literally a circle of friends, without any hierarchical connotations' (1977, 261) was the dominant informal network. Moore contradicts himself a page later by referring to an individual who had 'jumped *shillal*' headed by two leading Egyptian politicians respectively, which hardly makes them non-hierarchical groupings.

27. See for example Chubb (1981, 70) for Italy and Wade (1985, 486) for India. The point is made by Chubb that in the case of Sicily, 'the public employee can ill afford to neglect his obligations to his patron once his own job is secure.' Career 'advancement, promotions and pay raises within the bureaucracy proceed almost exclusively on the basis of political favouritism.' The employee's fate is thus directly linked to the continued political success of his protector, which in turn depends upon his own continued support (1982, 99).

28. In Algeria, Egypt, Jordan, Morocco, Tunisia, Pakistan and Turkey.

29. For an overview of this issue see Bottomore, 1964, 76–84. To what degree bureaucrats act independently of a political base is of course an empirical issue. Cruise O'Brien, for example, stresses the scope of independent action of the Senegalese bureaucrat (1975, 12, 172–173).

30. Kaplinsky postulates that 'the "national" interest in Kenya is most clearly articulated by the Central Bank and by middle level officers in most ministries and parastatals (1980, 99).' This lower tier of 'technocrats' and 'middle-level officers' in the Central Bank and in most ministries and parastatals is sometimes thought to challenge the dominance of the bourgeoisie (Kitching 1985, 128; Langdon 1980, 7,9).

31. 'In cases of severe conflict which is publicly defined as being along class lines or around a particular interest which sharply differentiates groups according to opposing interests, a measure of 'interest-group solidarity' may hold. But in the long sweep, the pressure of politicization and the strain toward establishing the vertical links necessary for maintaining or winning power, the lines are likely to be blurred and to be constantly shifting' (Chalmers 1977, 33).

32. For example for Guasti it is axiomatically true that clientele relations are class relations: 'The clientelistic structure ... serves to maintain the dependency of each class on those above it' (1977, 422).

33. Nor are 'class explanations, however covertly', reintroduced into the discussion (Flynn 1974, 144) if it is admitted that clientelist networks are established by the centre (149), that exchange relationships involve individuals of higher and lower socio-economic status respectively, or that the basis of the patron-client ties is inequality (142).

34. A class *an sich*.

35. A class *für sich*.

36.   Flynn (1974, 150) and Cammack (1988, 79) simply assert that clientelist politics can only be fully understood when seen as an important mechanism of class control imposed from above.

37.   Sandbrook (1985, 90) equates sultanism with absence of traditional legitimacy. This, quite clearly, is wrong, even if legitimacy does become tenuous. Weber had argued that 'scarcely anywhere does the political authority of the patrimonial prince rest exclusively upon the fear of his patrimonial military power' (1968, 1020). However, apparently the situation did approach this state in the Near East, 'the classic location of "sultanism"' (1020). Weber however classifies sultanism still as legitimate rule, whereas the tyrants of ancient and medieval cities 'perceived themselves, and were perceived everywhere, as specifically "illegitimate rulers"' (1317). Neither did they come to power through legitimate means, nor did a sufficiently strong tradition develop in support of their claims.

38.   Kasfir's notion that the thrust of Weber's analysis permits us to think of patrimonialism solely as a material exchange based on interest (1987, 56) is clearly a misreading of Weber.

39.   Personal rule is authoritarian by definition (Jackson and Rosberg 1982, 23; Sandbrook 1985, 89–90), associated with the absence of bureaucratic constraints and with 'personal ascendancy', personal domination, often with personality cults (Young and Turner 1985, 89).

40.   E.g. Ergas (1987, 5).

41.   Jackson and Rosberg attempt to explain differences of personal rule among different countries (1982, 75). Thus they distinguish between the 'prince' who 'tends to rule jointly with other oligarchs and to cultivate their loyalty, cooperation and support', and an autocrat who 'tends to dominate the oligarchy, the government, and the state without having to share power with other leaders' (79). Those two pragmatic rulers are opposed to the 'prophet', a visionary wanting to reshape society in ways consistent with his ideology (79). Last, there is tyrannical rule which 'involves a high degree of uncertainty, insecurity, and at least potential instability ... not only legal but also all moral constraints on the exercise of power are absent' (80). Other subtypes were used by Springborg, for example, who distinguished between exclusionist and inclusionist types of regimes, represented by Nasser and Sadat respectively, the latter identified by 'severely restricting both the pathways leading into and the actual number of individuals admitted into the political elite' (1979, 50). Our concern here is with the causes and consequences of personal rule and clientelism in general.

42.   In the extreme, if the norm of reciprocity is internalized and an 'unrepayable debt' is incurred,   loyalty is assured to the end of a lifetime (e.g. Landé 1977a, xvii).

43. The writers who stress the importance of loyalties also stress the importance of the possibility that a voter will switch allegiances. Wolf, for example, holds that it is 'this potential competition of patron with patron that offers the client his leverage, his ability to win support and to insist on its continuation' (1977, 175).

44. Not surprisingly, the personality of the ruler becomes of prime importance for the explanation of political events (Jackson and Rosberg 1982, 27).

4   Clientelism and the Causes of Administrative Corruption

Thus far we have portrayed a clientelist political system as being based on informal relationships between politicians and their supporters who exchange political backing for material benefits. Patrons and clients, as we have seen, form factional networks which favor the provision of private over collective goods, subvert the legitimacy of governments and introduce a high level of politicization and thus reduce the stability of political institutions. Where factionalism is rampant and institutionalization wanting, patron-client networks are extended to every institution of political significance to ensure the necessary political support, and the level of state autonomy tends to be low. The picture is not quite complete, however. One of the salient features of developing countries is the high level of administrative corruption which is greatly fostered by clientelism, but which also reinforces the political behavior that promotes clientelism.

Clientelism promotes corruption in a variety of ways. It tends to lead to an administrative structure several of whose features encourage corruption: discretion in administrative decision making; organizational disarray; contradictory rules and regulations; a low level of morale in the public service; the expansion of the government sector beyond the optimal size; low degree of legitimacy of the institutional arrangements; and powerless anti-corruption agencies. These traits survive because of the politicians' interest in expanding patronage politics.

Corruption is either overlooked in the analysis of policy generation and policy failures, or its analytical importance is negated. One way of denying the relevance of corruption is to reject the applicability of the conventional definition of corruption and thus to attempt eliminating the problem by a definitional twist. The first section of this chapter defends the concept of corruption, with all its moral connotations, against its detractors who see it as just another harmless social phenomenon unnecessarily vilified by Western cultural imperialists who imposed this alien notion on an unsuspecting Third World.[1]

The second section deals with changes in the level of corruption. Like any other rational action, corrupt acts will be performed only if expected future benefits exceed the expected future costs. Such costs include not only material costs, but also the distress of acting against the dictates of conscience. Furthermore, overall costs are not limited to the cost of punishment by the authorities, but include the cost of social sanctions as well.

The third section looks at the administrative features which traditionally have been held responsible for the emergence of corruption, both by reducing the costs of corruption and increasing the benefits: the state of the anti-corruption agency; the departure from the Weberian ideal of a fully documented decision making process based on impersonal abstract formal rules administered by adequately trained personnel; and the size of the government sector. However, all these variables are heavily influenced by political decisions, and thus changes in corruption cannot be a consequence of administrative processes only. An explanation of changes in the level of corruption must therefore include political factors as well.

Section four argues that political clientelism promotes the administrative characteristics that generate corruption. Thus it is in the interest of patronage politics to introduce rationing and discretion into the administrative system, and political criteria into employment and promotion procedures, to expand the scope of state activities, and to frustrate efforts to foster allegiance of the public servants to the state. But the political structure may be in turn a function of the behavior of the public. Hence the public's willingness to support politicians who engage in legislative and administrative corruption can be a major contributing factor to administrative corruption.

The final section argues that endemic corruption reinforces clientelism in a number of ways: it strengthens self-seeking behavior in politics, undermines the legitimacy of government, and provides incentives for corporations to seek to integrate themselves into clientelist networks. Moreover, it undermines the implementation of reform programs which may be necessary to reduce political clientelism.

4.1 Definition of Corruption

By what standard are we going to judge whether an act is corrupt or not?[2] There are three alternatives[3] violations of formal duties of office for the sake of private benefit, or public-office-centered definitions; what public opinion deems to be corrupt, or public opinion definitions;[4] and actions contrary to the public interest, or public-interest-centered definitions.[5]

Both public opinion and public interest definitions presuppose some kind of agreement on normative questions - either what constitutes the public interest,[6] or what constitutes corruption. Because such agreement is unlikely, both public opinion and public interest definition are of limited practical use.

The failure of public interest and public opinion standards to have many practical implications has led most students of corruption to adopt a public-office-centered definition.[7] Nye provides the most popular of such definitions:

behavior which deviates from the formal duties of a public role because of private-regarding (personal, close family, private clique) pecuniary or status gains; or violates rules against the exercise of certain types of private-regarding influence (1967, 419).[8]

However, a discussion of corruption cannot restrict itself to the public office definition and therefore to administrative corruption. Indeed, in a clientelist framework, administrative corruption is likely to be a consequence of actions by both legislators and the public. Such actions are not covered by the public office definition, but they can be contrary to the public interest and therefore corrupt in the wider sense of the term.[9]

4.1.1 Criticism of the Public Office Standard

It is often said that the public office standard is inappropriate, particularly for Third World countries, and therefore ought not to be applied. Allegedly, this is because corruption sometimes serves the common good and therefore advances the public interest. In addition, since public opinion does not always condemn individuals who make personal gains by breaching public office rules, the public opinion standard deviates from the public office rule. Moreover, the public office definition is inappropriate because different societies have different rules and because it precludes the discussion of corruption in pre-bureaucratic systems. Furthermore, the definition contains a conservative bias by endorsing government action. The public office standard is of course not beyond criticism, but the conceptual weaknesses are different ones, and they do not seriously impair its use in practice.

4.1.1.1 Corruption Fosters the Common Good

It is the contention of a group of revisionists that because corruption might be socially beneficial, the blanket condemnation of administrative corruption is premature, and therefore the prevailing morally-laden definitions of corruption ought to be replaced by value-neutral ones.

The target of the revisionists' attack is the 'moralizers'[10] who, it is said, are convinced that corrupt behavior 'is always against the "public interest"' (Leys 1965, 219), but failed to produce any evidence for their claim 'that the results of nepotism and all other forms of what they call corruption ... are serious and bad' (216). This apparently puts them 'in a direct line of descent from the viewpoint of the missionaries who were dedicated to the suppression of native dancing' (217). The moral stigma which corruption carries, argue the critics, may be entirely misplaced because it may lead to improvements in welfare. Corruption therefore must be removed 'from the realm of the moral (and unspeakable) to the neutral (and researchable)' (Caiden and Caiden 1977, 302).

As often happens in such debates, the revisionists significantly distorted the 'moralist' case. In fact there is little evidence that Wraith and Simpkins, who apparently constitute the 'moralist school' - at least in Leys' attack - thought that corruption was always bad. They found that the economic effects of corruption 'may not be very considerable' (1963, 16), that corruption may not reduce efficiency (172), but that the sums involved in corruption 'would have brought considerable benefits to people' in Africa, and that corruption in high places becomes a handicap to foreign aid and investment (172). Leys is not the only one who exaggerates the distance between the moralists and the revisionists.[11] Ben-Dor, for example, credits the revisionists for breaking away from 'the wholesale condemnation of corruption as a totally undesirable and harmful phenomenon by the earlier, or moralistically oriented generations of writers on the subject' (Ben-Dor 1974, 64).

In order to rescue corruption from moralistic prejudices, the revisionists introduced a series of what Heidenheimer calls 'market-centered definitions' (1970, 5). In fact these tend to be public office definitions in disguise, as they introduce such terms as 'extra-legal' or 'quasi-property rights'. Leff, for example, defines corruption as 'an extra-legal institution used by individuals to gain influences over the actions of the bureaucracy' (Leff 1964, 8). Hence a corrupt act is one outside the law. The same is true if we say that corruption 'involves a shift from a mandatory pricing model to a free-market model' where the public office becomes 'as a locus of quasi-rights which are traded by the incumbent in order to maximize his welfare' (Tilman 1979, 347). By 'quasi-rights' Tilman presumably means rights illegally appropriated by the incumbent. Hence we are back again at the public office definition.[12] Not mentioning the existence of rules and regulations hardly improves the matter. Saying that a 'corrupt civil servant regards his public office as a business, the income of which he will ... seek to maximize', that his office then becomes a "maximizing unit", and the 'size of his income depends ... upon the market situation and his talents for finding the point of maximal gain on the public's demand curve' (Van Klaveren 1970, 39) still leaves the problem that 'somewhere there is an authority that distinguishes between the rules applicable to public officials and those applicable to businessmen operating in the free market, or that there are certain characteristics that distinguish a "black market" from the free market' (Heidenheimer 1970, 6). Market-centered definitions then do not escape from the shadow of public office definitions.

Still, even if the revisionist attempt at establishing an alternative definition fails, their plea for the study of the consequences of corruption is obviously sound, as is their criticism of the poverty of the analysis of the 'moralists'.[13] It is also trivially true that some corrupt acts are likely to have socially beneficial effects sometimes, for example when corruption undermines the implementation of policies which decrease welfare.[14]

What the revisionists overlook is that corruption involves a special kind of a social loss. It undermines the effectiveness of public administration in its day-to-day operation[15] and the implementation of all policies, including those which are socially beneficial.[16] Revisionists fail to appreciate[17] that society undoubtedly has an interest in the efficient working of government machinery, and it is hardly sensible to destroy that machinery because it has been put to bad use.[18] The socially optimal course of action is to improve its operation, not to sabotage it. It is for this reason that corruption is *prima facie* against the public interest. The public office definition then becomes a special case of a public interest definition.

Hence there does seem to be good reason to believe that there is a justification for a moral rule that public office holders ought not to be corrupt. Public opinion, therefore, is right to condemn corruption. The fact that there are circumstances where breaking the rule may lead to welfare gains should surprise no one. It is in the nature of moral rules that their application sometimes leads to sub-optimal outcomes. Lying will sometimes be the welfare-maximizing course of action, but it does not follow that society should therefore abandon the rule that one ought not to lie.

4.1.1.2 Cultural Relativism

It is sometimes said that in some countries public opinion does not condemn violations of public office rules, which implies a serious deviation between public opinion and public office standards. This divergence between legalistic standards and public opinion is thought to be particularly serious in the Third World.[19]

The most extreme view maintains that 'in developing non-Western societies' existing moral codes frequently 'do not agree with Western norms as to what kinds of behavior by public servants should be condemned', and that therefore public opinion in Third World countries often does not condemn corruption (Bayley 1966, 721). This is a difficult argument to sustain, given the popularity of anti-corruption rhetoric throughout the Third World.[20]

A less extreme view contends that public opinion and public office standards deviate because of a conflict of values between 'traditional society' and Western bureaucratic norms: 'in most less developed countries, there are two standards regarding such behavior, one indigenous and one more or less Western, and the formal duties and rules concerning most public roles tend to be expressed in terms of the latter' (Nye 1967, 419). Similarly, Caiden and Caiden argue that:

> The issue is one of conflict of values. Against the Western, impersonal, and universalistic norms of bureaucracy are set the values of kinship and

reciprocity. Are these to be denied validity, and the public servant who fulfils their expectations to be considered corrupt? 1977, 302).

Such value conflicts may well exist, and people may indeed be torn between conforming to traditional and to bureaucratic obligations. But the existence of a value conflict is not the same thing as saying that there are no norms conforming to our public office definition. The conflict of values which has been postulated may explain a greater *incidence* of corruption, but it implicitly accepts that the public office standard does find public support, however weakly.

The Caidens put forward a related cultural relativism argument. They deny that corruption is a meaningful concept for acts which have become sufficiently widespread. Corruption to them is a 'divergence from an acknowledged standard' 1977, 304), and 'Once corruption ... becomes sufficiently widespread as to constitute a normal rather than an exceptional model of behavior, it ceases to exist' 302). This is not necessarily true. Norms as ideal standards may survive even if they are habitually disregarded. Corrupt Indian administrators who operate in an environment where corruption is endemic, 'to a man, were apologetic about the prevalence of corruption'. They 'deeply shared a sense of guilt' (Somjee 1974, 185).

The cultural relativism argument fails to establish that there is a widespread disparity between public office norms and public opinion in Third World countries. Moreover, it is likely that the differences in public attitudes to corruption between the First and the Third World are exaggerated for a different reason. Attitudes to corruption are not only a function of the strength of norms relating to the duty of public office. Even in the West it is debatable whether the public condemns corruption mainly because it involves a breach of public office regulations as such, or because such behavior is seen as conflicting with other norms. People may condemn corruption, for example, because they believe that the government ought to act as trustee for the community and therefore act in the interest of the community as a whole,[21] or they may believe in principles of equality. On both these grounds they may object to corruption involving the amassing of riches by the political elite, or to being discriminated against.[22]

Hence individuals in the Third World may denounce corruption even if they do not value the impersonal standards of bureaucratic decision making, and are unable to perceive the importance of distinguishing between the private and public spheres. Indeed, they are likely to denounce corruption for the very same reasons as people in the West. Holding overarching norms such as equality is a sufficient condition for opposing corruption; one does not need a sophisticated notion of the importance of modern bureaucratic systems to do so. Cultural relativism arguments for the acceptability of corruption in Third World countries on the grounds that people lack a sense of the importance of the bureaucracy are therefore highly questionable, and are probably based on a misunderstanding as to why people condemn corruption in the First World.

4.1.1.3 Rules are Different in Different Societies

Public office definitions of corruption are sometimes criticized because rules and regulations are likely to be different in different societies: nepotism may be forbidden in some societies but a perfectly acceptable practice elsewhere. 'Likewise, the acceptance of unsolicited gifts is not allowed in some states but it is in others; or at least it is permitted for some officials but not others' (Caiden 1988, 8). The unquestionable fact that substantive formal rules differ between societies and through periods in history has led some commentators to the conclusion that such 'differences thwart the acceptance of legal, moral and public-interest definitions' (8). This does not follow. What matters is not the substantive content of the rules and regulations, but the fact that there are rules and regulations, and that they are broken. Thus by linking corruption 'to the duties of the public office, it is possible to speak theoretically about corrupt practices under *all* kinds of constitutions where the concept of the pubic office has been reasonably developed' (Heidenheimer 1970, 13).

4.1.1.4 Absence of Rules

The public office definition is sometimes attacked because, in terms of the definition, corruption cannot occur in the absence of formal rules and regulations. It is, 'in effect, the creation of bureaucracy' (Caiden and Caiden 1977, 304), and in pre-bureaucratic systems 'by definition, corruption does not occur' (Van Klaveren, quoted in Heidenheimer 1970, 10), for it presupposes a social structure in which the separation between the public and the private sphere either has been carried through in actual fact, or else has been generally accepted by society as a criterion for proper conduct on the part of the civil servant (Wertheim 1970, 197). First of all, the distinction between bureaucratic and pre-bureaucratic societies is likely to be exaggerated. For example, prohibitions against low-level extortions of purveyors can be found in the Magna Carta, and thirteenth century statutes of Westminster prohibited officers from taking rewards beyond what the king allowed (Peck 1990, 5–6). Pre-bureaucratic societies are more likely to be an analytical than a historical reality.[23]

Moreover, even if pre-bureaucratic societies do exist the claim that corruption is absent in such an environment is wrong. What has been asserted is, loosely speaking, that an official is corrupt if he breaks formal rules and derives personal benefits from the breach. This does not imply than an official who does not break rules is not corrupt.[24] Hence those who sold state offices in seventeenth-century France, for example, may well have been corrupt, even if they did not violate any formal rule and regulation.[25] The public office definition is simply inapplicable in such cases,[26] but that does not support the conclusion that corruption was absent.

4.1.1.5 Conservative Bias

It is sometimes held that the public office definition implicitly sanctions 'whatever standards of official conduct happen to prevail' (Scott 1972, 5; Gardiner 1993, 115–117). This is not so. What has been asserted is that a person who acts corruptly by breaking rules and regulations in order to gain privately is ordinarily acting immorally, since corruption tends to undermine the efficiency of the state machinery and therefore is against the public interest. The argument does not imply that an individual who follows rules and regulations does act morally. An official may be acting immorally by implementing immoral rules and regulations. The public office definition does not sanction such conduct.

Nor is an individual who breaks rules automatically considered corrupt according to the public office definition, as a corrupt act presupposes a private gain.[27] An individual whose conscience dictates such a course of action therefore is not corrupt as long no benefit is accrued. A border guard who allows members of a persecuted minority to pass the border in breach of formal rules will only be considered corrupt if a personal advantage ensues.[28]

4.1.1.6 Problems with the Definition

This is not to suggest that there are no problems with Nye's definition. It is superior to most other definitions because there is a reasonably clear borderline between an act that is corrupt and one that is not.[29] By referring to *formal* duties of office it avoids the vagueness that goes with references such as the 'general duties of office' (McMullan 1961, 184), the 'misuse of authority' (Bayley 1966, 720) or 'accepted norms' (Huntington 1968, 59).[30] Still there is an ambiguity about what Nye means by 'private-regarding'. As Scott has pointed out, it should not be too narrowly conceived and include the politician who, from motives of loyalty, 'illegally diverts public funds to his ethnic association or political party' (1972, 4). Problems with operability emerge if rules and regulations allow for discretion which then may be employed for private gain.[31] However, since in most settings rules and regulations specify how discretion is to be employed, the damage seems to be limited.

More important is the objection that there may well be some tolerance towards some petty administrative corruption. Heidenheimer introduced the distinction between 'black corruption', condemned by a majority consensus of both elite and mass opinion, 'grey corruption' which only some elements of the public - usually the elites - may want to see punished, and 'white corruption', widely regarded as tolerable, where the majority of both elite and mass opinion probably would not vigorously support an attempt at punishment (1970, 26–27). The shades from white to black may indeed vary from one society to another. The existence of white corruption in the form of artificial padding of overtime work, various reports concerning their expenses, and petty bribery such as the custom of the 'bottles basket' presented to civil servants by their clients has been postulated by Werner for Israel (1989, 263–264). Nepotism also may belong to this category in some societies.

Last, Nye's definition is based on a consequentialist view of morality and therefore is not concerned with the motives of the actors. If a civil servant, for example, breaks a rule with the intention to improve welfare, but a close relative gains without the civil servant being aware of it, he is corrupt according to our definition, but probably not according to the view of the public.[32] More seriously, the definition does not consider the nature of the private gain. There is some evidence that motives do play a role in the public's assessment of corruption. Johnston finds that a transgression by a treasurer who keeps a 5 percent cut for himself is judged significantly more objectionable than one where the proceeds are used to pay a hospital bill (1989, 752). For example, would it be considered corrupt to take a bribe and use the proceeds to save the life of a close relative? By taking account of motives, public office definitions might be saved from this charge. Since motives cannot be observed, however, this comes at the cost of making such definitions inoperable. In addition, the potential gain from integrating motives into the definition is of limited relevance since, in practice, few acts of corruption are motivated by pure altruism.

To summarize: the much reviled conventional public office definition stands up fairly well against the criticisms leveled against it. There are *prima facie* reasons to believe that corruption is detrimental to the public interest; there are few reasons to believe that the usefulness of the concept is restricted to industrialized societies; and it does not have the conservative bias attributed to it by its critics.

4.1.2   Corrupt Legislators and Public Corruption

The public office definition is designed to deal with administrative corruption, and so operates exclusively in the sphere of 'derivative power', the sphere of the 'agent' who violates formal rules laid down by the principal. If politicians legislate for their own benefit, they are not considered corrupt according to this definition. The standard therefore 'does not cover political systems that are, in Aristotelian terms, "corrupt" in that they systematically serve the interests of special groups or sectors' (Scott 1972, 5).[33]

At this stage, the public interest definitions of corruption become relevant. According to those, any action by politicians which violates the public interest is deemed corrupt, and any preference of factional over communal interests becomes an expression of corruption (Dobel 1978, 964–966). Such strict standards find some support in public opinion. Pork-barreling, for example, was thought 'modestly corrupt' by a group of Canadian students, presumably because violates the public interest (Gibbons 1989, 771).

As has been pointed out, the public interest and public opinion notions are difficult to define. It does not necessarily follow, however, that they are empty sets. There is hardly anyone who believes that President Mobutu's appropriation of large chunks of Zaire's state revenue for private purposes is either popular or in the public interest and therefore not corrupt, even if this action did not violate rules nominally in force. More importantly, as has been established before, there is one case where the public interest definition does yield a determinate result. As the efficient operation of public administration is in the public interest, and breaching rules and regulations for private benefits tends to undermine its operation, such breaches are against the public interest. The justification for using the public office definition, therefore, rests in part on its correspondence to the public interest definition.

The public interest definition opens up the possibility that members of the public may act corruptly too. The support of a politician becomes corrupt if it is done with a view to the expected share of the spoils from administrative corruption: better access to government services, jobs, and so forth.[34]

The circle closes here. Members of the public who support clientelist politicians who break rules and regulations with a view to personal gain are corrupt themselves. To what degree this public interest definition corresponds to public opinion is far from clear, but at least it has the advantage of consistency. There is no reason, for example, why one would condemn politicians for violating public office rules or for acting against the public interest, and not the voter who backs those actions by supporting the politicians.

Moreover, as will be seen later on, administrative corruption is closely related to public corruption. In a democratic clientelist system, the expectations of the voters guide the behavior of politicians at least to some degree, and voters expecting particularistic benefits in violation of administrative procedures generate the political forces which induce administrative corruption.

4.2   Causes of Administrative Corruption

In order to assess the effect of clientelism on administrative corruption, we need to ascertain the causes of corruption. The conventional economic analysis is to stipulate that individuals perform a corrupt act if the benefits derived from it outweigh the costs. The level of corruption therefore is likely to increase if the benefits from acting corruptly rise and the costs fall.

Costs may be both material and non-material, an example of the latter being the opprobrium that a corrupt official may incur. These costs can be of three kinds: formal punishment meted out by the body politic, informal punishment by society at large, and by the psychological cost an individual experiences by acting against his or her conscience. The level of corruption will alter therefore with the probability of being caught and convicted and the severity of punishment, with the severity of social sanctions, and with the attitudes of those liable to engage in corrupt acts.

In many cases corrupt acts involve two or more individuals. To use Johnston's terminology, we have to deal with 'transactional' as well as 'unilateral' corruption (1982, 11). In economic terms, an explanation of the level of corruption has to deal with public officials who supply property rights in breach of rules and regulations as well as by members of the public who demand them.

Neo-classical models of the causes of changes in the level of corruption generally attempt to explain levels of corruption exclusively by reference to corrupt officials. This is unsurprising given the inheritance of the economics of crime (Becker 1968). Indeed, it is difficult to talk about the 'demand for crime'. Transactional corruption, however, cannot be explained using this approach.[35]

Moreover, neo-classical models of corruption focus exclusively on the expected costs of punishment by the authorities, the probability of being caught and convicted, the sentence and losses of earnings if employment is terminated. Whereas there is little doubt that fines constitute a cost to an administrator, the cost of loss of employment is less clear-cut.[36] If an official finds alternative employment after being sacked from the public service, then the opportunity cost in terms of lost earnings may well be small. That poverty is the fate of corrupt officials is not self-evident. Of the dozen corrupt Ghanaian officials interviewed by LeVine who lost their positions after the fall of Nkrumah only two were technically unemployed, 'but even these admitted they had stable sources of income, in both cases deriving in part from investments and contacts made during their terms of office' (LeVine 1975, 40).

Part of the failure of neo-classical analysis comes from neglecting the effect of social sanctions which may accompany the revelation that an individual acted corruptly. Such social sanctions may lead to both psychological costs and monetary losses. Non-material costs include suffering from expressions of disapproval by society, material costs the reduction in re-employment prospects if a person is dismissed, or reduced profits if a firm loses contracts to governments or private firms as a consequence of a conviction for corruption. The presence or absence of social sanctions, as in the case of LeVine's administrators, has a significant effect on the overall costs of corruption.

Neo-classical analyses assume moreover that tastes are constant, and thus attitude changes are eliminated from the analysis of variations in the level of corruption at the outset. Attitude changes, such as to what constitutes black or white corruption, might well influence the level of corruption.

The analysis put forward here leads to an equilibrium analysis where, at a given set of environmental conditions, a particular level of corruption will prevail. This, however, may not be the case. One explanation of why corruption increases is based on the distinction between black and white corruption (Heidenheimer 1970, 26–27). White corruption is socially accepted and will neither cause great pangs of conscience nor elicit social sanctions. In a version of the slippery slope argument, Werner held that 'The acceptance of white corruption as being "legitimate" will, in turn, tend to spill over to perceptions of other types of corruption. The grey and black shades become progressively lighter, and a momentum is established' (1989, 265). Left unchecked, white corruption becomes a growth industry. As corruption is universal, but has been contained in different countries at various levels over extended periods of time, the slippery slope hypothesis has limited applications.

4.3   Changes in the Level of Corruption

Changes in the level of administrative corruption are generally attributed to the nature of the administrative system. However, the administrative characteristics which cause corruption can be a reflection of the political structure, particularly of political clientelism. Clientelism may in turn be a function of public corruption - the willingness of the public to support politicians who engage in legislative and administrative corruption.

4.3.1   Nature of the Administrative System

Corruption is often seen as a consequence of the nature of the administrative system itself, or more specifically, the state of the anti-corruption agencies, the efficiency of the administrative system, and its size. Changes in these variables alter the level of corruption by modifying costs and benefits of corrupt acts.

4.3.1.1 Anti-corruption Agencies

The most obvious influence on the costs of corruption comes from anti-corruption agencies. Whereas neo-classical corruption models explain changes in the level of corruption in terms of the state of anti-corruption agencies and the cost of administrative punishment, outside that school it is not usually believed that these agencies are able to decrease substantially the *level* of corruption (Rose-Ackerman 1978, 220). Thus sceptics noted long ago that Indian figures 'suggest that both corruption and law enforcement efforts were increasing' at the same time (Hager 1973, 202).[37] Indeed, McMullan's pronouncement that he was unaware of any campaign to root out corruption 'which had any lasting effect, or indeed has even led to many prosecutions' (1961, 198) has lost only some of its force.

The few effective anti-corruption drives, as in Singapore and Hong Kong, were successful because by the time they were launched they were supported by public opinion (Klitgaard 1988, 103–121, 126–133), in the same way as the laws which were enacted in nineteenth century Britain 'have run a little ahead of public opinion as a whole, but they certainly had majority opinion behind them before they became laws, and the abuses which were finally swept away were the abuses which only a minority were continuing to commit' (Wraith and Simpkins 1963, 175). Moreover, anti-corruption drives need the support of the politicians in power. An anti-corruption strategy 'that involves only the organizational level is doomed to failure. It is not worth the paper it is written on because there is no will to enforce it or follow it through' (Caiden 1993, 266). Even worse, 'the frequent public and private campaigns to eliminate corruption and factionalism ... tend to be applied selectively to the detriment of particular individuals and clans and to the advantage of others' (Cruise O'Brien 1975, 171).

The greater the level of corruption, the smaller the effect of anti-corruption drives. There are a number of reasons for this. First, the detection of corruption becomes more difficult. This may be the result of corrupt officials muddying the waters: as corruption expands and more files are inaccurate, are being 'misplaced' and 'lost', it becomes increasingly difficult to establish cases against corrupt individuals, and detection becomes more difficult as corrupt officials form coalitions mutually protecting each other. For example, in its analysis of the genesis of corruption, 'the Chinese communist press attributes part of the blame to the existence of cliques or clientelism inside the party and state bureaucracy. Since 1977 almost every case of "aggravated corruption" publicized by the Chinese press in the mainland unearthed an extensive network of vertical (clientelist) and horizontal (dyadic) personal networks' (Liu 1989, 502).

Second, the general climate of corruption pervading the public sector may have an effect on the law-enforcement agencies. As Pashigian (1975) has pointed out, the number of bribes offered to law-enforcement agencies is closely tied to the degree of corruption in the administration at large. The usefulness of anti-corruption agencies declines rapidly as those charged with eliminating corruption are 'themselves tainted with it; indeed, under such circumstances, both investigations and remedial legislation tend to be ineffective and pointless, or to become elaborate exercises in hypocrisy' (LeVine 1975, 80).[38]

Third, an anti-corruption drive will be less effective because social sanctions are likely to become less severe. Convictions for corruption are increasingly seen as accidents of life without having any stigma attached to them. Indeed, the skill in managing complicated corrupt processes and the connections developed may increase a person's earning power outside the bureaucracy. It comes as no surprise that LeVine's former leading officials did not end up poor and unemployed. If the severity of social sanctions declines as corruption expands, the effectiveness of the official punishment is undermined by the reduction in the severity of social sanctions.

As corruption becomes entrenched, therefore, it becomes increasingly difficult to eradicate. Such was the environment in the U.S.S.R. where 'illegal rewards of various kinds, from private use of public resources, from gifts, from "undeserved" bonuses, seem to have acquired a quasi-legitimate status because "everyone is doing it"' (Lampert 1983, 279). The battle against minor transgressions in particular might simply be abandoned, as in the case of Werner's 'bottle basket', where the prevalence of this type of bribery meant that courts found themselves quite helpless in attempting to weed it out (Werner 1989, 264).

It is certainly true that the state of the anti-corruption agency is one of the factors influencing corruption. However, its effectiveness depends crucially on the state of public opinion and on the political support it receives. Moreover, it will become increasingly powerless the more corruption becomes endemic.

4.3.1.2 Efficiency of the Administrative System

A whole host of issues which are generally thought to govern the costs and benefits of corruption can be summarized under the heading of efficiency of the administrative system. An efficient administration, for our purpose, is one which follows Weber's classical rules: decisions are impersonal and based on abstract formal rules (and in practice precedents) according to established procedures, and they are fully documented. The jurisdiction of each official is well defined and officials are adequately trained.

Where chains of command are unclear, responsibilities vaguely defined, and files tend to get 'misplaced', the control system suffers and the costs of punishment are reduced: 'Illicit gratification and bribery thrives on slow and uncertain process' (Braibanti 1962, 370). For example, the prevalence of inefficient employment procedures is likely to foster nepotism and partisan appointments. Moreover, these inefficient administrative procedures affect the administrative culture and attitudes of staff. They prevent the achievement of administrative aims and undermine morale. Inefficient employment procedures often put officials into positions where they are unable to cope (1962, 367).

A similar argument is sometimes put in terms of discretion. Discretion implies that rules for decision making are absent and precedents are irrelevant or non-existent. As discretion increases, control begins to slip from the upper echelons of the bureaucracy (LeVine 1975, 95–96), and arbitrariness and the possibility of favoritism and opportunities for unilateral as well as transactional corruption are introduced.[39] Hence the larger the degree of discretion, the higher is the level of corruption (Rose-Ackerman 1978, 111).

If the demand for goods and services exceeds supply at the official prices, an official is forced to apply some system of rationing, which by its very nature involves discretion. Indeed, rationing is seen as a major cause of corruption (Tilman 1979, 346). Katsenelenboigen attributes the widespread corruption in the U.S.S.R. partly to government 'setting prices which are lower than the required prices of equilibrium on some consumer goods', which therefore become scarce (1983, 229). In the same vein, DiFranceisco and Gitelman explain the difference in the level of corruption between the Soviet pension agencies and the housing agencies 'by the fact that almost all who are entitled to pensions receive them, whereas the housing problem is perhaps the most difficult one in the daily life of the Soviet citizen' (1989, 477–478).

An extreme case of a violation of the Weberian norms occurs if rules are contradictory or impossible to implement, and breaking some rules becomes unavoidable, a problem particularly virulent in planned economies (Kramer 1989, 458; Liu 1989, 498). Thus if in the U.S.S.R. plan targets were not met, the temptation to cover up for failure by means of report-padding was very strong (Lampert 1983, 279). The strong temptation was matched by a low probability of punishment: the chances that a complaint would be taken up by the administrative superiors of an organization were very slim indeed. Local party officials knew that certain forms of illegality were necessary and that some leeway must be given to management if targets were to be met (281). The problem, however, is not confined to planned economies (Campbell 1977, 251). As Scott pointed out, a typical Indian entrepreneur or trader 'must pick his way through a plethora of state and local regulations that are at best confusing and at worst contradictory' (Scott 1972, 13).

The level of corruption is likely to rise if training is inadequate, or if insufficient time has been devoted to shift the allegiance of the civil servant from society to the state. Again, any decline in administrative competence is likely to reduce the effectiveness of the control structure and therefore the cost of punishment. Moreover, the lower the degree of allegiance to the state, the fewer inhibitions that prevent breaking rules officials are likely to have. In most Third World countries, the rapid localization of the civil service after independence, combined with its substantial expansion, inevitably called for upgrading civil servants, introducing crash-courses, and lowering entry requirements (Werlin 1972; Price 1975, 301–32). In addition, the process precluded the pursuit of strategies to shift the allegiance of civil servants from traditional groups to the state (Werlin 1972).[40] These factors have undoubtedly increased the level of corruption.

Three main organizational arguments are sometimes put forward to explain the level of administrative corruption: wage levels, the size of the government sector, and the degree of centralization.

It is widely believed that the level of wages is inversely related to corruption (Smith 1989, 429; Katsenelenboigen 1983, 230; Clarke 1983, xi, Wade 1985, 486).[41] More specifically, it is usually said that if wages do not provide for an adequate standard of living, corruption becomes widespread. But what constitutes an adequate standard of living? There are obvious cases, such as when officials have not been paid for some time. Indeed, it is not difficult to understand the behavior of a policemen who resorts to extortion and pockets some fines under these circumstances. Beyond that, it is difficult to judge what constitutes an adequate standard of living. Perhaps more important is the level of income relative to other groups. For example, a fall in the level of income of government officials relative to those in the private sector may result in lessened allegiance because of disappointed expectations.

It is often said that as the size of the government sector increases so does corruption (Huntington 1968, 61). Increasing regulation or nationalization adds new opportunities for corruption (62). For example, Wade refers to the 'large regulatory and allocative role of the state' as one of the causes of India's corruption (1985, 486). Two issues have to be distinguished. First, assume that the government produces and distributes goods and services which were in the past produced and distributed by the private sector. The assertion that an increase in the government sector leads to additional corruption then becomes partly a definitional problem. Quite clearly the opportunity set, or the demand for corruption, expands as well as supply. The number of corrupt acts increases even if the same practices prevail as previously in the private sector. The second issue then seems to be whether the private sector is better able to curb such practices than the public sector. It has been suggested that such structural features as greater fragmentation of authority and multiplicity of aims lead to an increase in corruption even in the absence of the definitional problem (Banfield 1975). Moreover, nationalized firms might be more exposed to political pressures. A typical example is provided by newly nationalized banks which were pressured to supply the ruling elite with loans in contravention of normal banking procedures.

There is another variation of the argument: it is not the absolute size of government, but the size of the public relative to the private sector which is the important determinant of the level of corruption: 'Foremost among the structural factor in new states is the tremendous relative importance of government in these nations as a source of goods, services, and employment' (Scott 1972, 12). The bureaucracy 'remains a most important avenue for wealth, status, and power' (77). It is by no means clear why 'the relative importance of government as a source of employment and social mobility' matters (1979, 102). As long as pay and conditions are the same as in the private sector, there is no reason for this desire to enter government employment. Rent-seeking and excessive demand for employment in the public sector occur only if employment conditions are more generous than elsewhere. Contrary to conventional wisdom, corruption may have been fostered more often by overly generous than by excessively miserly employment conditions. More generally, Tilman argues that 'the predominance of governmental activity in the new states, and the corresponding low level of activity in the private sectors, clients with demands unsatisfied by the mandatory pricing system of the government bureaucracy are likely to have fewer non-official alternatives open to them than would be the case in the more developed states' (1979, 347). Tilman simply throws the argument back to the rationing problem. If under the mandatory pricing system demand can be satisfied, then corruption does not vary with the size of government.

It is sometimes thought that 'deductive reasoning suggests that a highly centralized governmental structure may not only make corruption possible, but necessary' (Smith 1989, 432). The deductive reasoning of others has led them to assert the opposite (Van Klaveren 1964, 195; Wraith and Simpkins 1963, 208). Quite clearly, the issue is moot, depending on secondary assumptions about the working of a particular bureaucracy.

In summary, the supply of corrupt acts depends on innumerable institutional factors which determine the costs and benefits of corruption to individuals employed in the public administration. Of these factors, the most critical are the state of the anti-corruption agency, the efficiency of the administration, and perhaps the relative size of the government sector. However, these institutional factors are not ultimate data, since political processes are largely responsible for the state of the anti-corruption agency, for the great number of complex and contradictory rules and regulations, for the increase in rationing as goods and services are not available at official rates, for the lack of training and thus of administrative competence, for the employment conditions and the size of the public sector.

Of course it can be argued that some of these features, such as the expansion of the government sector, benefit the bureaucrats, and that therefore they are a result of the bureaucracy pursuing their own self-interest. But it is not a sufficient explanation because it still needs to be explained why the political process accommodates such bureaucratic pressures.

4.3.2   Clientelism and Corruption

Clientelism provides an explanation of why politicians allow the development of features conducive to corruption: the decay of the anti-corruption agency, and the administrative features that favor corruption. With clientelism, it is in the interest of politicians that administrative procedures deviate from Weberian rules by the large scope of discretion, by rationing, by contradictory rules and regulations, and by employment and promotion procedures not based on qualifications and performance. Moreover, politicians gain from the overexpansion of the government sector.

Clientelist politicians, as we have seen, have an incentive to replace collective with private goods. Goods and services provided by the government are not a compensation for political support if everyone else gets the same goods and services on the same terms. A Weberian administration where everyone who satisfies certain objective criteria has access to particular benefits stands in the way of remunerating political supporters. If politicians want to ensure that government benefits are received mainly by the faithful and the well connected, they have to resort to such practices as rationing and discretion.

Moreover, contradictory rules and regulations impossible to implement become sources of revenue through extortion. Health and safety regulations which are entirely unenforceable, for example, afford opportunities to harass, exploit, and politically neuter local shopkeepers. This is probably one of the reason why such stipulations, normally considered to be anomalies, remain on the books for lengthy periods of time. Practices like rationing, discretion and establishing contradictory rules therefore become tools in the quest for political power.

Among the goods and services provided by the government, administrative positions are of particular importance. Politicians will tend to fill administrative positions with friends and supporters, until, as in Sicily, 'over the years, a massive influx of relatives, friends, political supporters, family, and friends of friends and of political supporters, without the least consideration of the applicant's qualifications for the job in question, other than family name or political loyalty, swelled the ranks of the regional administration to gargantuan proportions' (Chubb 1982, 94). Not only does the bureaucracy become inflated by the great number of underqualified staff reducing the competence of the administration, but the morale of existing staff sinks under the dual onslaught of political appointments and the increasing arbitrariness of decision making. As the Weberian rules of employment, training, and promotion are increasingly violated, subjective barriers that prevent individuals from engaging in corruption are increasingly eroded. Clientelism not only clashes with the Weberian bureaucratic efficiency norms but also undermines the effectiveness of the anti-corruption agency. Positions in the bureaucracy may become prebends, assigned by leading politicians to relatives and political followers with the tacit understanding that the incumbents are allowed to exploit them for private gain. Even more importantly, as corruption is sanctioned by the politicians in power the anti-corruption agency will be virtually powerless in most cases.

Finally, as will be shown in the following chapter, clientelism has a tendency to expand the size of government beyond what is socially optimal in order to broaden the scope for patronage. This again has a tendency to increase the level of corruption.

So far we have looked at how clientelism encourages bureaucratic features that promote corruption. There are, however, other channels through which clientelism affects corruption. It undermines both the strength of social sanctions and attitudinal barriers to violating rules and regulations. Clientelism epitomizes a state where legislative corruption is rampant, and where legislative measures are introduced with the manifest intention of benefiting supporters, independent of their contributions to the public good. In such a political environment, both the public and the administrators will have few inhibitions to promote their self-interest and break rules and regulations. Similarly, such an milieu is unlikely to strengthen social sanctions against corrupt behavior.

4.3.3   Public Corruption and Clientelism

Up to now, administrative corruption was attributed to the behavior of politicians. However, clientelism might be at least partially a reflection of the value orientations of the public at large. It may be that people 'vote for whom they think can give *them* the most favors in a particularistic way' (Wade 1985, 487). In that situation, 'politicians will find it difficult to provide effective inducements without violating formal standards of public conduct' (Scott 1972, 93).

Indeed, in the framework which has been outlined, public corruption, the willingness to maximize one's own self-interest through the support of corrupt politicians, is an essential pillar of clientelism. Thus the behavior of the public bears a heavy responsibility for the level of administrative corruption. It follows that it is too simple to argue that a system which 'permits public participation in the formulation of policies' and where 'public institutions are responsive to public concerns' minimizes corruption (Ouma 1991, 477).

4.4   Corruption Reinforces Clientelism

Clientelism not only promotes corruption, it is also sustained by it. A high level of administrative corruption is likely to promote cynicism towards politics and thus reinforce the self-seeking political behavior associated with clientelist politics. Moreover, it has been shown earlier that corruption facilitates the absorption of corporate groups into clientele networks. As administrative decisions are less and less guided by general policy rules, it becomes more important to influence decisions at the output stage, and the leading members of corporations have an incentive to join the political patron-client networks, to abandon the contest for collective goods and enter the scramble for private benefits.

4.5   Conclusion

The chapter argued that the concept of administrative corruption based on a public office standard is unnecessarily reviled: there is a *prima facie* case that corruption violates the common good; critics have failed to establish that public opinion in the Third World condones corruption; the concept does not have the alleged conservative bias attributed to it; and the fact that rules and regulations are different in different societies and formal rules are sometimes absent does not invalidate the concept.

In general, the level of corruption will depend on the cost and benefits of corruption. These in turn are heavily influenced by the nature of public administration: the state of the anti-corruption agency; the efficient organization of the public administration in general; and the size of the government sector. Whether such features are allowed to develop and flourish will in turn largely depend on political decisions.

Clientelism suggests why it is in the interest of politicians to make political decisions that encourage administrative corruption. Clientelism facilitates corruption because of the need to provide particularistic benefits for supporters. Providing particularistic benefits to maintain political power tends to lead to rationing and contradictory administrative rules; an increase in the size of the government sector; a decrease in the effectiveness of the anti-corruption agency; and a high level of legislative corruption, which undermines individuals' inhibitions about engaging in administrative corruption.

In a fully fledged clientelist system we would expect corruption to be endemic. As it is widely and systematically used by the political class to shore up political support, and therefore is sanctioned at the highest level, there are few barriers to its spread, and it permeates all spheres of administration, including the law enforcement agencies and the judiciary. 'Wrong-doing' becomes the norm, and behavior 'according to notions of public responsibility and trust' the exception[42] (Caiden and Caiden 1977, 306).[43]

If clientelism reflects the preferences of the individual voter, then administrative corruption becomes ultimately a reflection of the behavior of the public. Voters support politicians who promise to provide particularistic benefits to their supporters, and in the process they create the administrative features responsible for corruption.

Corruption in this environment is systemic. It is not random behavior of deviant individuals that is observed in all societies, but an integral part of the working of the political system. It is this which makes corruption in many Third World countries different from its counterpart in most industrialized nations. Many observers of corruption feel the need to point out that corruption exists in both the developed and the less developed world. The statement is true, of course, but it is also trivial and misleading. It is trivial because there is bound to be corruption, as there is bound to be crime. It is misleading because what matters economically, socially, and politically is not the fact that there is corruption, perhaps not even so much the fact that levels of corruption are different, but that it constitutes a major pillar of the political system.

Notes:

1.   Another attempt to protect respectable social science from dealing with corruption is to equate it with rent-seeking in the manner of Evans: 'Rent-seeking, conceptualized more primitively as corruption, has always been a well-known facet of the operation of Third World states' (1992, 144). Clearly, rent-seeking is not the same as corruption. To call someone's pilfering of government stores rent-seeking would

surely be absurd.

2. The definitions are applied for different kinds of activities. In order to make these points, we are not following the conventional distinction between administrative and political corruption, where administrative corruption is concerned with what administrators do, and political corruption with the misdeeds of politicians. Administrative corruption applies to all public roles where action is circumscribed by public rules and regulations, to politicians and administrators alike. Thus contravening rules relating to the election process and tampering with census figures are elements of administrative corruption. Legislative corruption, on the other hand, involves the process of policy generation, including the establishment of administrative rules and regulations.

3. See Heidenheimer (1970) and Scott (1972, 3).

4. The term was explicitly used by Scott (1972, 3–4). One way of advancing the understanding of corruption is to investigate what public opinion believes to be corrupt. Indeed, a common empirical approach is to use such a study to arrive at a public opinion definition of corruption. Peters and Welch proceed on this track by trying to determine the elements of an act which the public perceives to be corrupt (1978, 974).

5. For example, it is said that a pattern of corruption 'can be said to exist whenever a power-holder who is charged with doing certain things, i.e., who is a responsible functionary of office holder, is by monetary or other rewards not legally provided for induced to take actions which favor whoever provides the rewards and thereby does damage to the public and its interests' (Friedrich 1966, 74).

6. E.g. Scott (1972, 2–3).

7. Leys falls into the trap of presupposing that a public office definition demands universal agreement about what constitutes the public interest, hence his objection that neither 'attitudes nor material conditions in these countries are focused on the support of a single concept of the national interest' (1965, 224).

8. As corruption corresponding to the public office definition is simply a sub-set of corrupt acts that is closely related to what public opinion condemns as corrupt, the definition ought to be chosen accordingly. Nye's position does this fairly well, whereas alternatives tend to suffer in this respect. Gains, for example, need not be monetary or even material (Bayley 1966, 720), hence definitions like McMullan's according to which a 'public official is corrupt if he accepts money or money's worth' (1961, 183–184) are too narrow. Nor is corruption tied to exchange, such as bribery; embezzlement or the padding of expense accounts generally violates rules and regulations, and indeed is considered to be corrupt by the public. US senators share this view; padding expense accounts, using public funds for personal travel, and

diverting money allocated for office expenses to personal activities ranked among the most seriously corrupt actions (Peters and Welch 1978, 977), and embezzlement ranked highest in the list of serious corruption in Johnston's American survey (1989, 750).

9.   Ideally, a satisfactory definition of corruption should be able to reconcile the different standards. Whereas conventionally the three types of definition are treated as competitors, they are in fact complementary, the public office definition being subsumed by the public interest definition, and the public interest and public opinion definitions coinciding to a large degree. The reason is not far to seek. One would expect moral rules in general and rules regarding corruption in particular to denounce those types of behaviour that are against the public interest. Moreover, it will be shown that breaking rules and regulations for personal gain is against the public interest, and that therefore the public office definition becomes a special case of the more general public interest definition.

10. The terms 'moralizing approach' was used by the 'moralizers' themselves (Wraith and Simpkins 1963, 172).

11. Who are the members of the 'moralist' school? Leys mentions only Wraith and Simpkins (1963), Nye (1967) adds Friedrich (1963; 1966) and K.T. Young.

12. Rottenberg's attempt founders on the same rock: 'Fundamentally, it seems to me that what corrupt people do is to sell rights that they possess *de facto* but do not possess legally' (1975, 612).

13. Indeed, for Wraith and Simpkins corruption 'is above all a moral problem' (1963, 17) which undermines altruistic human intercourse by introducing self-seeking behaviour into each nook and cranny of society, and there the analysis rests.

14. For a criticism of the revisionist position see Kurer (1993).

15. Arguments that corruption increases administrative efficiency are dealt with in section 3.1.

16. As Foltz has pointed out: 'Particularly in the crucial field of economic development, reform measures which may threaten individual power bases are regularly blocked by local politicians' (1977, 245).

17. E.g. Leys (1965) and Leff (1968).

18. Bureaucracies have lately become fashionable again as their importance for the process of economic development has been rediscovered (Evans 1992), especially the postulate well-known to Adam Smith that even market-driven reforms require an efficient regulatory framework (e.g. Robbins 1952).

19. For empirical evidence for developed countries see Gibbons (1989, 773).

20. Including in Africa and India, to take the two examples singled out by Bayley. In a more recent example, 55 percent of respondents of a survey in Sierra Leone 'considered corruption as second only in

importance to the ongoing rebel war' (Kpundeh 1994, 154).

21. The notion is obviously older than that of bureaucratic rule. For example, the popular theory of kingship 'suggested that the king was a landlord who, like other landlords, had responsibilities to society and was answerable to the community for the exercise of his privileges' (Abercrombie and Turner 1982, 401).

22. 'Politics and policymaking are, after all, complex, distant and unfamiliar worlds to most people' (Johnston 1989, 745). As Chibnell and Saunders pointed out, both elites and ordinary citizens engage in the 'social construction of reality' (1977), devising their own conceptions of political ethics. Hence popular conceptions of corruption are unlikely to conform to formal definitions of corruption.

23. Evidence from the early seventeenth century contradicts those historians who suggest that the distinction between public and private was only sketchily established in the early modern period (Peck 1990, 161, 184).

24. In other words, the criticism involves the fallacy of denying the antecedent.

25. As Scott seems to claim (1972, 7).

26. It is of course still true that it is not very helpful, that 'it virtually forecloses discussions of corruption in pre-bureaucratic systems' (Heidenheimer 1970, 9), but that is a different issue.

27. Something Gardiner (1993, 116) in his criticism of legalistic definition overlooks. Equally, Klitgaard misses the point when he describes 'corrupt' managers who allocate funds in breach of rules and regulations in order to better achieve the aims of the organization (1988, 32–33). This is not a case of corruption, since the managers do not benefit materially from the breach.

28. An act is corrupt, however, if rules and regulations are violated and the transgressor gains thereby, even if the act results in a welfare improvement.

29. Lowenstein's criticism of public office definitions is beside the point. According to him, public office definitions are 'said to be "operational" because bribery laws are relatively "precise and consistent", or "generally clear-cut"' (1989, 33). The central contention of his article then becomes that 'at least as far as political bribery is concerned, the law in the United States is neither "precise and consistent", nor "generally clear-cut"' (33). Lowenstein's position is based on a misreading of Scott, who writes that public office definitions rely heavily on 'legal norms in defining corruption' (1972,4). The legal norms Scott refers to are evidently not bribery laws, but the 'formal duties of a public role' which usually are fairly precise and consistent (4).

30.   Gardiner alters Nye's definition: a corrupt act becomes one which deviates from 'normal' instead of 'formal' duties of a public role (1993, 112). Gardiner then goes and criticises Nye's definition for the vagueness implied by 'normal' duties!

31.   For example, rules about which bids to accept often allow some discretion, and it becomes sometimes difficult to determine whether corruption, often in terms of political favours, was involved in the allocation of contracts.

32.   Similarly, the crime of corruption requires generally 'corrupt intent' in American law (Lowenstein 1989, 30).

33.   See also Rogow and Lasswell (1970, 54) and Friedrich (1966, 74).

34.   On the next level there is the case of members of the public who promote corrupt legislation. Scott simply applies the public office definition and argues that a powerful lobby's ability 'to secure passage of a law that greatly benefits its members does not in itself constitute corruption unless it can also be shown that the lobby bribed legislators or otherwise violated formal norms' (1972, 5). Dobel, on the other hand, takes what is essentially a public interest perspective and argues that in a corrupt state civic loyalty and virtue, 'the ability and willingness of the citizens to act spontaneously or disinterestedly to support other citizens or communal institutions' (1978, 963), have broken down. As in the case of the legislator, the actions of the public can only be considered corrupt if the definition is extended to a public interest one.

35.   Recent discussions on the optimal level of punishment remain in this vein (e.g. Leung 1991; Shleifer and Vishny 1993), although Andvig and Moene claim to deal with demand for corruption. However, the demand depends on search costs which in turn are a function of the relative number of corrupt officials. Hence 'supply directly induces demand' (1990, 66). This is not a demand analysis in the conventional sense, which at the very least has to integrate the benefits of corrupt acts to consumers.

36.   Examples of studies where this exceedingly questionable assumption plays an important role in the analysis are Cadot (1987, 231) and Andvig and Moene (1990, 66).

37.   During the period under review by the Santhanam report.

38.   One of the problems with Lui's argument is that the anti-corruption agency is supposed to be unaffected by corruption. It is viewed not as part of the general administration, but as a *deus ex machina*.

39.   This is not to say that some degree of discretion is not inevitable or even desirable in public administration.

40.   It is interesting in this context that there is a long populist tradition which declared that attempts to alienate officials from traditional society and shift their loyalty to the state are socially harmful (e.g. Brownsberger 1983, 228).

41.   For a critical view see Braibanti (1962, 371).
42.   The use of public office 'for private enrichment is the normal and accepted practice in African states' (Andreski 1979, 277). Corruption becomes 'a fact of life that one cannot avoid and that had best be mastered' (Waterbury 1989, 344).
43.   Caiden and Caiden define this as systemic. It is more accurately described as endemic.

5 Clientelism, Policy Failures, and Economic Growth

This chapter deals with the economic consequences of two salient features of clientelism: corruption and the expansion of state intervention. The chapter shows that a government that maintains power through clientelist exchange is likely to encounter the familiar problems associated with an inward-looking development strategy: excessive waste through rent-seeking, the neglect of infrastructure, a misallocation of government services, an overstaffed and inefficient public administration, a large and inefficient parastatal sector and private sector regulations which reduce welfare. These factors impede growth through low savings and investment rates.

Corruption in a clientelist setting is less innocuous than some revisionists would like us to believe. The revisionist case is built on the implicit assumption that policy formulation is independent of corruption. However, corrupt politicians must be assumed to take into account potential corrupt gains when they formulate policy. Moreover, the apologists' case that corruption enhances the efficiency of the public administration is flawed. Nor will licenses and contracts generally be allocated to the most efficient producers if politicians not only maximize bribe revenue, but take into account political support as well. Misallocation of resources, impaired productivity, lack of investment and a slower rate of economic growth are therefore intimately connected with the prevalence of clientelism and corruption.

5.1   The Revisionists

We have already encountered the revisionists, whose aim it was to rescue corruption from the prejudices of moralizers. In their overall assessment of corruption they did not present a unified front. In the main, they rejected the *a priori* denunciations of corruption and deferred judgement on the ground that it had at least potentially beneficial effects.[1] Of this group Leff was prepared to go furthest by arguing that 'the consequences of corruption for development are not as serious as is usually assumed. At the same time, it may have important positive effects that are often overlooked'. Consequently corruption 'may not be a problem at all' (1964, 13).

The analysis of this monograph, on the other hand, leads to the unequivocal conclusion that, at least in a clientelist environment, corruption has detrimental effects on economic development. Why are the conclusions so different?

5.2   Private Sector Regulation

5.2.1 The Revisionist Fallacy and the Regulatory Process

The revisionist case is strongest where a government attempts to introduce policies that reduce welfare, and where corruption prevents their adoption or implementation. In these circumstances corruption may indeed be welfare improving.[2]

The revisionists put forward two arguments: corruption improves the choice of a policy, and it may undermine the implementation of measures detrimental to welfare. For example, corruption may improve policy choice 'if business groups are otherwise at a disadvantage in articulating their interests to the government, and if these groups are more likely to promote growth than is the government, then their enhanced participation in policy formulation [through corruption] can help development' (Leff 1964, 8). Moreover, 'corruption may provide the means of overcoming discrimination against the members of a minority groups, and allow the entrepreneur from a minority to gain access to the political decisions necessary for him to provide his skills' (Nye 1967, 420).[3]

Furthermore, corruption may alleviate the *consequences* of sub-optimal policies by undermining their negative effects at the execution stage. Hence 'corruption helps to mitigate the consequences of ideologically determined economic devices which may not be wholly appropriate for the countries concerned' (420) and therefore 'may serve as a means for impelling better choices' (Bayley 1966, 727).

However, even if it is true that corruption may sometimes alleviate the consequences of sub-optimal policies, this does not mean that corruption is socially beneficial overall, because corruption will subvert the implementation of all policies, including those that are optimal. Thus, there might have been very many sub-optimal policies in Nkrumah's Ghana, but the official government purchasing policy was certainly superior to a practice where 'the size of the commission rather than the usefulness of the purchases was the determining factor in many governmental transactions' (Werlin 1973, 174), and materials were purchased which were simply not needed (175). To take another example, there is no particular reason to doubt that the official policies and administrative aims on canal irrigation in Southern India are reasonably sensible. However, as a consequence of corruption economic planners and farmers 'have recurrently been dismayed' finding 'that canal systems operate substantially below the expected level of performance' (Wade 1982, 287). Nor is there much reason to believe that many of the safety procedures which were undermined by corruption, such as in rail transport, have been deficient (McMullan 1961, 182). Thus the fact that corruption is sometimes advantageous does not establish that it is socially beneficial on the whole.

There is, however, a more fundamental problem with the revisionist's case. They assume that sub-optimal economic policies are pursued because the government is incompetent or suffers from ideological bias.[4] Such revisionist reasoning implies an initial stage where politicians draw up sub-optimal policies because of ignorance or ideological predilections. It ignores the possibility that anticipated gains from corruption enter the deliberations about policy from the very outset. Revisionists are caught up in the fallacy of assuming that the state of the world in which particular corrupt practices take place is determined independently from corruption.

In a clientelist system, corruption does affect policy-making. Policies are selected and implemented with a view of generating income and political support. Hence licensing, tariffs, quotas, and nationalization of industry are seen as means to generate revenue which then can be appropriated by the politicians in various ways including bribes and kickbacks, or which can be left to clients as remuneration for political support. Here the sub-optimal policies which lead to a distortion in the price structure and to welfare losses become a consequence of corruption. From this viewpoint, the revisionist case breaks down. If the sub-optimal policies are a result of corruption, then it makes little sense to credit corruption with alleviating negative allocative effects for which it was responsible to begin with. If a system of licenses was created to increase corrupt gains, then Leff's argument that the competitive pressure of a bidding procedure will increase efficiency founders. If discriminatory policies are designed because of expected monopoly gains by clients, corruption generates misallocation to begin with and may at best alleviate further welfare losses.

The revisionist claims are based on inconsistent behavior on the part of the government. Revisionists discuss the case where politicians are corrupt, but their decisions on policy remain unaffected by potential corrupt gains. In other words, politicians initially behave in a perfectly honest manner while sitting down discussing policies but get enmeshed in corrupt practices immediately afterwards. Only then can it be assumed that sub-optimal policies are the result of considerations other than corruption. This is not to say that sub-optimal policies may not result from incompetence or ideological bias, but that, as soon as corruption is allowed for, it must be presumed to constitute one of the elements in decision making from the very outset.

Indeed, there is widespread agreement that corruption does influence policy making. Thus LeVine discovers empirical support for this suggestion in the Ghana case, where 'fostering projects ostensibly designed to be economically profitable but actually designed to conceal diversion of capital to corrupt fees or procurement of cost-plus contracts and suppliers' credits ... most closely describes the visible situation in Ghana during the Nkrumah period' (1975, 101). Scott finds that patronage considerations are often reflected in the structure of development programs (1972, 121). The process of nationalization in Indonesia in the late 1950s and '60s 'was as often motivated by the desire of important cliques for new fields of patronage and revenue as by a set of nationalist of socialist policy goals' (82).[5] Similarly, the goals of reorganizing and centralizing the cocoa trade in Ghana 'corresponded closely with the desire of CPP leaders to maximize the political utility of government employment and expenditure' (130). Fieldhouse (1986, 94) observed that in Africa particular policies developed because of their prospect as tools of patronage politics: 'Licensing of all kinds is desirable because licenses can be used either as rewards or as threats. Price controls to balance over-valued currencies are preferable to rational monetary policies because they can be used selectively ... Such practices have become endemic'.

Thus the revisionist assumption that corruption and policy formulation are independent is neither theoretically sound[6] nor supported by empirical evidence. It therefore makes little sense to credit corruption with hampering the implementation of sub-optimal policies which it helped to shape.

In conclusion, the revisionist case that there is no *a priori* case against corruption finds little support. First, as has been argued before, corruption negatively affects the operation of the public administration; second, it is true that corruption may undermine the introduction and implementation of sub-optimal policies and thus be welfare-improving, but since it does not distinguish between optimal and sub-optimal policies, it sabotages the adoption of all alike; third, the distortions in the economy which corruption may alleviate are as likely as not the result of corrupt decisions to begin with. However, it remains to be shown that corruption in a clientelist setting is heavily responsible for the misallocation of government funds, a bloated public administration, the inefficient provision of services, the bias against infrastructure projects, the overexpansion of the government sector and the overregulation of the private sector.

5.2.2 Allocation of Licenses and Contracts

Clientelism leads us to expect that licenses and contracts will be allocated to politically well connected but inefficient producers. This, according to the revisionists, is not true. Leff, for example, believes that 'bureaucratic corruption also brings an element of competition, with its attendant pressure for efficiency, to an underdeveloped economy. Since the licenses and favors available to the bureaucrats are in limited supply, they are allocated by competitive bidding among entrepreneurs ... Hence, a tendency toward competition and efficiency is introduced into the system' (1964, 11). Thus competition ensures, the revisionist's argument continues, that licenses and contracts will tend to go to the low-cost producer.[7] How plausible is this claim?

One obvious rejoinder is that the secrecy surrounding the allocation of contracts and licenses will often prevent this process from operating effectively since it presupposes 'auction-like conditions' like unimpeded information flows and free access to the bidding process. But officials who allocate licenses and contracts may seek to limit the size of the illicit market 'to what might be considered safe levels', and permit entry 'only to a small clique of trusted friends and relatives who need not be the most efficient producers' (Alam 1990, 90).[8]

Even if the bidding process is fairly open and there is a reasonable degree of information available, the revisionist case still does not generally hold. Revisionists analyze the behavior of an isolated individual administrator who decides whether or not to grant a license or a contract. In a patronage system, however, officials are often part of a clientele network, and it is generally the patron, the politician in power, who makes decisions, at least those of substance. This patron, however, is not interested in bribe revenue only.

When does the inclusion of political support in the objective function matter? Let us look at two scenarios. First, assume that maximizing bribe revenue also happens to lead to the greatest amount of political support. Suppose that political support depends exclusively on the amount of money transferred to clients; in other words, clients sell their support to whoever offers the greatest cash-transfer. In this scenario, maximizing bribe revenue also maximizes political support. Here, the revisionist story re-emerges: contracts are allocated to the most efficient producer who is able to pay the largest bribe.

In the second scenario, clients are not only interested in money transfers, they also care about employment. Take the situation where a client firm is a relatively inefficient producer. The patron may decide to maximize bribe revenue and to allocate the contract to the more efficient outsider. The income from the bribe might then be partly or wholly used to compensate the client firm for the loss of the contract. It may well be, however, that this bribe revenue is insufficient to recompense the clients for the loss in employment if alternative employment opportunities are not readily available. Take the case of a firm that is located in an area where a patron has his power base. Such a firm may have to shut down because of the loss of government contracts which have been awarded to a more efficient producer. In this situation, it is very likely that the additional bribe revenue that can be extracted from the more efficient producer is insufficient to maintain the same level of political support, even if all of it is distributed in this particular constituency.[9]

There is therefore no particular reason to believe that corruption leads to an optimal allocation of licenses and contracts.[10] Indeed, trading off between political gains and bribe revenues has been observed repeatedly. Licenses are sometimes given to the favorites of the government and sometimes in exchange for bribes (Andreski 1979, 276). Similarly, clients often receive preference in bidding for local public works contracts; but simultaneously large contracts go to outsiders who are then expected to pay large bribes, sometimes through 'consultancy companies' expressly set up for the purpose of 'laundering' illegal payments (Scott 1972, 127, 129).[11]

5.2.3 Regulation and Rent-seeking

Clientelism is likely to diminish welfare through regulations that serve mainly political purposes and lead to widespread rent-seeking behavior. Through regulations, a government is able to generate rent which it is able to distribute among its members and supporters. A politician maximizing his welfare will impose a particular regulation if the benefits he derives from it exceed the costs. Thus when the overall net benefit, in terms of political support and income, is positive, he will introduce the measure. These benefits and costs are not directly related to economic criteria, so regulations will be introduced which have little economic justification.

Welfare-reducing regulations imposed to shore up the wealth of the rulers and their political support are a widespread phenomenon. Thus borrowers would be advantaged by the removal of interest rate controls, but retaining those controls provides an avenue for patronage (Rimmer 1984, 262). 'From the point of view of both officials and politicians, it is better to expand the rules and regulations than to reduce them, for this increases the number of citizens in the category of applicants' (Wade 1989, 104). From this perspective, import substitution strategies are seen as just another method of generating rent for the protected and subsidized industries. Clientelism, therefore, has a tendency to generate the distorted regulatory environments of many Third World countries.

The existence of rent will in turn lead to rent-seeking behavior as people begin 'to employ resources in attempting to obtain or prevent such transfers' (Tullock 1981, 48).[12] There are two types of rent-seeking activities: those aimed at changing the legislative system,[13] and those that compete for the rent provided for by the existing system of regulations.[14]

Resources employed in obtaining rent-seeking activities constitute a pure welfare loss, because rent seekers are prevented from engaging in productive activities. For example, Krueger assumes that rent in the upper echelons of public sector employment leads individuals to consume too much education in order to be able to compete for jobs where higher education is a prerequisite (1974, 293). More importantly, much of political activity is pure rent-seeking behavior. Krueger makes what she thinks is a conservative estimate of rent in India of approximately 7 per cent of GDP and in Turkey of 15 per cent. If the same amount of resources is invested in competing for this rent, then this corresponds to the welfare loss to society.[15]

In a clientelist environment characterized by the relentless pressure to increase benefits to the clients one would expect rent-seeking activities to be widespread, both to change the legislative structure in order to increase the total amount of rent available in the economy, and to influence the distribution process. The difference from the conventional story of Tullock and Krueger is not so much the fact that rent-seeking is ubiquitous, but the way it manifests itself: not through organized interest group activities, but through diffuse pressures originating in the patron-client networks. Indeed, the high degree of politicization of a clientelist regime is a manifestation of this incessant struggle for rent.

Clientelism is therefore likely to generate a private sector which is governed by regulations many of which have little economic rationale and where licenses and contracts are allocated to inefficient but politically well connected producers. A consequence of such a regulatory regime is the explosion of wasteful rent-seeking behavior.

5.3 Efficiency of the Public Sector

In a clientelist environment, private and public sector alike will be afflicted by distortions. Goods and services will not be distributed to those who need them most but will go mainly to patrons and their clients. Goods unsuited to clientelist exchange, such as infrastructure investments, will be under-provided. We are likely to encounter a bloated and inefficient public sector, and government finances are probably in disarray.

5.3.1 Production and Distribution of Government Resources

It has been noted already that clientelist politicians have few incentives to produce public goods such as infrastructure projects which serve the public at large, clients and non-clients alike. They will prefer to provide particularistic benefits which can be withheld from non-clients and therefore can serve as a remuneration for political support (Scott 1977b, 143).

But how is a given amount of goods and services distributed? Are they likely to be allocated where the benefits are largest? In a clientelist world, patrons attempt to channel goods and services mainly to clients. Pork-barreling ensures that services are located mainly in areas where there are disproportionate numbers of clients: roads are not built where traffic is greatest, but where patrons have their power base. Pork-barreling is supplemented by corruption: party brokers provide 'selective access to agricultural loans, scholarships, and places in schools and universities, patronage employment, hospital treatment, fertilizers' (1972, 135), loans are made to the most loyal farmers, not to the most efficient (129), and the police 'guard effectively only the houses of important people or of those who pay them, while ordinary citizens have to rely on self-defense' (Andreski 1979, 281). A party might resort to handouts pure and simple, as in the case of a Malaysian village improvement scheme the benefits of which were distributed only to strongholds of the ruling party (Scott 1985, 221), and allocated within villages mainly to party stalwarts and faithful (1985, 220–233). All these practices lead to a distribution of goods and services not according to where they are most needed, but where political support is most heavily boosted.[16]

5.3.2 Financial Distortions

It has been shown so far that the government will ensure the production of goods and services favored mainly by clients and that it will favor private over collective goods. At the same time, it has an incentive to shift the financial burden to non-clients by reducing user fees to clients, and to introduce price discrimination in favor of clients. To bring the issue into focus, take the example of a small but efficient hydro-electric power station supplying electricity exclusively to a particular constituency. What is the likelihood that an optimal investment and production decision is going to be taken?

First of all, is it going to be built at all? If it serves only non-clients, then it is likely to be built only if full costs are going to be retrieved, since the government is unlikely to commit general revenue to service non-clients. However, even if full costs are to be recovered, non-clients may have to wait a very long time until it is built. The waiting period may reflect capital scarcity and the sheer inefficiency of the bureaucracy.

If the power station serves clients only, one would expect their representatives to clamor for government subsidies. In fact, from the point of view of the clients and their representatives, the optimal solution is to finance the plant through general taxation and keep charges low. Charges below cost of production will lead to the over-use of electricity. Moreover, if clients do not pay total (social) costs, they will call for a plant even if overall social benefits are negative. Thus power plants may be built which reduce welfare.

Let us alter the example and assume first that the power station serves both clients and non-clients, and, second, that there are no central government funds involved. It will now be in the interest of the clients to apply price-discrimination: to impose different rates for clients and non-clients. This will generally result in non-optimal production as well as consumption decisions because the low charges induce clients consume too much electricity, and the high charges to non-clients induce them to consume too little.

Clientelism, as this example illustrates, leads to distortions in the price structure and to inefficient production decisions.

5.3.3 The Efficiency of Public Administration

What is the effect of clientelism and corruption on the efficiency of public administration? Whereas it is the contention of this monograph that corruption reduces the quality of labor inputs, revisionists take the opposite view. According to them the 'opportunity for corruption may actually serve to increase the quality of public servants if wages in the government sector are below the competitive level' (Bayley 1966, 728). Corruption is supposed to bring 'elasticity and humanity to rigid bureaucracies. It may also increase the caliber of public servants because corruption brings with it opportunities for supplemental income' (Werner 1983, 148).[17]

However, such an outcome is unlikely if jobs are allocated with a view of increasing political support. This not only reduces the pool from which officials are drawn (because non-clients do not have access to government jobs); in addition, the quality of the staff suffers even more because the major consideration in employment and promotion decisions is the usefulness of an individual's appointment in terms of political support. As Andreski writes of Africa, 'the allocation of posts in public services ... is mostly determined by criteria which have nothing to do with fitness for the job' (1979, 281). Thus we often find that although the administration is overflowing with personnel, there is a chronic shortage of employees with technical skills (Chubb 1982, 100). Corruption, therefore, is unlikely to increase the quality of the bureaucrats.

Labor productivity is likely to be low for other reasons as well. First, we would expect staff *levels* to be mainly determined by considerations other than efficiency. Governments will be mainly concerned with allocating resources to different kinds of pork-barrel and patronage uses where the patron's benefit from the additional dollar of government revenue is largest. Since public employment is a very effective way of gaining and maintaining political support, it is hardly surprising that, in developing countries where clientelism dominates, government organizations are 'overstaffed with redundant personnel' (Sandbrook 1985, 126). Overstaffing is not only wasteful, but will tend to reduce the efficiency of government services.

There is the further revisionist claim that corruption leads to increased work incentives. The starting point for the argument is Trivedi's contention that corruption is simply a means of allocating scarce resources, and an efficient one at that. Due to congestion, 'government service has become rivalrous', and because civil servants have a large amount of discretion they can exclude some consumers (1988, 1389). Payments to officials are simply a rationing device to allocate a given quantity of government services because of congestion. If this is the case, the given amount of services may indeed be allocated optimally.

Trivedi's argument assumes that corruption has no effect on the supply of services. As soon as corruption is allowed to influence the quantity of services the officials supply, the argument breaks down. And indeed, in practice this seems to be the case. Thus Myrdal quoted the Santhanam report commissioned by the Indian government which claimed that 'certain sections of the staff concerned are reported to have got into the habit of not doing anything in the matter till they are suitably persuaded ... [T]his custom of speed money has become one of the most serious causes of delay and inefficiency' (Myrdal 1968, 953). The supply of services, as one would expect, is not independent of corruption.

However, even assuming that corrupt officials determine the supply of services, it has been said that corruption leads to improvement in services. In Lui's model, the official will set the service time such that it maximizes bribe revenue.[18] 'He will not choose a speed that is too slow because too few customers will want to join the queue or pay any bribes. He also will not choose a speed that is too fast because when waiting cost is very low, many people will have less incentive to pay bribes' (1985, 773). Suppose that, before any bribing occurs, his service time was below that which maximizes bribe revenue: After bribery is permitted, the server has the incentive to speed up the system rather than to slow it down.[19] The contrary of Myrdal's hypothesis is therefore possible (773). This is undoubtedly true, but does not invalidate Myrdal's *empirical* observation based on the Santhanam report that the 'popular notion ... that corruption is a means of speeding up cumbersome administrative procedures, is palpably wrong'

(Myrdal 1968, 953). In fact, far from contradicting Myrdal, Lui's findings provide a theoretical underpinning for Myrdal's empirical observation.[20]

Lui's argument continues: the proposition 'is useful in showing that it is unlikely for the server to slow down the system when bribery is involved. Assuming increasing marginal cost for the speed, with no bribery, the optimal strategy for the server is to do nothing at all. In other words, the service rate ... is infinitely large. If bribery is allowed, the speed can only be faster or remain the same. ... [T]he contrary of Myrdal's hypothesis is true' (1985, 773-774). The assumption is, of course, that the official was flouting his contractual obligations to begin with by doing no work at all, or at least very little.[21]

To clarify the issue, it is helpful to introduce a point made by Leff. 'Empirically, inefficiency and corruption may appear together, and may blend into each other. Both as a policy problem and for analytical purposes, however, it is important to distinguish between two essentially different things' (1964, 8). Leff might have had in mind Lui's bureaucrat who is stimulated to exertion by corrupt gains. But can we really separate inefficiency from corruption? Is it not rather the case that inefficiency and corruption not only 'may appear together, and may blend into each other', but that they generally do? In both cases officials break rules and regulations, even if the lazy official is not corrupt according to our narrow definition since his indolence neither increases his income nor his status. What this shows is the limitation of a narrow definition, since it is entirely arbitrary to draw the line between corruption and its absence where acts break rules and regulations for monetary and status gain only. There is no particularly good reason why an act which breaks rules and regulations to decrease one's workload deserves to be categorized differently. The two types of behavior therefore relate not to 'essentially different things', but essentially the same thing: to breaking rules for personal benefit, separated only by an arbitrary definition. As a consequence, it is difficult to imagine a circumstance where an honest but slack bureaucracy's performance is improved by corruption. Leff's and Lui's case can safely be discarded. Corruption is unlikely to increase the efficiency of a bureaucracy.

5.3.4 Overexpansion of the Government Sector

Clientelism may lead to the expansion of the government sector beyond its optimal size. The transfer of productive capacity from the private to the public sector is likely to result in a fall in efficiency as the same employment practices as in the public administration in general become the norm in the newly nationalized firms, and the managers of parastatals perceive their positions mainly as prebends.[22] But why would politicians advocate such a transfer?[23]

If we take conventional predatory state models, such a transfer is entirely inexplicable.[24] For example, Findlay and his collaborators[25] attempt to determine the expected size of the predatory state[26] if the ruler maximizes revenue by altering the tax rate or the size of public employment. But if the ability to tax is unconstrained, the size of the public sector will be optimal: since all surplus above a given amount of income can be extracted from the public, 'the ruler will make sure that the government sector is of that [optimal] size which maximizes output and therefore tax revenue' (Wellisz and Findlay 1988, 63). In other words, the ruler ensures that the economy operates along the production possibility frontier because any deviation from it results in lost tax revenue.

It is acknowledged that the conclusion is somewhat odd: 'Surely the fear today is the opposite, that civil liberty and private initiative are threatened by an excess of government' (Findlay and Wilson 1987, 298). How do they explain this development? According to them, 'bureaucracies have evolved into monolithic institutions in their own rights, Frankenstein monsters that have somehow got out of control' (298).[27]

The hypothesis put forward here is a different one: the pressure to expand the bureaucracy emanates from the politicians, not the bureaucrats. The politicians connive in overstaffing the bureaucracy because it increases political support.

Indeed, examples where the clientelist picture is the more accurate are not difficult to come by. Such bureaucracies teeming with superfluous manpower have little similarities to the orderly and planned growth of Parkinson's empire-building bureaucrats to which Findlay refers. Moreover, politicians have been directly involved in the expansion of the staff. Such is the case of the Sicilian administration where, over the years, a massive influx of relatives of politicians, their 'friends, political supporters, family, and friends of friends and of political supporters, without the least consideration of the applicant's qualifications for the job in question, other than family name or political loyalty, swelled the ranks of the regional administration to gargantuan proportions' (Chubb 1982, 94).

Moreover, the expanding scope of government activities cannot be solely or even mainly due to the desire of bureaucrats to expand their agencies. In the Sicilian story the sphere of public intervention progressively widened into the areas of the economy and of civil society previously under private control: banks, hospitals, social security and health insurance programs, public-controlled or public-supported industries, job placement, etc. In each case an independent bureaucratic structure was created that tended 'to impede rather than facilitate the satisfaction of individual needs' (74). There is little doubt that the massive expansion of the state sector was allowed to take place because of its political expediency.

It is the fundamental flaw of these predatory state models that they cannot explain why something might be politically expedient, since rulers do not have to concern themselves with politics in the conventional sense at all.[28] How to gain and maintain power is not an issue: a ruler simply maximizes output, which also maximizes tax revenue (Wellisz and Findlay 1988, 63).[29] As soon as we introduce the possibility that a politician is also concerned with political support, the argument breaks down: a politician may then forego revenue for political support, thus choosing a sub-optimal position from an efficiency point of view.

A case in point is that of government agencies that derive their justification from their contribution to patronage politics. By scrapping statutory marketing, for example, the generality of farmers would benefit. However the government prefers to pay low prices and support agriculture by public works projects and subsidization inputs (Rimmer 1984, 262). Similarly, many agricultural programs in Africa derive their justification from their contribution to patronage politics. They increase political support by judicious allocation of selective benefits (fertilizer subsidies, use of tractors, etc.) to particular groups of farmers, even though the overall social benefits are negative (Fieldhouse 1986, 94).

The gains to politicians from nationalization are considerable. The resources of the nationalized firms are now available to increase their income and their political support: board of directors positions become open to them and their followers, and less important clients can be appointed further down the hierarchy. Suppliers can now be chosen more for their political sympathies or their personal connections than for the price and the quality of their wares,[30] and the price of output can be manipulated to suit political ends. Not surprisingly, considerable pressure is exerted through the networks to expand the size of the government. The land reclamation scheme of Tahrir province in Egypt provides an example where an a group of former officers 'not only had an interest in pressing the government to reclaim ever increasing amounts of land, but also to retain the land under state control' (Springborg 1979, 56).

This does not mean that nationalization is the only course of action that clientelist politicians will contemplate. An alternative to nationalization which might improve the welfare of the patrons even more is to take over the firms themselves, a practice universal in Africa, and usually done in the name of nationalism, 'indigenization' or 'Africanization'.[31] Here it is quite obvious that a transfer of ownership is in the interest of politicians and their clients (even if it involves losses in productivity) if, as is generally the case, the firms are acquired below market prices and with the help of subsidized loans.

Thus clientelism tends to reduce the quality of labor employed in the public administration, to lower the level of performance of the public administration - even taking into account the low quality staff - and to expand the state sector at the expense of the private one, even if this leads to a welfare loss.[32]

5.3.5 Rent in the Public Sector

The argument here presupposes that those employed in the public sector will generally earn rent. This rent component of the remuneration may not show up as a wage differential between the private and the public sector, but may take other forms such as the ability to earn an income through bribes and kickbacks, or favorable employment conditions like nominal workloads or the absence of the skill requirement normally associated with such positions.

The existence of rent in the government sector has been questioned on *a priori* grounds. Beenstock believes that 'certain types of corruption may not reflect market imperfections e.g., where bureaucrats are paid low wage rates and the commissions they hope to earn through corruption are effectively the competitively determined supply price for their labor' (1979, 16). Similarly, Rose-Ackerman thinks that 'the promise of corrupt gains may lower the salaries which the government must pay to attract job applicants' (1978, 61). The underlying assumption is, of course, that competitive bidding reduces employment conditions to a competitive level.

In a clientelist environment, government employment is provided as a means of remunerating clients for their political support. That employment, however, provides a compensation for political allegiance only if rent is earned. After all, no one is indebted to a politician if he or she receives what could have been got in the free market anyway. For this reason, one would expect politicians in power to prevent employment conditions to fall to the competitive level.

It has been assumed so far that the threat to the rent earned in the public sector originates from competition for jobs that brings on a deterioration in employment conditions. Alternatively, administrators might have to transfer the gains to their superiors. Such a process is described by Wade in his investigation of canal irrigation in southern India. In order to be appointed to a desirable position, officials have to transmit substantial sums to those in charge of transfers.

> One is thus led to visualize a special circuit of transactions, in which the bureaucracy acquires control of funds, partly from the clients and partly from the state treasury. These funds are channeled upwards to higher ranks and politicians, the latter in turn using the funds for distributing short-term material inducements in exchange for electoral support (1989, 101).

Still, as one would expect, not all rent is extracted (Wade 1989, 87), and the income of officials remains above the competitive wage. Thus both empirical evidence and theoretical considerations lead to the conclusion that employment in the public sector often does convey rent.

5.3.6 Government Finances

Clientelism will have repercussions on both government expenditure and government revenue. On the expenditure side there is the continuous pressure by clients to expand government benefits, including government employment. This is a rational course of action because most of the additional personal benefits an individual derives are largely financed by others, mainly non-clients.[33] Thus it is hardly surprising that there are few barriers to demands for particularistic benefits.

To take an example: clientelism in southern Italy has been characterized by the 'perpetual escalation of its costs' (Caciagli and Belloni 1981, 39). One reason has been the notable increase in the number of persons aspiring to patronship, which heightened considerably the competition for control of the client market (39). Added to this increased competition was 'the growth of client "political consciousness" defined as greater awareness of the power of the client and the increasing competition for clients' (39).

Simultaneously, the tax base tends to shrink. Clients may be taxed lightly to begin with, and the corrupt tax administration ensures that only a fraction of the tax revenue is collected and even less of it delivered to the public till. The tax base is undermined even more by the transfer of productive capacity from the profitable, and tax-paying, to the unprofitable government sector.

The over expansion of state services, coupled with the vast, expensive, and inefficient administrative structure, has obvious financial consequences. An increase in expenditures and a shrinking tax base generate mounting government budget deficits. This means that either government indebtedness increases or - if those deficits are financed by printing money - inflation starts to soar.

5.4   Economic Growth

What is the effect of such an economic environment on economic growth? The clientelist approach leads us to expect that the anti-market inward-looking strategies brought about by clientelism significantly handicap economic development. Again, this contrasts with the revisionist stance that corruption 'may result in increased allocations of resources away from consumption into investment' (Bayley 1966, 728), thus promoting growth.

5.4.1 Savings and Investment

Corruption may increase savings if it redistributes income to people with a relatively high propensity to save. As little is known of relative propensities to save of those who lose and those who gain, the overall effect of corruption on savings is ambiguous, as the revisionists well recognized (Bayley 1966, 728).

But even if corruption causes savings to increase, it by no means follows that investment increases, since the money made by corrupt means 'more often than not finds its way to Swiss bank accounts, casinos on the Riviera, speculation or just plain conspicuous consumption rather than to productive investment' (Ben-Dor 1974, 71). The massive capital flight from Third World countries supports this position.

Corruption in itself provides a good reason to transfer capital abroad. In general, whether an investment is made at home or abroad will depend on the relative size of expected future returns to capital and, in the main, risk differentials.[34] Corruption, it will be shown, both reduces returns and increases risk.

The ubiquitous regulations and their arbitrary and inefficient implementation reduce the return to investment through the additional transaction costs in the form of paperwork, the time spent in procuring licenses, and the cost of administering the regulations themselves (Bayley 1966, 725).

Perhaps even more important is the effect of clientelism and corruption on risk and uncertainty. First, there is the risk of being caught and convicted by some anti-corruption agency acting autonomously. In standard neo-classical models, as we have seen, this is treated as the main risk factor. However, given that corruption is sanctioned at the highest level, there is little risk of being bothered by the authorities as long as political protection lasts.

The main threat then comes not so much from the anti-corruption agencies, but from the withdrawal of political protection as a consequence, for example, of political upheavals.[35] In its aftermath, earnings from past corrupt dealings are liable to be confiscated, and thus an individual has an incentive to shift his savings abroad where funds are less easily accessible. Savings will be invested domestically only if the return on investment compensates for this particular risk. If the risk is considerable, few of the savings derived from corruption will to be invested domestically. Since in a clientelist state corruption is all-pervasive and therefore nearly all profits are tainted by it, this type of risk is high, and capital flight might well turn into a flood if the political system is unstable.

Next, there is the risk of extortion. Individuals may always be threatened with being dragged to court if they misbehave politically or do not satisfy the predatory demands of politicians and officials. But, where rules and regulations constantly change and bribes and kickbacks are constantly re-negotiated, uncertainty becomes substantial. Ekholm Friedman describes the difficulties of a firm operating in the Congo: 'There is no legal system to protect their interests. The management does not know from one day to the other which rules are operative. New laws and taxes are introduced and they may have to pay fines for "crimes" the meaning of which they do not understand. All this makes the situation uncomfortably insecure. Besides, the political elite is continuously attempting to plunder their profits' (1992, 231).[36]

Transaction costs, risk and uncertainty not only lead to substantial capital outflow but also prevent capital inflow. Moreover, investments by indigenous owners as well as foreign investors are biased towards short-term high-yield ventures.[37] Long-term investments are hardly forthcoming at all. Moreover, often little equity is committed to those long-term projects that are realized, and the risk of failure is frequently borne by the government which underwrites the loans.[38]

Not only does clientelism lead to a loss of savings which seep abroad, the savings which remain available to the national credit system are often used ineffectively. In a clientelist system credit tends to be allocated according to political and not economic criteria and therefore ineffectively. Moreover those politically well connected often successfully avoid repayment.[39] Such practices are by no means limited to the elite. The Burmese peasants connected to the governing party 'were almost universally in default on agricultural loans they had received as party supporters. They assumed the loan was a gift for clientship, and knew that a government dependent on their votes could scarcely press matters' (Scott 1977b, 143).[40]

There is little doubt that clientelism reduces the flow of investment spending by generating a great deal of uncertainty.[41] The negative effects of uncertainty on savings and investment have been pointed out for centuries;[42] Weber's comments are perhaps the best known. He thought that the 'unpredictability and inconsistency' associated with the environment we have been describing may be compatible with some kinds of capitalist enterprises such as trading firms, but that industrial capitalism involving long-term planning and commitment on account of the large quantity of sunk capital required 'is altogether too sensitive to all sorts of irrationalities in the administration of law and taxation' (1968, 240, 1095).

5.4.2 Clientelism and Growth

After these considerations, one would hardly expect to find a positive relationship between clientelism and growth. Still, there is the empirical observation from the US: 'Corruption, even when it was most blatant in nineteenth-century America, apparently did not retard economic development. Indeed, the epoch of the big city boss coincided with the period in American history of most rapid economic growth. This has suggested to some scholars that corruption actually facilitated economic development' (Werlin 1973, 172). This experience, however, is hardly relevant because machine politics did not pervade the whole of the political system, which is more aptly described as containing pockets of clientelism in a sea of pluralism. Nor did machine politics spread and become endemic and systemic. Hence even if it was damaging, it would hardly show up in the overall US growth performance.[43] More generally, as Ben-Dor has pointed out, if the revisionists' arguments are right, it would be necessary to demonstrate that corruption correlates highly with periods of rapid economic growth: 'Yet it does not seem that the countries undergoing the quickest processes of economic development (Japan, West Germany, Israel) demonstrate anything resembling this pattern' (1974, 70).[44]

5.5   Conclusion

Revisionists attribute beneficial effects to corruption because it blunts ideological fervor and ignorance. This claim becomes increasingly implausible as we enter the world of clientelism, where policies are aimed at increasing political support and personal income, and corruption becomes a widely used tool in the service of these aims.

Clientelism generates particularistic benefits suitable for clientelist exchange. One set of such particularistic benefits is derived from the anti-market inward-looking regulatory framework at least partially aimed at generating rent. Thus it is in the interest of a clientelist regime to introduce import substitution regimes and institute systems of licensing into every nook and cranny of the economy. An overregulated economy is therefore often explained at least partly by the desire of politicians to generate rent for themselves and their clients.

The second set of particularistic benefits suitable for clientelist exchange is the goods and services distributed by the government. As collective goods are unsuitable for clientelist exchange, governments tend to replace collective with private goods. In particular, infrastructure suffers, together with other services which have public goods character but no special political importance.[45]

Clientelism leads to an expansion of government beyond the optimal level. As the private costs of many goods and services provided by the state to clients approaches zero, the demands for benefits steadily increases. The deviation of private from social costs, particularly severe with private goods, leads to an unrestrained demand by clients for material benefits. If the government responds to these pressures, government expenditures are higher than warranted.

The overextension of the state is exacerbated by the tendency to transfer production processes to the state sector in order to increase the power of patronage, even if overall output is going to be reduced as a consequence.

At the same time, much of these resources is spent on the administration itself, since one of the 'goods' most coveted by clients is government employment. Many of the resources the government controls are therefore frittered away through financing an increasingly inefficient administration. Moreover, misallocation is exacerbated because much of the output the government produces is channeled primarily towards the clientele of the politicians in power. Since, at the same time, infrastructure expenditure declines, the government has little to show for the vast amount of resources it absorbs.

Government finances will tend to come under pressure for several reasons. Apart from the growing expenditures, the losses of the prebendalized parastatal sector have to be absorbed. Corruption tends to erode the tax base as clients are able to exempt themselves from paying taxes, and the tax administration itself becomes increasingly corrupt and inefficient.

The situation is likely to worsen in the long run. Capital flight and the lack of substantial foreign and domestic investment undermine economic growth and therefore future tax revenue. The failure of investment to grow is of course not limited to the 'modern' sector of the economy: the same damage is inflicted on the 'traditional' sector through the distortions of prices and taxes and the insecurity in the political environment.

Clientelism is not conducive to macroeconomic stability. The increase in government expenditure, coupled with a very narrow tax base, inevitably leads to budget deficits. These deficits can generally be financed only by printing money or borrowing from abroad.[46] Neither solution is satisfactory: printing money kindles inflation and borrowing from abroad leads to foreign indebtedness.

The main task of this monograph is to explain a set of policy failures: overregulation of the private sector, the bloated bureaucracy, the large size of the government sector, budgetary problems, the neglect of infrastructure, a low rate of investment and a high degree of allocative inefficiency. It should be obvious by now that the policies are closely tied up with clientelism. Corruption, as has been shown, is a consequence of clientelism, and the combination of these 'terrible twins' determines to a large degree the kind of policies pursued by the government and the nature of their implementation.

It has been said that countries which pursue highly restrictive import licensing practices 'are also countries that are likely to be found having established large numbers of inefficient ... parastatal enterprises, to have agricultural pricing and other policies that greatly discriminated against farmers, and to have stringent credit rationing at negative real interest rates. Those same countries that have excessive and antigrowth levels of intervention in labor and capital markets, and in major productive sectors of the economy, also generally have delivered woefully inadequate levels of infrastructure services' (Krueger 1993, 14, 29). This correlation between 'the types of economic policies pursued with regard to various facets of economic activity' is not accidental. Many of these features have a common cause in a particular political structure: political clientelism.

Notes:

1. Similarly, Bayley attempts 'to show that corruption in developing nations is not necessarily antipathetic to the development of modern economic and social systems; that corruption serves in part at least a beneficial function in developing societies' (1966, 719). Nye goes on to speculate about the social and political conditions under which corruption is likely to be beneficial (1967, 423). Not all of the revisionists challenged the doctrine that corruption had negative economic effects. Colin Leys, for one, still subscribed to the traditional conclusion that an effective public service is a precondition for economic development (1965, 228).

2. Along the line of the functional dysfunctions of the functionalists (Merton 1957, 72–82).

3. The factual truth of these claims is contested by Waterbury (1989, 345–354).

4. Bayley, for example, argues that governments 'have no monopoly upon correct solutions; governments are simply one among many bureaucratic institutions which may do stupid things' (1967, 727). Nye attributes the prevalence of suboptimal economic policies to the experience of imperialism which 'has led to a systematic bias against the market mechanism' (1967, 420). Leff takes the example where 'the government consists of a traditional elite which is indifferent if not hostile to development, or of a revolutionary group of intellectuals and politicians, who are primarily interested in other goals' (1964, 10).

5. For Thailand see Scott (1972, 70).

6. See also Appelbaum and Katz (1987, 685). A different interaction was outlined by Johnson, who argues that governments use private firms to collect a 'corruption tax'. The private firms are able to collect such a tax 'by obtaining monopoly rights *cum* special concessions from the government and will share in the tax proceeds by not handing over ... all the monopoly rent realized' (1975, 55). By doing this, governments are able to reduce the risk of criminal procedures against them, and reduce public opprobrium which diminishes the chances of re-election. A deadweight loss then results from 'x'-inefficiencies and from allocative inefficiencies due to monopolization (56). Thus corruption *causes* suboptimal policies. Johnson's scenario is different from the clientelist one, where anti-corruption agencies are of little consequence.

7. Leff for example argues that 'in the long run, the favors will go to the most efficient producers, for they will be able to make the highest bids which are compatible with remaining in the industry' (1964, 9). Similarly, Beenstock claims that 'the most efficient supplier will tend to win the contract' (1979, 23), assuming that all salesmen are equally dishonest and are equally discreet (22).

8. Similarly, officials might discriminate among suppliers on the basis of friendship (Lien 1990, 155).

9. It is assumed here that firms and individuals who work for them face exit and entry costs, that alternative employment opportunities at the going wage are scarce, and that firms are unable to sell any amount of output at a well defined market price (in other words, markets are imperfect).

10. In addition, the most efficient firms may not participate in bidding because they may be especially averse to corruption as such or to the risk associated with it (Johnson 1975, 56).

11. Ben-Dor concludes that rather than facilitating the survival of the fittest, 'corruption often creates groups of entrepreneurs whose major resource is the knowledge of the workings of the relevant segments of the bureaucracy and the network of acquaintances - and thus the potential availability of important favors - in the offices of government' (1974, 71).

12. Tullock's paper, which contains all the central ideas of the later literature (Krueger 1974; Bhagwati 1982, 989), was published in 1967.

13. In Tullock's classic case, governments do not impose protective tariffs on their own, they 'have to be lobbied or pressured into doing so by the expenditure of resources in political activity' (1981, 44).

14. Bhagwati suggests a distinction between rent-seeking and 'directly unproductive, profit-seeking (DUP) activities'. He wants to restrict the term 'rent-seeking' to 'lobbying activities which are triggered by different licensing practices' (1982, 990). It is difficult to see that such a distinction warrants additional jargon.

15. The assumption here is that people will seek distributive rent until the average wage from rent-seeking is equal to the average wage elsewhere.

16. Some arguments can be dismissed out of hand. Bayley, for example, argues that 'In underdeveloped countries the tangle of popular pressures involving traditionally antagonistic groups frequently causes government to award contracts, scholarships, privileges, and jobs according to mechanical quota systems. Since talent and ability are very often unevenly distributed through these societies, this policy is not in the direction of optimum efficiency. Corruption .... might very well offset this pervasive influence' (1966, 727). There is no particular reason to believe that corruption leads to an outcome that is superior to quotas.

17. Referring to Nye and Bayley.

18. Shleifer and Vishny (1993, 607) argue that the reason for the absence of corruption in the passport office in the US is the ability to obtain passports from various officials who are prevented from colluding. This is obviously incorrect, since a revenue-maximizing rational official not threatened by official sanctions will not issue a passport without some returns. The level of bribes will never be zero under their assumption.

19. Leys makes the same point slightly differently: 'Where bureaucracy is both elaborate and inefficient, the provision of strong personal incentives to bureaucrats to cut red tape may be the only way of speeding the establishment of the new firm' (1965, 223).

20. Sometimes a parallel is drawn between the corrupt official and waiters, who 'have a two-part wage rate where the first part is fixed and the second part reflects the number of services provided. Indeed, in some respects the second part will be conducive to allocative efficiency since it is a form of marginal cost pricing - the better the service, the bigger the tips' (1979, 17). Unlike the official, however, the waiter has limited control over supply. Only if the waiter were allowed to determine the number of customers and to auction off places would the parallel hold.

21. Lui also misinterprets Myrdal. Myrdal's statement was based on an empirical observation which cannot be refuted by a theory.

22. For example: the Congolese executive 'in charge of a state enterprise ... acts from a predatory position and for him the enterprise is only a means of personal enrichment' (Ekholm Friedman 1992, 232). In Sicily in 1973, of the 414 executive positions all but a handful were political appointees. 'These positions have been widely used by political figures to engage in rampant patronage hiring as well as favoritism and corruption in buying and marketing practices' (Chubb 1982, 118).

23. From the point of the politician nationalization is appropriate until the losses of political support as a consequence of price increases and rationing resulting from decreasing efficiency outweigh the gains in personal income and political support through the additional scope for patronage.

24. In the introduction we have dealt with Lal's explanation of policy failures. Lal's analysis is a development of North's study of the predatory state. The ruler aims to maximize his net income, which in turn is a function of the tax system and the total output produced. These two categories 'are not completely consistent. The second objective implies a completely efficient set of property rights to maximize societal output; the first attempts to specify a set of fundamental rules that will enable the ruler to maximize his own income ... This fundamental dichotomy is the root cause of the failure of societies to experience sustained economic growth' (1981, 24–25). The maximization is 'constrained by the opportunity cost of its constituents since there always exist potential rivals to provide the same set of services' (23). 'If the wealth or income of groups which close access to alternative rulers is adversely affected by

property rights, the ruler will be threatened' (28). Findlay's models are an outgrow of this approach.

25. Findlay and Wilson (1987); Wellisz and Findlay (1988); Findlay (1991).

26. The model is actually more restricted than the situation discussed here. The government sector is confined to the civil service, which does not produce final goods.

27. The same is true for Przeworski and Limongi (1993, 59).

28. The failure to deal with politics is closely related to the type of method used in these models. Methodological individualism is abandoned: 'The state is the unit of analysis, not the citizen, the politician, or the bureaucrat' (Grindle 1991, 49). It is then possible to abstract from the messy process of competition for power and rent.

29. Thus Margaret Goodman's study of Yucatan shows that corruption, rather than benefiting the efficient producer, 'may protect the incompetent and reward the inefficient' (1974, 152). When the entire henequen industry declined, '*hacendado* bureaucrats were able to use the connections they had made through years of government contacts plus bribes in the right places, to sell their factories to the federal government at an inflated price' (152). Thus the government 'bought out producers who were neither efficient nor experimental' (156).

30. The contrast is somewhat too stark, because even if no nationalization takes place some of these benefits can be extracted by extortion. Private owners can be forced to part with some of their profits, and followers can be placed in these firms.

31. See chapter 6.

32. The latter conclusion, coupled with the tendency of clientelism to lead to an over-regulation of the private sector, sheds some doubt on the contention attributed to the revisionists that corruption strengthens 'the private vis-à-vis the public sector' (Werner 1983, 148). Clientelism and its accompaniment, corruption, are more likely to weaken it.

33. The more general the benefits, the less the deviation of private from social costs. If having a scholarship for a child means that everybody in the same category gets one, taxes might increase and the scholarship will have some private costs attached to it. If the scholarship simply means beating the system by using connections, it has no private costs. For a more formal treatment see Olson (1965).

34. More precisely, differences in the discount rate which reflect differences in risk assessment.

35. Such as the events in Ghana, mentioned in the preceding chapter, when Jerry Rawlings had eight leading military figures, including three former heads of state, executed for skimming public resources at an extraordinary pace (Young 1982a, 5–6).

36. Similar conditions prevailed in Sekou Toure's Guinea, where 'laws and decrees were heeded only as long as they were being mentioned on the radio. They were easily promulgated and as easily forgotten with the

changing needs of the government and the mood of the president. But they were not rescinded. If a particular decree was in the interest of a certain government official, it was enforced and those unaware of it paid dearly' (Azarya and Chazan 1987, 124).

37.   'One would expect prudent businessmen, for example, to invest in long-range activities that tie up fixed capital where instability and uncertainty abound. The rational course, instead, is for the businessman to minimize his risks by concentrating on short-run, high liquidity, commercial transactions. And this is precisely what the majority of entrepreneurs in underdeveloped nations do' (Scott 1972, 84).

38.   The increased risk leads firms to prefer loans, contracted services and sales of technology to equity investment. It the government picks up the equity, risk and uncertainty are shifted from the foreign investor to the state. This may have disastrous consequences, as in the case of Zaïre after the fall in copper prices in 1974 (see Young 1982a, 248).

39.   For example: 'In Sicily ... the most influential banks are publicly controlled and have constituted major centres of power for the Christian Democratic Party ... This political domination of the banks ... has meant that the fastest and surest way to secure a loan has been to have an influential politician vouch personally for the client's reliability' (Chubb 1982, 120).

40.   Similar problems exist in the government sector: investment is reduced by embezzlement of government funds destined for investment, or when loans granted for investments are used to boost consumption spending (Alam 1989, 451).

41.   It is, however, exactly in the area of investment spending that revisionists think their case that corruption has socially beneficial effects is strongest. The first instance they have in mind is where certain categories of investment are limited to members of a particular group who do not take up the opportunities. Corruption then provides a means to overcome these legal obstacles, and investment increases (Werner 1983, 148). Then there is the contention that corruption may increase the degree of control the entrepreneurs have over an inherently unstable environment and render it more predictable, and thus 'corruption can increase the rate of investment' (Leff 1964, 11). However, if our analysis is correct, the factors which inhibit investment are consequences of clientelism and corruption.

42.   E.g. J.S. Mill in Kurer (1991, Chapter 3).

43.   In addition, as Werlin points out, the relative size and importance of the public sector in countries like Ghana is vastly different from the US at the turn of the century (1973, 177).

44.   The argument does not suggest that clientelism and corruption necessarily imply zero growth or even economic retrogression. Moreover, corruption may not have the same effects in a non-clientelist environment. Thus it has been argued that in Tunisia 'concern for

building political clienteles has not been a governing consideration in the state's distribution of discretionary benefits in the industrial class' (Bellin 1994, 431), nor has 'concern for personal gain on the part of the state elites' (432). The economic system was described as 'cronyism', or 'the provision of preferential treatment to one's chums' (432).

45. As opposed to the media, for example.
46. The possibilities of borrowing domestically tend to be limited in the countries we are concerned with.

6   Pathological Clientelism: Africa

This chapter focuses on the interaction between political and economic change. Clientelism can lead to a situation where, after each change of government, a large-scale reallocation of property and quasi-property rights takes place. This is likely to happen where the social position of the members of the political class is insecure and they thus have an incentive to engage in the winner-take-all politics widely observed on the African continent. Such changes in property rights lead to systematic instability which goes beyond the uncertainties attributable to the arbitrary decision making innate to all clientelistic systems.

In a clientelist environment the private sector of the economy tends to rely on the state to an extraordinary degree, with most business activities affected by arbitrary decision making resulting from corruption and from regulations which favor discretion over rules. Corruption implies that regulations including tax laws, licensing, and health and safety regulations are only selectively enforced. Thus costs and revenues of businesses crucially hinge on arbitrary decisions by government officials even where rules exist. In a clientelist environment with endemic corruption, private sector activities tend to need the continuous support of government functionaries.

As a consequence of this extraordinary degree of state dependence, any political change threatens significant economic consequences if the new government embarks on a program of redistribution of government favors. Such a redistribution is likely to happen in a faction-ridden clientelist environment where rule by the political class lacks legitimacy. Thus security of property is likely to be low. Indeed, if such an environment prevails it is difficult to talk about a capitalist economic system in any meaningful way. Capitalism, as understood by most writers, presupposes both a high level of security of property and much scope for market operations. By contrast, the success of typical African 'entrepreneurs' depends on political protection. Because their fortunes hinge on the connections provided by particular clientele networks that happen to dominate government, the economic system is more accurately described as 'client-capitalist'.

How can a fully developed capitalist system emerge from client-capitalism? The conventional account suggests that economic develop-ment increases the political influence of the bourgeois class, which is then able to ensure stable and secure property rights. Such a path, however, is barred by a clientelist environment, which tends to obstruct the growth of an independent bourgeoisie capable of successfully pro-moting its group interests. An alternative process of transformation envisages that the ruling class which dominates both state and private enterprise introduces reforms of property arrangements. This class undoubtedly has an interest in stabilizing property arrangements but is likely to do so only if its position as a class is secure, and it will be suc-cessful only if it is able to contain intra-class competition.

Machine politics has been observed to dominate African political processes since the time of independence (Zolberg 1966), and it has since become the conventional wisdom that African politics is domi-nated by clientelism.[1] Moreover, the African development experience has been particularly disastrous. As we have seen in the last chapter, clientelism is likely to have contributed to the malaise by generating inefficiencies in the public and private sectors of the economies, and by reducing the level of investment.

However, there are many countries where clientelist politics has not had such calamitous economic consequences, such as India, or where indeed where economic growth has been rapid, as Thailand. It is argued that the pathological African situation is largely the result of political instability feeding through to economic instability because changes in government have tended to lead to a significant redistribution of property and quasi-property rights.

The chapter begins by contending that, as a consequence of clientelism, the ownership structure and the profitability of firms depend on political connections. The second section continues by showing that this dependence engenders insecurity of property because the ruling class tends to engage in large scale redistribution of business opportunities after changes in political power, partly because of intra-class competition and partly because of the precarious position of the ruling class as a whole, a class whose rule lacks legitimacy. Section three leads to the obvious point that insecurity of property reduces growth. The fourth section argues that an economic structure characterized by state dependence and insecure property rights is different in kind from fully developed capitalism, but constitutes a kind of 'client-capitalism'. The economic arrangements imply that a bourgeois class in the conventional sense cannot evolve, since the political power of the bourgeoisie presupposes secure property rights. The fifth section looks at possible routes of a transition to capitalism where property arrangements are more secure and market processes operate to a much larger degree. Such a transition presupposes a political transformation where the ruling class has managed to contain intra-class competition and acquired security of tenure as a class. The last section looks at some competing views of African development: it questions the notion that primitive accumulation is something belonging to the past and that the state plays a beneficial role in economic development.

Since much of the chapter deals with insecurity of property and quasi-property rights, we need to define what is meant by quasi-property rights. These consist of privileges which are not legally sanctioned: bureaucrats' 'right' to misuse their position to increase their income through bribery and extortion; businessmen's preferential access to credit or foreign exchange; their ability to escape prosecution if they break the law; or informal agreements about tax assessments or customs duties and import regulations. Such privileges are not necessarily illegal, but may reflect incomplete, unclear or contradictory rules and regulations. Not only are these quasi-property rights precarious, but property rights are equally so. Insecurity of property rights may result from frequent changes to rules and regulations and from the absence or arbitrariness of the enforcement of legal claims. Since we are concerned with the economic and social consequences of uncertain economic conditions, insecurity of property and of quasi-property rights will not always be distinguished in what follows.

6.1   **Stability of Property Rights and State Dependence**

A clientelist political structure suggests that patrons will use the system of laws and regulations, including their power of patronage, to increase wealth and income of themselves and their clients. Thus ownership of means of production will often be acquired with the help of the state, and profit opportunities will frequently result from specific state intervention. This leads to an extremely heavy dependence on the state, a situation which is exemplified with exceptional clarity by post-colonial Africa.

6.1.1 The State and the Process of Accumulation

That African states were instrumental in re-shaping the ownership structure after independence is well established.[2] First, the governments organized a redistribution of assets from foreign to domestic interests, mainly through indigenization laws, coupled with the provision of easy credit to nationals.[3] To take the example of Nigeria, indigenization decrees have 'significantly shifted the balance of ownership in the Nigerian economy from foreign to domestic capital' (Beckman 1982, 37). They

> provided a windfall for a sprinkling of fortunate Nigerians. Share prices of public companies were undervalued ... In private-company transfers, it was clear that Nigerians were often rewarded lucratively for cooperating in transfer arrangements advantageous to the foreign firms ... [P]ossession of adequate funds was not a prerequisite. Private acquisitions were financed primarily by credit (Schatz 1977, 61).

Second, 'profit opportunities mainly involved the manipulation of the state' (Sandbrook 1985, 137, 67) which provided cheap credit, subsidies and protection from domestic and foreign competition. State regulations may have lowered the costs of production of specially selected firms through subsidies such as the provision of cheap credit or other inputs, or they may have increased revenue by protection.

One of the important ways of acquiring capital throughout Africa was through provision of cheap credit through innumerable loan schemes to indigenous businesspeople, and through political pressure on banks to lend to well connected individuals (Sandbrook 1985, 68). More specifically, credit policies underwrote large amounts of real estate speculation: The great 'land grab' was not limited to the country but proceeded in the cities as well, where 'state sponsored credit and loan schemes' allowed members of the dominant class to 'speculate in real estate at state expense' (Diamond 1987, 591).

Subsidies were not restricted to credit, but included other inputs as well. The government of Senegal 'curried favor' with powerful religious leaders 'by giving them privileged access to publicly subsidized inputs: fertilizers, mechanical equipment, land carved out from forest reserves' (Bates 1981, 111), and similarly in Nigeria and Ghana 'big commercial farmers have ... been able to obtain privileged access to subsidized credit, fertilizer, equipment and so on' (Diamond 1987, 591).

The profits of domestic producers and domestically owned firms are significantly affected by protection. Protection of domestic producers benefits local as well as multinational firms operating in a particular country (Iliffe 1983, 77). Zaire is one of many countries where favorable tariffs 'have eliminated competition for domestic industry' (MacGaffey 1987, 195). But in addition to protection from foreign competition, domestically owned firms were protected from competition from firms owned by foreigners as access to particular sectors of the economy began to be restricted to citizens (Sandbrook 1985, 68; Schatz 1977, 3). Typically restrictions first affected retail operations, and were extended later to wholesale business (Swainson 1977, 41ff) and to other areas of the economy.

Third, corruption provided a means of acquiring capital as well as profit opportunities through illegitimate practices in allocating licenses, permits, grants, and government contracts. Graft, therefore, becomes 'an important factor in the growth of an indigenous owning class' (Szeftel 1982, 4).[4]

> Opportunities for corruption were legion as officials were called upon to exercise more authority - grant permits and licenses, tender contracts, regulate commercial transactions, direct corporations and invest public revenues (Sandbrook 1985, 67).[5]

Credit agencies and the construction industry became especially notorious for corruption. In Nigeria the problem of political manipulation 'was of such overriding importance in the case of the regional loans boards that all other difficulties fade into relative insignificance. In the main, the regional boards were political instruments' (Schatz 1977, 230, 161–162). In the construction industry, the 'most important process through which political corruption took place involved the power of high-level politicians to manipulate safeguard procedures. When they wanted to favor particular contractors or groups of contractors, political leaders were able to exert virtually irresistible pressure on their subordinates to distort or simply ignore these procedures' (189). But the allocation of contracts according to political criteria was not limited to construction: 'Whatever the motivations of Shell-BP, there is no doubt that members of the political class were frequently favored in business relations and jobs with foreign firms for political reasons' (163). In Zaire's singularly blatant case, those who held political power 'used their position in the state to gain access to economic resources ... in an essentially illicit or semi-licit manner in recognition of the politically illegitimate character of their conduct' (MacGaffey 1987, 46).

Thus we find that the ownership structure is mainly the result not of market operations and competition, but of state intervention.[6] But the dependence of the private sector on the state goes beyond the original acquisition of capital.

6.1.2 The Process of Profit Creation

Not only are businesses the creation of politics, but ongoing business success hinges crucially on the cooperation of those in power for the continued flow of privileges: the fortunes of the few local 'monopolistic or oligopolistic businessmen' 'are closely tied to state favors and to the continued domination of the political class of which they are part' (Diamond 1987, 588).[7] Hence the 'embryonic bourgeoisie' 'is not only recent in origin but thoroughly dependent on the state for protection from foreign capital, control of the labor force, loan capital and so on' (Sandbrook 1985, 72).[8] This need for the continued flow of privileges in the form of licenses, permits, access to credit, and favorable government contracts leads to the 'quite exceptional' 'dependence on the state and proximity to political power' (Young 1982b, 81).[9]

At this stage we have to deal with MacGaffey's argument that in Zaire a 'small local capitalist class outside the state' is emerging (1987, 3). What she does show is that there are owners of businesses who do not hold public office (56–57, 66, 4).[10] But that fact alone does not make them 'outside' or independent of the state. In contrast to her own claim she shows that the survival of these 'outsiders' *does* depend on the state: her autonomous producers are only 'relatively independent of politics', because to get anything done 'it is necessary to have connections of some sort' (57) and ordinary people 'must seek to be clients of influential and powerful patrons' (209).[11] The entrepreneurs therefore are hardly 'independent entrepreneurs' (68), 'the embryo of a true national bourgeoisie' (66).[12]

This all but destroys MacGaffey's case of the informal sector of the economy purportedly challenging 'the importance accorded to the state in the literature on class formation in Africa' (24). While it may well be true that the 'expansion of the second economy in Zaire is an indication of the difficulty the state has in controlling the extension of capitalist relations of production and their social reproduction', it does not follow that it 'is thus a measure of the decreasing significance of the state for class formation' (22).[13] Even if formal controls disintegrate, 'economic activities' are not 'independent of the state' (24) and producers do not necessarily become 'autonomous' (25). Indeed, one can turn the argument around and say that those businesses transgressing the law are even more dependent on special favors by the local administration, if only for the special favor of not being shut down! To turn these businesses into a 'true indigenous bourgeoisie' (1) is very far fetched.[14] Thus businesspeople are either clients of the state or dependent on discrete government decisions for their continued profits as much as they rely on the market.

Thus clientelism in Africa has led to a situation where not only the ownership of firms has been heavily influenced by state intervention, but the rate of profit earned by private sector enterprises depends to an extraordinary degree on discretionary decisions by the state .

6.2 The Absence of Security of Property and of the Ruling Class

State dependence is not in itself responsible for the climate of insecurity, even in a clientelist environment. Indeed, one would expect steady symbiotic relationships between businesses and their protectors to develop. These will ensure a high degree of stability as long as the administrative personnel of the government remains unchanged. Thus property arrangements can remain undisturbed for extended periods even if administrative decisions are based largely on discretion and rules and regulations are irregularly enforced. Even a change in administration may not lead to a redistribution of business opportunities if the incoming administration decides to leave the economic gains of the outgoing administration undisturbed.

The crucial question then becomes: under what conditions will it be in the interest of the incoming administration to accept existing property and quasi-property rights? Why might it abstain from replacing a large number of supporters of the outgoing administration with its own supporters, both in the public administration and in the government-owned enterprises? Why will it refrain from extracting revenue from firms associated with the outgoing administration and reallocating business opportunities to itself and its clients? Before addressing these questions, some terms need to be qualified.

6.2.1 The Ruling Class

Who are the members of a ruling class? The two most common answers to this question are contained in Mosca's narrow and extended definitions. Callaghy's definition of a political aristocracy correspond's to Mosca's narrow definition that encompasses only the minority in whose hands is the 'management of public affairs' (1929, 50). Other writers employ Mosca's extended version.[15] Thus Sklar's definition includes 'businessmen, bureaucrats, leading politicians and members of the learned professions' (1979, 546; 1965, 204), Cohen's 'nationalist leaders, including the bureaucratic and military elites, professions and businessmen' (1972, 255), and Markovitz's 'the top political leaders and bureaucrats, the traditional rulers and their descendants, and the leading members of the liberal professions and the rising business bourgeoisie. Top members of the military and police forces are also part of this bureaucratic bourgeoisie' (1977, 208). Both Mosca's versions will be employed at various times.

What does it mean to talk of a particular set of individuals as a class? At the minimum, its members must have a common interest, such as holding on to political power or political influence.[16] However, they may not perceive themselves as forming a distinguishable entity and are not necessarily aware of their common interest. Moreover, even if people are aware of their common class interests, they may not act on that awareness, perhaps because their individual interests are more pressing, or because of constraints which prevent organizational efforts.[17] An ideal historical process is usually postulated according to which individual members of a class become aware of their common interests, and in due course develop stable organizations to promote these objective interests.[18]

The upshot is that we have to distinguish three different kinds of classes. They are, in ascending order of cohesion: classes united only by the common interests of their members, or classes-in-themselves; classes-for-themselves where members are aware of these interests; and classes whose members consciously pursue their common goals and in the process establish permanent organizations, in short classes which have become groups. For us here, a ruling class means those individuals influencing government decisions directly or indirectly (Mosca's extended version) who have a common interest in maintaining their influence on political power, without necessarily exhibiting class-consciousness or acting as a group. They constitute a class according to the weakest of the three definitions cited.

6.2.2 Conditions for an End to Winner-take-all Politics

Why might incoming administrations not engage in winner-take-all politics? A possible answer is suggested by the theory of repeated games: an incoming administration may expect to alternate in power with the outgoing administration, and so displacing each other's followers after each change of power might not be an optimal course of action. The process of continual displacement is costly not only for the individuals displaced, but for most people belonging to the ruling class, since the process of displacement threatens the economic and social gains of all its members. Hence a consensus might emerge that it is in the interest of all parties to stabilize property rights. If such a consensus is sustained by the necessary trust that each party in power will keep its part of the bargain, winner-take-all policies may indeed be abandoned.

The evolution of the necessary element of trust is helped if the ruling class has developed into a community[19] where the individuals belonging to it are linked through affective ties. Such a feeling of community may develop if both the incumbents and those who replace them are socially connected and share a distinct set of values. Not only do social connections and the affective ties that grow out of them increase the level of trust, but the welfare of the loser becomes part of the welfare of the winner and thus provides an additional reason why an incoming administration might want to abandon redistributive strategies.

There is a further condition ensuring the stability property rights. So far the threat to the social position of a member of the ruling class came from within that class. Thus if individuals belonging to the ruling class are able to agree to refrain from ousting each other from their social and economic positions, their class membership is safeguarded. However, there is also the risk that the class as a whole might be swept away. Thus the degree to which patrons will engage in predatory behavior will also depend on the degree of security of tenure enjoyed by the ruling class as a whole.

The security of tenure of the class as a whole will be greatly affected by the degree of legitimacy of its rule. The lower the degree of legitimacy, the greater the probability that major sections of the ruling class will be ousted. The degree of legitimacy of a clientelist regime, as has been shown earlier, is not bolstered by a widely shared ideology. On the contrary, it is undermined by large scale corruption and the grossly inefficient delivery of public services, combined with the impoverishment of most of the population. In such a situation the ruling class might well feel insecure, fearful of being swept away in some major upheaval. Hence the insecurity of the ruling class *qua* class adds to the temptation to accumulate as much as possible during its tenure.

Winner-take-all politics is likely to be abandoned, therefore, if the legitimacy of the ruling class is high and intra-class competition is low because of the prevalence of shared values, affective ties and mutual trust.

6.2.3 Absence of Conditions of Stability

Whether the prerequisites for stable property rights exist in Africa is disputed. Social 'closure', makes it increasingly difficult to gain membership of the ruling class (Young 1982b, 82), a process which would help the development of group formation. On the other hand, the legitimacy of clientelist regimes tends to be low and major upheavals are not infrequent.[20]

However, claims have been made that a ruling class has emerged that does act as a group. Thus Sklar chides social scientists who 'have been relatively slow to recognize the appearance of dominant classes in modern African societies' (1979, 533). His own study of Nigeria during the final decade of British rule had found an emergent or new and rising class, 'one that was engaged in class action and was characterized by a growing sense of class consciousness' (533).[21]

Sklar's point was taken up by Diamond (1988), who argued that the 'abuse of public responsibilities and resources for personal enrichment' is 'not the random expression of individual greed;' it is 'the deliberate, systematic effort of an emerging dominant class to accumulate wealth and to establish control over the means of production, at public expense' (41).[22] These processes of 'enrichment' and 'entrenchment' are interpreted as class action, as 'collective action to increase or reduce social inequality and domination, or to strengthen or weaken the means whereby the domination of a privileged stratum is maintained' (41).[23] However, the fact that individuals promote their personal interests which also happen to be the interests of their group does not establish that they are endowed with class consciousness or are engaging in class action. Thus competitive producers increasing the prices of their products because their cost of production has gone up are not engaging in class action.

That talk of a ruling class acting as a group in Africa is premature is supported by Diamond's own evidence: the Nigerian ruling class is riven 'by ethnic, regional, and religious cleavages, by shifting partisan and factional divisions, and by continual civil-military tension', united only by 'a shared taste for extravagant consumption and acquisition financed by access to state power' (1993, 219). Intense competition among politicians is likely a mark of limited class-consciousness. Diamond attempts to avoid this conclusion by a sleight of hand. Without any warning, we are suddenly confronted with 'the struggle among the political classes to control the narrow resource base of an under-developed economy and state' (1988, 45). Instead of a single dominant class we now have three, Northern, Yoruba and Igbo: 'From its base of political power in the regional government, the emergent dominant class in each region competed with the other two for the resources and opportunities of class formation' (51).

Not only do we now have three ruling classes, but these ruling classes are also racked by intra-ethnic contests.[24] The bitterness of such conflicts is obviously not an indication of the existence of a class-for-itself, but of its absence. Indeed, Diamond relates the depth of the friction between different individuals and groups to their fear of losing political power, followed by 'a traumatic decline in income and status, a return not to some respectable level of comfort and security but to a marginal social position' (283), which in turn is seen partly as an expression of the winner-take-all aspect of Nigerian politics. Intra-class competition and the redistribution of property after a change in power are indications that we are not dealing with a class acting as a group.

The African situation, then, is characterized by a situation where winner-take-all politics predominate: shared values and affective ties have not made strong inroads on intra-class competition. Moreover, the legitimacy of the ruling class is low and therefore its members cannot feel secure in their social position.

6.2.4 Stability of Property Rights

The combination of state dependence and winner-take-all politics of the African continent has the predictable consequences for the security of property. Not only are African businesses reliant on the state for their profits, but the flow of privileges on which business success hinges can by no means be taken for granted; individual membership of the bourgeoisie 'is contingent upon remaining within the orbit of established political authority; a fall from political grace can be exceedingly costly' (Young 1982b, 82). A change in government or in factional power thus leads often to a large scale redistribution of business opportunities. As the incoming administration replaces the members and supporters of the outgoing one in the economic as well as the political realm, the old beneficiaries of government largesse, even if they do not lose their privileges, are forced at least to renegotiate terms.

The two best known cases where political change led to massive relocations in the economic realm are Uganda and Kenya.

> With each change of regime, those prominent officials who had accepted the patronage of one government lost all their investments and sometimes their lives. Northerners who profited from the first UPC[25] government were force to abandon their investments by Amin and his henchmen.

Nubians and other northwestern Ugandans who received Indian businesses did not hold on to them for very long. The few who did succeed were forced to flee after liberation. Further political struggle among factions in the interim post-liberation governments gave returning refugees who joined the government access to state funds until they were forced to flee once again. One class fragment after another, each ethnically defined, was dispersed (Kasfir 1984, 100; 1987, 57).[26]

The Ugandan events are the most dramatic, but similar incidents are documented elsewhere. Thus when the dominance of the class faction identified with Kenyatta was challenged by the group represented politically by the Kenya People's Union,[27] its economic and political base was eliminated. A similar upheaval occurred after Moi came to power (Currie and Ray, 1984), this time at the cost of the Kikuyu, Kenyatta's major base of support. 'By 1983, the Kikuyu were a minor force within Moi's system of personal rule. The President surrounded himself with the leaders of smaller tribes who, in turn, used the state apparatus to displace the Kikuyu bourgeoisie. Based as it was on patronage and force, Kikuyu dominance proved vulnerable to the turns of political fortune' (Sandbrook 1985, 71).

However, not only major political upheavals such as changes of government lead to a redistribution of business opportunities. The flow of formal privileges is also threatened by changes in the balance of factional power, or even by 'the downfall of a political patron' (Harsch 1993, 39). Equally or perhaps even more precarious are the privileges derived from corrupt dealings. The loss of an important contact in immigration, customs, or the tax office can have significant effects of the profitability of an enterprise.

Since political change leads to widespread economic change, property arrangements are extremely unstable. Ownership is never secure as the regulatory framework is in constant flux, because either regulations themselves or their administration is constantly changing. Political clientelism, combined with the insecure position of the political class, ensures that security of property is very low.

6.3   Pathological Clientelism and Growth

From what has been said in the last chapter there is no need to elaborate on the detrimental economic consequences of such a high degree of insecurity of property. The negative effect on the level of investment, particularly on investment involving long term commitments, is too obvious to be overlooked. The heavy disincentives to invest in long term capital-intensive projects mean that many of the savings accumulated in a country are sent abroad, and that any investments within the country are either extremely profitable, short term, or financed with very little equity, thus shifting the risk to the lender, and often to the government of the particular country who underwrites the loan provided by international lending agencies. The level of investment forthcoming in such an environment is unlikely to generate enough economic growth to raise people's standard of living. Indeed, in Africa it failed even to maintain it.

6.4   Client-capitalism

Marxist writers in particular have scanned Africa for decades in the search for capitalist development, and often concluded that it progressed apace. However, from a clientelist perspective it must be questioned whether African economic systems are capitalist in any meaningful sense. Indeed, it is more likely that the economies we observe constitute a distinct type of economic system, a structure which might be termed client-capitalism.

But what constitutes capitalism? According to some writers in the Marxist tradition, the crucial factor that defines capitalism is the employment of wage labor. Sender and Smith, for example, attack those who have misgivings about the 'existence and importance of the bourgeois class in Africa' for their superficial understanding of capitalism, and quoting Lenin, for upholding a 'conception of capitalism [which] has not advanced beyond the commonplace vulgar idea that a capitalist is a wealthy and educated employer who runs a large machine enterprise' (1986, 79). This view, however, leaves out essential aspects of a capitalist system.

6.4.1 Definition of Capitalism

Marx clearly defines capitalism in terms of the existence of wage labor (1976, 874, 557, 439). In the African literature, however, this is all too often taken to be a sufficient condition for the existence of the capitalist mode of production. For example, it is said that the development of a free market for labor 'is the specific definition of what constitutes capitalism: namely, a form of organization of production in which the direct producers sell their labor power since alternative means of survival are increasingly constrained' (Sender and Smith 1986, 35). Similarly, the growth in 'the share of wage and salary employment in total employment' is equated by Leys to 'an extension of capitalist relations of production' (1978, 246). Iliffe's statement is even more uncompromising: by arguing that capitalism centers on the exploitation of the labor power of free wage labourers, 'African capitalism is by definition identical to capitalism elsewhere' (1983, 4).[28]

It is questionable whether Marx would agree. The position implies that any institutional arrangement in the sphere of circulation is compatible with capitalism. However, Marx clearly thought that both secure property rights and an accumulation process based on the operation of competitive market forces were necessary ingredients of a capitalist economy.

Following the beaten path of classical economics, Marx identifies the capitalist mode of production with 'capitalist' private property (1976, 940), and contrasts secure private property with original or primitive accumulation.

Marx introduced the concept of original or primitive accumulation in order to explain the origin of capital (873).[29] This pre-capitalist mode of accumulation was based mainly on force, often force derived from the power of the state (874, 915–16). He draws attention to such practices as 'the discovery of gold and silver in America, the extirpation, enslavement and entombment in mines of the indigenous population of that continent, the beginnings of the conquest and plunder of India', the conversion of Africa into a preserve for slavery (915–916), the expropriation of rural producers (877–895), and the forcing down of wages by acts of Parliament (896–904). The latter in particular makes it clear that primitive accumulation *may* include overriding market decisions using state power in order to favor particular individuals or groups.[30] Profits derived from privileges granted by the government therefore *may* signify primitive accumulation, and not of fully developed capitalism.

Moreover, Marx locates this marketing process in a competitive environment. 'The division of labor within society brings into contact independent producers of commodities, who acknowledge no authority other than that of competition' (477). 'Free competition makes the immanent laws of production confront the single capitalist as a coercive force external to him' (1962, 286 - my translation).

Competition is of structural importance in Marx's theory because it is part of the explanation of the process of capitalist accumulation. The capitalist is 'fanatically intent on the valorization of value; consequently he ruthlessly forces the human race to produce for production's sake. In this way he spurs on the development of society's productive forces' (739). This process of developing the productive forces succeeds only because competition forces low-cost producers out of business.

6.4.2 Capitalism in Africa?

Thus there are two criteria which characterize advanced capitalism: the predominance of the market over primitive accumulation through direct government intervention, and the existence of a set of well defined and reasonably stable property rights in which competitive market operations can be conducted. The question then becomes whether these conditions are satisfied in a particular environment, such as contemporary Africa, or whether primitive accumulation in an environment of high insecurity of property is a more apt description of that reality.

Any answer to this question involves matters of degree: property rights are never perfectly defined or stable and the scope of market operations is restricted everywhere. Even so, it is possible to identify at which end of a spectrum an economic system is operating by estimating the prevailing degree of security of property and whether the process of accumulation is more closely related to primitive accumulation than accumulation through profits derived from a competitive market.

Let us compare Marx's businessperson to an African. As defined by Marx, capitalists are free to organize their business, buy inputs solely on the basis of economic criteria, and rely on a well organized distribution system; their success depends on the price and quality of their product, and their operations are embedded in a reasonably stable regulatory framework. An African business, on the other hand, often depends for its survival largely on the goodwill of the government: for special protection, for subsidies, for the general license to operate the business, and for licenses to import inputs and export the final product, and to obtain foreign exchange. It depends on special considerations when it comes to the provision of necessary government services such as telephone and electricity, on not being fined for sometimes inevitable or imaginary transgressions of laws and regulations, on having its taxes assessed through bribery, perhaps even on selling its output to the government or a government agency through a tendering procedure which is arbitrary and corrupt. The list could easily be extended. African businesses operate constantly under conditions where market decisions are overridden by the government, and where the control over the business environment is severely limited because of the unstable and unpredictable nature of political decision making. This, quite clearly, is not the capitalist of Volume 1 of *Das Kapital*.

If the argument has been valid so far, the widely held assumption of 'the dominance of the capitalist mode of production in most African countries' (Swainson 1978, 360) breaks down. Hence even if it is agreed that the modern sector of African economies has expanded rapidly in recent decades, it is still possible to disagree with Warren's conclusion according to which 'empirical evidence suggests that the prospects for successful capitalist development in many underdeveloped countries are quite favorable' (1980, 9), or with the assertion that 'the reality of capitalist development in many African countries can no longer be ignored' (Sender and Smith 1986, 130). Markovitz's eulogy on the power, determination and ingenuity of African businesspeople which 'shook their societies' (1977, 231) fails on similar counts. It is not the businessmen who shook African societies, but the politicians and their clients who used political power to acquire interests in businesses whose success is based on precarious privileges granted by the state (51–53).[31]

6.4.3 Reasons for the Absence of Capitalism

It has been argued by a number of writers that the economic structure encountered on the African continent has little to do with modern developed capitalism. Schatz, for example, describes Nigerian entrepreneurs as 'pirate capitalists': 'For the most vigorous, capable, resourceful, well-connected, and "lucky" entrepreneurs (including politicians, civil servants, and army officers), productive economic activity ... has faded in appeal. Access to, and manipulation of, the government-spending process has become the golden gateway to fortune' (1984, 54). Similarly, Callaghy argues that 'Zaire is not in a "bourgeois phase" at all. The current situation is prebourgeois' (1986, 186). The reason why Callaghy, like Schatz, thinks that capitalism is absent is that 'the political aristocracy in Zaire does not invest its ill-gotten gains in productive, as opposed to merely profitable, ways' (186, 185).[32]

However, this notion of why capitalism is absent is superficial and misleading. First, the argument is shallow because these capitalists are not inherently different from their counterparts in developed countries. Rent-seeking is a universal phenomenon, and one would expect everywhere that firms seek rent for as long as it is profitable. The reasons why these 'pirate-capitalists' invest in the way they do is the nature of property arrangements, determining the relative profitability of different economic activities, including rent-seeking. Second, even if these capitalists did invest in productive activity instead of engaging in 'discretionary consumption and real estate speculation' (Joseph 1984, 25), that would still not necessarily turn them into capitalists. The major difference from conventional capitalists lies not in the nature of their investment decisions, but in the nature of the environment they operate in, the sphere of circulation, characterized by a combination of dependence on the state which underwrites their profits through regulation and corruption and the instability of property and quasi-property rights. It is this crucial difference which defines what will be called client-capitalism.[33]

6.4.4 Client-capitalism and the Bourgeoisie

Client-capitalism, therefore, defines an economic system where business opportunities and the rate of profit are heavily influenced by changing and arbitrary political and administrative decisions. Thus businesspeople confront insecure and badly defined property rights, and the personal ties to officials which stabilize this environment are threatened by political instability which translates directly into economic instability. There is another feature of such an economy which is important for our purposes, however: the productive capacity of the country will be owned largely by the political class, and an independent bourgeoisie is largely absent and is prevented from emerging by the insecurity of property rights.

It is hardly surprising that the personnel of the state benefited disproportionately from the transfer of ownership from foreigners and minorities to nationals and majorities after independence. Thus the upper echelons 'of the civil service, along with the politicians and the business partners of these two groups, avidly exploited the new economic opportunities' (Sandbrook 1985, 67). In Zambia, a substantial pro-portion of those with the most extensive agricultural landholdings had come from, or continued to occupy, the upper ranks of the ruling party, government and parastatals, and many had benefited as recipients of loan funds from government institutions (Baylies and Szeftel 1982, 200). Bates describes the tendency of members of the political elite in Kenya to use government programs to acquire large agricultural holdings: 'Foremost among these new landholders, of course, were the President and his family' (Bates 1981, 108). In Zaire, the majority of new owners were politicians and administrators or their friends and relatives, the most powerful acquiring the most extensive holdings (MacGaffey 1987, 46; Young and Turner 1985, 326–350). Indeed, Zaire's wholesale transfer of ownership of foreign firms almost exclusively to the political elite only constitutes the most extreme case of 'parasitic capitalism' (Iliffe 1983, 80). The major beneficiaries of indigenization, regulation and corruption were those wielding political power and the bureaucracy. Thus there is a great overlap between owners of the means of production and the personnel of the state (Leys 1978).[34] 'It is of interest that across all sectors of enterprise and at all levels of scale, African owners can be characterized frequently by a close association with UNIP (the ruling party in Zambia at the time)' (Baylies and Szeftel 1982, 199).

Political supporters benefited too. In Nkruhmah's Ghana, the government loan program, for example, 'became a weapon in the struggle to build a pro-government organization in the cocoa-growing region and to counter growing resistance to the government's pricing policies' (Bates 1981, 109). In Senegal political considerations bolstered the economic position of the politically powerful Marabouts. The process of transferring parts of the economic surplus from the community to members of an emerging class occurs

> on a wider scale through the system of patronage operated by political parties and, particularly by the ruling party ... The administration of loan funds would again appear to be an important way in which the system operates and through which loyalty to the Party is rewarded (Baylies and Szeftel 1982, 198–199).

This leads directly to the familiar conclusion that political processes determine economic processes.[35] As Balandier put it: 'It is participation in the exercise of political power that gives economic power, rather than the reverse' (1970, 168). Unlike in Western industrial societies, 'wealth or status do not customarily precede power; rather power and status are isochronous, while wealth more often than not increases with power' (Cohen 1972, 247).[36] Thus we finally have arrived at Sklar's conclusion that 'class relations, at bottom, are determined by relations of power, not production' (1979, 537)[37] where a political ruling class or protoclass 'emerges out of the patrimonial administrative state and creates an economic base for itself using the state apparatus, without necessarily having any major prior accumulation' (Callaghy 1984, 52).

Moreover, the redistribution process often not only bypassed the existing bourgeoisie, but even discriminated against it. Accordingly the principal beneficiaries after independence in Zambia 'were often not so much the existing bourgeoisie but the incumbents of high office or high salary positions' (Baylies and Szeftel 1982, 196). In the Sudan, although the indigenous Sudanese business sector 'was, within the limits of its historical experience, efficient and hardy, it was not allowed to play a significant role, in the hurried development efforts of the 1970s, either by politicians or by foreign investors and advisers' (Tignor 1987, 211).

The merchants in Mali rioted precisely because the state discriminated against them (Meillassoux 1970, 106). Not only did political power beget wealth, it tended to destroy wealth not begotten by political power.[38]

This impotence of businesspeople is illustrated by the experience of a rich cocoa farmer in Ghana, who, when asked why he did not try to organize political support among his colleagues for a rise in product prices

> went to his strongbox and produced a packet of documents: licenses for his vehicles, import permits for spare parts, titles to his real property and improvements, and the articles of incorporation that exempted him from a major portion of his income taxes. "If I tried to organize resistance to the government's policies on farm prices," he said while exhibiting these documents, "I would be called an enemy of the state and I would lose all these" (Bates 1981, 117).

The power of the bourgeoisie in developed capitalist countries, on the other hand, is based on much more secure property rights and a marketing process which allocates resources according to non-political criteria to a much higher degree.[39] Thus the income and wealth of the bourgeois class is protected from the predatory inclinations of the politicians by constitutional guarantees of property rights, a legislative process ensuring some degree of protection against arbitrary and unstable legislation, and bureaucratic procedures which are generally enforced. This shelter allows an individual to accumulate wealth independent of the political sphere, wealth which in turn provides the basis of political power.

Without secure property rights the bourgeoisie's vantage point from which to engage in class action and decisively influence political processes is largely absent. This of course does not mean that we do not find powerful businesspeople in Africa, only that their power is primarily derived from their political connections, and not from their ability to operate successfully in markets.

Moreover, as we have seen earlier, even where corporations or interest groups have emerged, they tend to be weak because of the propensity of the state to coopt their leaders and integrate them into personal clientele networks. Hence organizations ostensibly with the purpose of furthering interest group or class benefits often degenerate into amalgams of personal followers interested in administrative decisions benefiting them personally. A bourgeoisie that is independent of the political system is thus unlikely to spring from a clientelist system. Client-capitalism, therefore, is a matter of state dependence and insecurity. The process of clientelist redistribution favors those with political connections. But most importantly, a substantial independent bourgeoisie able to engage in significant organized political action is unlikely to emerge as long as businesses depend for their economic survival on the political support of individual members of the ruling class.

6.5 Transition to Capitalism

How can such a pathological form of clientelism transform itself? How can a capitalist system emerge in which security of property is high and the bourgeoisie powerful? These latter developments are related, as we have seen, since it is the security of property which provides the springboard for the ascendancy of the bourgeoisie.

A transition along the traditional pattern of Western Europe would involve the formation of a bourgeois class that achieves political ascendancy and thus is able to transform the legal structure and establish a system of property rights conducive to capitalist development. However, such a path of development is barred precisely because of the absence of secure property rights.[40]

Sometimes a different pathway to capitalism is envisaged: the African political class transforms itself into a bourgeoisie. Such a view is expressed by Callaghy: a 'political aristocracy' composed of individuals holding top or medium level administrative, political and military positions (1984, 182–183) is in the process of emerging in Africa. This 'transethnic' class, according to Callaghy, is not 'completely coherent and unified' (185) but 'usually fragmented into various competing factions' 'composed of sets of partially interlocking, partially competing patron-client networks' (192). However, as it 'builds an economic base for itself' it 'slowly manifests increasingly genuine bourgeois characteristics' (51).

Such a transformation might occur if in the process the nature of property rights is transformed. However, that would require a political transformation which leads the ruling class to abandon winner-take-all policies, which in turn presupposes the moderation of intra-class competition and a high degree of security of tenure of the class as a whole.[41]

6.6   Competing Views on African Development

Client-capitalism implies that the political class uses state power to acquire an economic base, but that this base is precarious. Thus businesses, mainly owned by patrons and clients, operate in an environment of extreme uncertainty, with the result that economic growth is impaired. Another consequence is that a transition to capitalism requires a political transformation: security of tenure of the ruling class and the moderation of intra-class conflict. This description is at odds with a number of analyses on Africa.

First, it differs from a conventional Marxist position that holds that the progress of capitalism is unproblematic because the capitalist mode of production dominates Africa already, and all that is needed to create a modern capitalist system is a continuous expansion of the sector of the economy which employs labor. On this account, political change is therefore not a prerequisite for the progress of capitalism in Africa. Given the importance of the institutional environment for economic development, and the fact that political arrangements are a vital element of this institutional framework, such a Marxist account leaves out a central part of the explanation.

Second, it is sometimes questioned that African development has been retarded at all. There is the optimistic Marxist view that economic development in Africa has been a success.[42]

> The evidence for the development of the productive forces ... in many African countries in the post-colonial period is overwhelming; the rate of change has been particularly rapid in comparison with Africa's own experience prior to World War II (Sender and Smith 1986, 94).[43]

Given that the standard of living today is lower than at the time of independence in large parts of Africa (World Bank 1990), such a position is difficult to sustain.

Third, different reasons for Africa's slow economic development have been postulated, such as the dependency theory and the 'articulation of modes of production' arguments.[44] Whereas dependency theory attributes the retardation of growth to the integration of the local economy into the world capitalist economic system, the argument here locates the causes for the lack of development squarely in the domestic sphere. Alternatively, the 'articulation of modes of production' theorists find the causes for the lack of economic development in the Third World in the persistence of pre-capitalist modes of production (Ruccio and Simon 1988, 148). Thus the failure of capital to separate direct producers from their means of production hampers the extension of capitalism beyond industry into agriculture and results in restricted and uneven development. There is little doubt that pre-capitalist modes of production, particularly in the rural sector, have significant effects on the process of economic development. What clientelism opens up, however, is the possibility that the cause for the lack of development lies in the modern sector itself, a possibility from which the 'articulation of modes of production' theorists have barred themselves by equating the sector of the economy where wage labor is employed to capitalism, progressive by definition.

Fourth, according to the position taken here African accumulation is closely related to what Marx called primitive accumulation. Leys takes the opposite view, asserting that primitive accumulation is a thing of the past: 'In Kenya the spectacular phase of accumulation through modern forms of plunder was probably the years from 1971 to 1975' (1978, 253). Since then, 'a small, older political stratum, heavily involved in the various forms of modern primitive accumulation, [is] increasingly giving way to a younger generation more equipped to dispense with primitive forms of accumulation and oriented strongly towards fully capitalist valorization of the inherited family capital' (258).[45]

Leys' argument, however, is based on a very narrow definition of primitive accumulation, limiting it to 'such practices as the commandeering of state-owned land and livestock or the semi-forcible take-over of expatriate farms or businesses' (1978, 253). Leys might well be right that these crude methods of primitive accumulation have died out, but that still leaves the more subtle and more important varieties in the form of the state granting and withholding economic privileges to particular individuals or groups - something, as we have seen, which is a form of primitive accumulation. Primitive accumulation through redistribution of equity, specific state intervention to provide business opportunities to particular individuals or groups, and accumulation through graft all show that primitive accumulation is still a widespread phenomenon throughout Africa. Nor is just voluntary decision by 'a younger generation' required to change the nature of these practices. Businesspeople may simply have no choice but to cultivate political connections in order to gain economic privileges if they want to stay in business. Primitive accumulation therefore is by no means a thing of the past.

Fifth, the existence of clientelism leads to an analysis of the role of the state which conflicts strongly with Marxist interpretations. According to conventional Marxist accounts, the state is an instrument of capital accumulation. Beckman, for example, concludes that the 'primary role of the Nigerian state is to establish, maintain, protect and expand the conditions of capitalist accumulation in general' (1982, 45), and Swainson follows the same textbook description when she writes that in Kenya one of the primary functions of the state 'in the economic sphere is to create conditions conducive to capital accumulation' (1978, 365).

Underlying this view is of course the traditional Marxist position that the state is dominated by a bourgeoisie[46] which uses its power to foster its class interest. The view may take either the crude form of the state acting as the executive committee of the bourgeoisie, or of a state which is "autonomous" but still acts in the interests of the bourgeoisie.[47] However, if we accept that we operate in a non-capitalist system where the bourgeois class in the conventional sense is absent, and the state is dominated by a political class engaged in maintaining power through clientelist exchanges, we are in a position to explain why it is that by no stretch of imagination the typical African state can be said to have encouraged capital accumulation.

Sixth, we have finally arrived at a point which at first seems paradoxical: the state helped very many people to acquire and set up new businesses, yet has retarded the formation of a bourgeois class and the emergence of the capitalist mode of production. If this analysis is correct, it is more likely to have generated a set of client-capitalists precariously living off rent, rather than Marx's capitalists or Schumpeter's entrepreneurs.[48] Even if it is accepted that 'corrupt patronage and close control of the bureaucracy' (Alavi 1973, 157)[49] had favored the institution of private property, that still does not necessarily mean that it thereby fostered the capitalist mode of production.[50] The state may well have transformed 'small traders, civil service clerks, and peasants - all poised at the edge of capitalism' into substantial business-people, but that alone does not turn them 'into a locally dominant bourgeois class' (Kasfir 1984, 84). In fact, state action which furnished individuals with capital and profits neither has fostered the capitalist mode of production nor the development of a bourgeois class.

6.7   Conclusion

Africa's political life is widely described as being clientelist, dominated by the exchange of material benefits for political support. This clientelist structure generates pressures to provide personal benefits to supporters, to expand the revenue base and to soften bureaucratic allocation. This means that patrons will use their political and administrative power to allocate business opportunities to themselves and their clients. However, their economic base is precarious. Business opportunities that are generated through regulatory processes and corruption can easily evaporate. Indeed, a change in government is likely to lead to a large-scale redistribution of property arrangements. Thus the security of property tends to be low.

This characterization has several implications which contradict widespread beliefs about the nature of the political economy of Africa. It implies first that much of the modern sector of the economies must be considered non capitalist, engaged in primitive accumulation. Clientelism has a tendency to tether businesses to the state by providing them with precarious property and quasi-property rights. The income derived from business activity is, as a result as precarious as the favors on which it is based. Businesses, therefore, operate in an extremely insecure environment, which is incompatible with fully developed capitalism.

The position of these client-capitalists *vis-à-vis* politicians is correspondingly weak. The dependence of businesses on the support of the state to provide capital and profit opportunities prevents the emergence of a capitalist class with a secure power base outside politics. Class organizations, even where they exist, are weakened by the focus on the provision of individual and not class benefits, by the cooptation and corporatization of class organizations, and by the integration of their leadership into patron-client networks.

Clientelism leads to a particular view of a possible transition to capitalism. If this analysis is correct, the development of capitalism is held back by the nature of the sphere of circulation, and the transition to capitalism will occur only if the sphere of circulation changes: when legislation and regulations remain stable and are administered in a predictable manner, thereby improving security of property. Only then will primitive accumulation be transcended and will pre-capitalist firms transform themselves into capitalist ones. This process is likely to occur if the ruling class becomes more secure in its tenure, and it is in the interest of incumbents not to manipulate existing property rights on a large scale.

The view put forward here thus locates the economic problems in the political structure. It needs to be stressed that there are many reasons for the failure of African economic development, and this view does not exclude additional explanations. Nevertheless, it is believed that the pathological kind of clientelism which has been described in this chapter is sufficient to stifle economic growth.

If it is accepted that clientelism can have such a negative effect, it becomes important to ask: what causes clientelism? That will be the topic of the next chapter.

Notes:

1.   Thus Joseph finds that the 'grid of Nigerian political society is an intricate and expanding network of patron-client ties, which serve to link communities in a pyramidal manner. At the summit of such networks can be found individual office-holders in the federal and state capitals' (1984, 28). Donal Cruise O'Brien writes that Senghor's friends have been nepotists, no doubt, but 'have shown an impressive aptitude for using the selective mechanisms of administrative patronage in establishing a framework for the government of the whole territory of rural Senegal. Tribal chiefs and notables, Moslem religious dignitaries, all have been incorporated into the government machine' (1979, 215; 1975, 149–185). According to Szeftel, 'Zambian politics are characterized by a clientelist form in which patronage constitutes an important mechanism through which political supporters often obtain access to state resources in return for helping patrons obtain access to public office itself' (1982, 5). Callaghy tells us that Zaire's regime is 'underpinned by extensive and complex patron-client relationships' which constitute 'the primary linkage between state and society' (1984, 30, 46, 185). And Kasfir holds that the 'control of political resources and their exchange for material benefits in order to maintain a following is ubiquitous throughout Africa' (1987, 54). 'One structural factor that binds together state, class, and ethnicity is the pervasiveness of patron-client relationships' (Young 1982b, 93). See also Clapham (1985, 55).

2.   For example: Baylies and Szeftel (1982, 197); R. Cohen (1972, 247); Sandbrook (1985, 67); Schatz (1984, 55); Swainson (1977, 39, 42).

3.   E.g. Swainson (1978); Schatz (1977, 3); Sandbrook (1985, 68).

4.   See also Sandbrook (1985, 68); Harsch (1993, 39).

5.   See also Baylies and Szeftel (1982, 197); Wolters (1984, 188).

6.   Cruise O'Brien remarked categorically: 'In Senegal at least ... money cannot be made in large amounts without effective access to political power' (1975, 12).

7.   It is not surprising, therefore, that the businesses of bureaucrats who doubled as entrepreneurs failed after they were 'removed from office' (Himbara 1993, 101).

8.   Or, as Joseph found, 'the relative ease of appropriation via state agencies militates against the establishment of a strong independent economic base outside the public sector' (1984, 25).

9.   See Fanon's eunuch capitalists (1966, 144); see also Young (1982b, 81).

10.   Or, in a more roundabout way, who are not part of the 'political aristocracy', defined in turn as individuals holding higher level public offices.

11.   As Azarya and Chazan point out, the 'parallel-system structures could not be sustained without some measure of formal collusion' (1987, 123).

12.   The more so as MacGaffey avoids testing her thesis by looking for political connections apart from the formal criteria of holding office.

13.   MacGaffey follows a well worn path: Says Kasfir: 'The better approach to the black-market economy is to define it as autonomous economic activity by predominantly illegal operators' (1984, 94). This again presupposes that black market activities are pursued without passive or active connivance of state officials, which is difficult to believe, particularly if many of the operators belong to the public sector to begin with.

14.   For the same reasons, neither does it follow that 'the weaker the state, the more likely the formation of such a[n independent] bourgeoisie' (Kasfir 1984, 12).

15.   Where Mosca includes landowners, the bourgeoisie, the petit bourgeoisie (1929, 300, 270), and 'the numerous class of people who find employment in the liberal professions, in commerce and in industry, and who combine moderate means with a technical and often scientific education' (1929, 377, 408).

16.   As opposed to their individual interest, which is to maintain their membership in the class.

17.   Which allow class action beyond intermittent protest.

18.   The classic case is of course that of the labor organizations.

19.   A 'Gemeinschaft' in the Weberian sense (1976, 21).

20.   Obvious recent examples include Liberia; Rwanda; and Sierra Leone, where two former presidents of the country, Siaka Stevens and Joseph Momoh, and some other leading former politicians had significant assets confiscated (Kpundeh 1994, 144).

21.   More cautiously, Kasfir observes that 'a common sense of class consciousness by class members' 'surely occurs, though episodically, in African politics among both privileged and unprivileged groups' (1987, 54).

22.   Diamond explicitly talks about a 'class-for-itself' that will 'have high degrees of class consciousness and social coherence ... as this is a precondition for the class action necessary to consolidate and preserve class domination' (1988, 31).

23.   Statement based on Sklar (1979, 547).

24.   Such as the conflict between two paramount figures of the Yoruba establishment, Chief Awolowo and Chief Akintola.

25.   Uganda People's Congress.

26.   For a detailed account see Kasfir (1984).

27.   Formed by a dissident group of KANU members, with a leadership based mainly on the Luo tribe which had a populist-left program.

28.   The list can easily be extended. Swainson (1978, 1977), never considers the possibility that her Kenyan businesspeople might not add up to a bourgeoisie.

29.   Which cannot itself be the consequence of capitalist accumulation.

30.   Marx also makes it clear that this primitive accumulation assumes different aspects in different countries (1976, 876).

31.   Markovitz does notice that politicians and civil servant engage ever more frequently and ferociously in business (1977, 236) and that 'African business rose anew and achieved unprecedented heights of prosperity and governmental power' (260), but does not take the analysis of the connections between government and business any further.

32.   See also Joseph: 'There is a contradiction that must be recognized between a system whose investible capital is diverted into discretionary consumption and real estate speculation and one which can be said to reflect "the growing coherence of bourgeois interests"' (1984, 25).

33.   A term suggested by Charles McCoy.

34.   See also Swainson (1980, 191).

35.   Swainson remains on conventional Marxist ground in arguing that it is important 'for our analysis of capitalism in Kenya to reiterate a fundamental proposition that the *production and exchange* of things is the basis of all social structures' (1980, 5).So secure is she in her conviction that 'individuals at the top of the political structure provide for the maintenance and expansion of capitalist relations of production', and that on the other hand 'there are those businessmen who have organized politically to further their own economic interests' (184), that she has absolutely no need to test the direction of the causation, though her book is shot through with examples of the importance of state help for capital accumulation.

36.   To put it differently, its standing in society 'is not rooted in control of property, wealth, or productive facilities' (Young 1982b, 81–82).

37.   See also Sandbrook (1985, 72).

38.   In the Congo, the entrepreneurial class 'that emerged in the 1960s, has been outcompeted by the political elite' (Ekholm Friedman 1992, 230).

39.   As Young points out of Western countries: 'There, the state always encountered potent forces that were outside its grasp and partly hostile to its growth - the feudal nobility and mercantile capital, and later, industrial and financial capital' (1982b, 82).

40.   Joseph draws attention to the relatively large size of the state sector and only a 'nominally' private sector in Nigeria, resulting in a '*rentier*' state dominated by 'drone capitalists' (1984, 22–25). Nevertheless, that a Nigerian bourgeoisie 'has emerged during the past half-century' 'should be a matter beyond dispute' (24–25). Joseph cannot have it both ways: capitalism and the bourgeoisie are inseparable twins and therefore if Nigeria is not capitalist then the emergence of a bourgeoisie is hardly beyond dispute.

41.   A similar argument is made by Scott when he contrasts the behavioral differences between the homogeneous Thai elite and the fragmented political elite of Sukarno's Indonesia: 'The institutionalization of intra-elite politics in Thailand approximated a restricted conflict in which losers could be participants in the next "round". The very rules of the game in Indonesia were in jeopardy and it was understood that losers might be eliminated altogether' (1972, 83). Moreover, the greater 'homogeneity' of the Thai elite made for a (comparatively) reasonably predictable environment for businesses. The consequences for investment behavior of this difference in security of property and quasi-property rights are obvious (1972, Ch. 4 and 5).

42.   The starting point of the debate is Bill Warren's optimistic assessment of the progress of capitalism in Third World countries generally, where 'substantial, accelerating, and even historically unprecedented improvements in the growth of productive capacity and the material welfare of the mass of the population have occurred in the Third World in the postwar period. Moreover, the developing capitalist societies of Asia, Africa, and Latin America have proved themselves increasingly capable of generating powerful internal sources of economic expansion and of achieving an ever more independent economic and political status' (1980, 189).

43.   The empirical evidence was questioned from the outset (e.g. McMichael, Petras and Rhodes 1974; Emmanuel 1974). Kaplinsky, for his part, has 'no doubt that capitalist relations of production have extended significantly over the years' (1980, 86). However, since the early 1970s, 'real capital incomes have stagnated and accumulation in industry has been financed by limited growth in agricultural

productivity, balance of payments deficits and the temporary boom in coffee prices' (90). Hence he seems to accept Warren's argument, but argues that it is likely to end because of structural problems. See also Leys (1978).

44.   E.g. Langdon 1987.

45.   One of the more puzzling positions is that of Ake. He talks about the capitalist sphere, where relationships of production are mediated and distorted. The 'distortion' relates to the overlap between race and class: capitalists are mainly Europeans while the working class tends to be African (1981, 61). Ake has no doubt that there is a 'capitalist class', although he accepts that they tend to accumulate their wealth through political corruption (179). Indeed, he goes on to say that 'capitalist accumulation tended to degenerate into primitive accumulation' (179). He does not seem to notice the conflict between primitive accumulation and capitalism.

46.   To Leys, for example, the 'indigenous capitalist class assumed the hegemonic place in a new "power bloc"' (1978, 260). The local bourgeoisie, it is said, managed to dominate the state and successfully used state power as a means to dominate foreign capital (Kitching 1985, 128; Leys 1978, 253).

47.   Despite all the debate on 'state autonomy', this fundamental point was adhered to. Bonapartism provides the point of departure, which originates in 'the inability of any one of these [classes and fractions in power] to raise itself to be the hegemonic class or fraction' (Poulantzas 1973, 302). It follows that the state of the Second Empire 'is thus relatively autonomous from the power bloc', but it still 'serves the interests of the bourgeoisie in its ensemble' (302); in fact, its relative autonomy allows it to rise beyond its factions and to organize the hegemony of this class as a whole (1969, 74). Alavi follows Poulantzas (1969), even though he insists on the difference between the Pakistani situation and that of Europe (1973, 146, 160). He argues that as a result of the colonial legacy the state was 'overdeveloped' relative to any social class (145). This meant that the 'bureaucratic-military oligarchy' 'acquires a relatively autonomous role and is not simply the instrument of any of the three propertied classes' (146), the metropolitan bourgeoisie, the indigenous bourgeoisie, and the landed classes (148). In a pluralist fashion, the bureaucracy mediates 'the competing interests of the three propertied classes ... while at the same time acting on behalf of all of them in order to preserve the social order in which their interests are embedded' (148). Hence despite this postulated autonomy, the state elite, as with Poulantzas, still acts in the interests of the bourgeoisie. For a critical view of Poulantzas see Miliband (1970). For a criticism of applying Alavi's overdeveloped state to Africa see Saul (1979); Leys (1976); Jackson and Rosberg (1986, 6).

48. As Sandbrook concludes: there is little development towards the classic risk-taking entrepreneur; they rely on 'an opportunistic exploitation of "insider" privileges in many cases' (Sandbrook 1985, 72).

49. As Alavi has argued in the case of Pakistan, an argument widely employed in the African context.

50. The same argument is implied by Szeftel (1982, 7–8).

7   Causes of Clientelism

It has been argued that the policy failures which devastated the economies of many Third World countries are at least partly the result of unbridled clientelism. Clientelist regimes often established themselves in the Third World through elections at independence. Some of those regimes with clientelist leanings were long lasting, such as in India; others were overthrown, often to popular acclaim, and the elimination of the excesses of clientelism was promised. Subsequently, clientelism continued to flourish in many places: whether competitive elections were held or some form of authoritarian government was established hardly mattered. The disastrous economic record of clientelist governments and their dismal failure to improve welfare raises the questions: why do people vote for political parties which promise particularistic benefits? how likely is it that this pattern is going to change? The likelihood of the success or failure of the current wave of stabilization programs will depend largely on the answer to this question. If it is true that clientelism is a major factor which causes inward-looking anti-market policies, then it may be that only the removal of clientelism is able to break the cycle of failed reforms. Thus policy reform and economic recovery may ultimately depend on political change.

Modernization theory sometimes embodies clientelism as an intermediate and 'transitional' stage as society moves from tradition to modernity. Clientelism, closely associated with parochialism, was expected to decline as allegiances shift from local community or urban neighborhood to social class. It was believed that the broadening of loyalties would tend to a replacement of individual-communal inducements by sectoral or class inducements (Huntington and Nelson 1976, 63). Although warnings were added that the 'ordering of stages need not be universal' (Landé 1977, xxxii), the ultimate outcome was hardly in doubt.

More recently, however, there has been a greater tendency to stress the permanence of clientelism. People in southern Italy continued to vote for the Christian Democrats 'as guarantor of a society that remains fundamentally clientelistic in its conception of the relationship between the citizen and the state' (Chubb 1982, 248). Instead of disappearing 'under the impact of modernizing forces such as the state and the market', Italian clientelism was a major force in shaping the modern Italian state (Graziano 1973, 3–4; Chubb 1982, 75; 211). Similarly, there are few indications that voting behavior has changed in countries like Greece,[1] India, and the Philippines, or on the African continent (Wade 1985; Landé 1977; Wolters 1984; Joseph 1984; Berman 1974).

Why do voters support clientelist politicians? The question is approached in the Schumpeterian fashion by looking at the electoral process as a market for policies where competing parties offer different policy packages, and the voter chooses the one which offers the greatest attainable benefits. The choice we are concerned with here, however, is not between slightly differing policy packages, but between different political styles: one where particularistic benefits are parceled out through clientele networks, and one where general benefits are distributed by a Weberian-type bureaucracy.

There are four types of potentially relevant explanations of why people support candidates that promote clientelist politics. First, clientelism may reflect the rational choice of a fully informed electorate maximizing its welfare. Second, voters may support clientelism because of particular failures in the 'market' of politics: voters have imperfect information, are caught up in prisoner's dilemmas, or simply do not have a choice. Third, unchanging value orientations prevent voters from pursuing their self-interest. Fourth, socio-economic factors promote clientelism: a social structure which obstructs the emergence of broad loyalties along group and class lines; poverty; and variability of income.

The first section of this chapter shows that clientelism has often been viewed as a reflection of the preferences of individual voters. The second section evaluates the hypothesis that clientelism is a true reflection of the preferences of utility-maximizing voters. This hypothesis implies that voters consciously choose candidates who operate along clientelist lines because expected benefits are largest. It is argued that such a case is unconvincing since the net benefits are likely to be negative, even for the average client. There are several reasons for this. Many of the benefits evaporate if opportunity costs are taken into account, and imperfect discrimination between clients and non-clients diminishes the benefits available to clients through patronage allocation. Furthermore, uncertainty about the outcome of elections lessens the value of the expected future benefits from clientelist voting. In addition, clientelism tends to diminish the benefits available for distribution generally. If patronage politics does not materially benefit the average voter, the commonly held position that clientelism is due to the excessive materialism of the voter is ruled out.

The third section looks at market failures that might induce self-interested voters to support parties offering fewer attainable benefits than their competitors: imperfect information, transaction costs and prisoner's dilemmas. In addition, market failures may impose constraints on the 'supply' side: the preferred policy package may simply not be offered. Of the market failure arguments, the imperfect information hypothesis was particularly popular, but it becomes increasingly unconvincing as the voters' experience with clientelism accumulates. Indeed, they often express their dissatisfaction with clientelism. Nevertheless, it is possible that voters are unable to perceive preferable alternatives. But perhaps prisoner's dilemmas play an even more important role in explaining the persistence of clientelism, since they may induce even rational and perfectly informed voters to support clientelism. They might be better off under an alternative political system, but the worst possible outcome is not being part of a clientele network when clientelism prevails. The section goes on to reject the elitist interpretation according to which the political behavior of the population simply mirrors the attitudes of the elite. Contrary to this belief, the evidence shows that attitudes of the elite are influenced by those of the public. The approach is useful, however, by bringing into focus the role of political entrepreneurship in the process of political change. The absence of political entrepreneurship, therefore, can be one of the reasons for the longevity of clientelism.

The fourth section reviews culturalist and structural positions. Culturalists stress the importance of unchanging value orientations that induce people to promote a kind of politics detrimental to their welfare. Structural arguments, on the other hand, focus on the absence of horizontal ties, on poverty and on variability of income, that encourage clientelist voting patterns. These factors in turn influence the severity of market failures such as the degree of ignorance and the prisoner's dilemma.

The fifth section explores some of the implications of clientelism for policy reforms in a democratic setting where clientelism reflects the voting behavior of the populace. It has been a central contention of the monograph that clientelism can be a cause of inward-looking anti-market policies. If that position is correct, clientelism is a major stumbling block to policy reform. In fact, a permanent departure from welfare-reducing policies calls for a change in voter behavior capable of altering the political structure. Successful policy reforms are possible only if the causes of clientelist voting behavior are removed: imperfect information, the prisoner's dilemma, barriers to political activity, elite attitudes, poverty and variability of income, and weakness of civic culture.

7.1   Clientelism as a Reflection of Voters' Preferences

The most popular view attributes the emergence and persistence of clientelism to the preferences of the voters. For example, Scott thinks that if,

> as with many "new" electorates, the desire for immediate tangible gain predominates, candidates will find it difficult to provide effective induce-ments without violating formal standards of public conduct. The pressures to win a majority following make it likely that, in the short run at least, a party will respond to the incentives that motivate its clientele rather than attempt to change the nature of those incentives (1972, 93, 107).

Clientelism, then, is caused by 'the patterns of political beliefs and loyalties that prevail among voters' (104).

In the same vein, Riley holds that 'there was, in the period [after independence], a contrast between individual expectations of the state and ... the "Weberian inheritance". Citizens regarded the prime duty of politicians to "help their people", and they viewed the efforts of politicians primarily in instrumental rather than ideological terms' (1983, 201). In India, efforts by politicians to create broad organizational support have usually failed 'because the ordinary voter has an extremely narrow range of public responsibility and is not willing to give time and effort without the promise of immediate material reward' (Bailey 1963, 135). Similarly, Wade finds the electorate 'primarily swayed by material and particularistic inducements' (1985, 486, 479): 'People vote for whom they think can give *them* the most favor, in a particularistic way' (487).[2]

However, why would voters endorse clientelism, even if they are 'swayed by material and particularistic inducement' (486), regard the prime duty of the politicians as to 'help their people', and view politicians' efforts 'in instrumental rather than ideological terms'?[3] If voters are rational benefit maximizers there are two possible answers: voting for particularistic benefits maximizes their welfare, or they hold the mistaken belief that it does so. These two possibilities are analyzed in turn.

7.2 Do Clients Benefit from Clientelism?

Clientelism might be chosen by well informed rational voters who wish to maximize their welfare. This implies that they must have the choice of representatives standing for clientelist politics, in short C-politics, and others who offer generalized benefits administered by bureaucratic rules, or G-politics.

What are the net benefits of a voter voting C? They consist of the benefits derived from the connections to a particular patron, and the costs are the opportunity costs, or the benefits foregone by not voting G.

Let us construct a very favorable case for C-politics. Assume that two parties compete in an election, a C- and a G-party. Moreover, suppose that the C-party is expected to win an election with 50 percent of the vote, and that the sum of government spending and taxes is 1. All government spending is allocated to clients, all taxes are paid by non-clients. All benefits are measured in terms of dollars spent by the government. The total benefits to clients then amount to 1, the net benefits to non-clients to -1. The outcome is unaffected by opportunity costs, which are zero in the case where the G-party wins. Thus a situation can occur where clients' net gains are positive. Therefore it can be rational for a typical client to prefer C-politics.

Payoff Matrix	C-party wins		G-party wins	
	Clients	Non-clients	Clients	Non-clients
Government spends on	1	0	0.5	0.5
Taxes paid by	0	1	0.5	0.5
Net benefit	1	-1	0	0

The payoff may increase if voters are poor, or their income varies in an unpredictable way. In this situation, clientelism sometimes provides an insurance against destitution. This was the case with the American machines, where 'it meant a great deal to an immigrant or laborer cast adrift in a *laissez-faire* state to know that when and if he needed help, the local ward boss would do what he could' (Scott 1972, 108). The same effect is believed to operate in the Third World. Thus insecurity of urban life for the poor, 'in the absence of the institutional assistance and legal protection (such as social security) available in more advanced nations, is in itself an adequate explanation for the tendency to seek best-placed friends and protectors' (Huntington and Nelson 1976, 128). Hence clientelism becomes a kind of 'social insurance' (Wolf 1977, 175). And, as in the case of the American machine, the clientelist politician becomes 'something of a social welfare worker not recognized by the profession' (Merriam 1929, 173).[4] To the degree that machines and patrons do offer protection against indigence superior to that of G-politics, the payoff from voting C increases.

Having made the strongest possible case why a rational benefit-maximizing voter might prefer C-politics, we now turn to the reasons why this possibility is rather remote. First, we have to question the relevance of two types of benefits which are sometimes used to explain the persistence of clientelism: protection and intermediation benefits. Protection benefits ensure that a person escapes punishment by the authorities for transgressing rules and regulations, and intermediation benefits occur when a client receives government resources through the intercession of a patron.

Protection benefits are often considered to be a particularly important attraction of clientelist politics. There are indeed cases where such benefits are real enough. Thus a patron may be able to deflect punishment from a client for transgressions which are punished in any society, such as traffic offences. However, protection benefits often include 'protection against ... illegal exactions of authority' (Wolf 1977, 174). Similarly, it is said that the benefits of the traditional middle classes in Palermo, largely the shop-keepers, consisted in protection from harassment for real or imaginary transgressions of rules and legislation by officials.[5] Protection from illegal and arbitrary exactions, however, resembles the benefits offered by a protection racket which protects an individual against being robbed by the racket itself. Thus 'protection benefits' of this kind cannot induce a voter to vote C, since protection would not generally be needed under an alternative political regime.

The protection argument is sometimes put in terms of security of property. The most obvious gain from a patron-client relationship, Scott tells us, is 'situations where public law cannot guarantee adequate protection against breaches of non-kin contracts' (1977, 133). This is undoubtedly true if the person cannot choose the political system. For example Bloch, in his writings on the origin of the feudal society, shows that the reason for the transfer of many freehold properties to the control of powerful individuals and institutions was the prevailing insecurity of life and property. Thus the French peasant of the village of Forez who transformed his freehold into a villein tenement on condition of being henceforth 'protected, defended and warranted' by a religious order 'doubtless thought he was doing something to his advantage' (1962, 246). There is little doubt that Bloch is right, but it is equally likely that this very peasant would have preferred to be protected and to keep his title.[6] He would have preferred a different political system, but did not have a choice. Thus these benefits do not explain why individuals prefer C to G where a choice between the two political styles is available.

Bureaucratic intermediation is generally thought to be another major attraction of clientelism. However, clientelism generates the need for intermediation by dislocating the bureaucratic mechanisms which largely obviate the need for it. Since G-politics largely does away with the need for patronage as a means to receive government benefits, it is difficult to believe that intermediation provides a major incentive to vote C.[7]

Mistaking all protection and intermediation for substantive gains leads to the claim that the strength of the Christian Democratic Party in Palermo was due largely to such benefits. Since the traditional middle classes and the urban poor constituted a major pillar of its power, and because they received next to no direct patronage spending, Chubb concludes that their allegiance must have been due to protection and intermediation benefits (1981, 83). The conclusion does not follow: such gains largely vanish if opportunity costs are taken into account, and therefore they cannot constitute a major attraction of clientelism.

Pork-barrel and personal benefits are real enough, however. Through pork-barreling, clients can gain disproportionate tax concessions and benefits such as roads, electricity supplies, clinics, schools, water supplies and the like. Discrimination in the allocation of such collective goods is of course widely practiced: 'whether it be Mayor Daley's Chicago or Awolowo's Western Region of Nigeria, the supply of such services ... can be, and is, tailored to the quest of political support' (Bates 1981, 113).[8]

However, pork-barreling is an inefficient way of remunerating clients for political support, since non-clients often cannot be excluded from consuming the benefits it provides. Pork-barreling, still in the realm of bureaucratic structures, therefore gives way to the provision of personal benefits and to administrative corruption. Personal benefits derived from patron-client relations typically include direct subsidies (including the reduction of taxation), employment in the government sector, and special access to government services such as health or education, credit and government contracts. Moreover, non-clients can be excluded from consuming collective goods on the same terms. Thus the existence of power lines in one's neighborhood does not guarantee access to the grid, nor does the availability of local heath services guarantee treatment. By dispensing these services not according to bureaucratic criteria to the public at large but through corrupt practices, targeting can be improved.

The quantity of potential benefits delivered to clients now crucially depends on the effectiveness of this targeting process. In our earlier example the whole of the government budget is spent on clients, whereas all taxes are paid by non-clients. In practice, the difficulty of distinguishing between clients and non-clients curbs efficient targeting. Clients will have to pay some taxes because it is infeasible to devise a tax system which exempts exhaustively one part of the population. This is particularly true where the bulk of tax revenue is derived from indirect taxes such as import duties. Moreover, some services will have to be provided where it is impossible to design a distribution system that restricts access, such as radio services and transportation.[9] Furthermore, factionalism and political instability may make it advisable to spread benefits widely in order to assure sufficient political support to maintain political power.[10] In addition, it may be necessary to spend some revenue on non-clients to avoid total disaffection.

The gain an average client can hope to receive from C-politics above what would have been received under an alternative arrangement thus amounts at best to some small additional amount of benefits forked out through the clientele network and perhaps some favorable tax treatment. But what are the losses?

The main loss is due to the shrinkage of the resources available for distribution. If economic growth declines as a consequence of C-politics, the tax revenue and the amount of resources available for distribution shrink. The shackling of the private sector means that alternative income opportunities become scarcer. The decline in the resources available for distribution is accelerated by the inefficiency of a bureaucracy which absorbs an increasing amount of the tax revenue. Moreover, such administrative failings can mean that many of the benefits become increasingly nominal. There is little gain in having privileged access to a hospital that has run out of medication, or to an electricity or a telephone system that hardly ever works. Furthermore, even if government spending is the same, benefits suffer because the goods provided are not those which lead to the greatest improvement in welfare, but those most likely to increase political support.

Considerable non-material costs of clientelism have to be added: the indignity of having to grovel before corrupt officials and politicians, and to actively support people one heartily despises in order to gain access to even the most basic government services, to be allowed to pursue one's business, or to get any bureaucratic decision taken at all.[11] These non-material factors are not irksome only to the rich: 'Indeed, one might even expect the sense of self-respect and the need to preserve one's dignity to be even more pronounced and cherished among the poor who, after all, have but little else' (Anderson 1990, 106).

What happens if we introduce more C-parties? If several C-parties compete, voting C becomes increasingly risky. Government resources will be distributed mainly to the clientele of the winning party, and the supporters of the defeated C-parties will be left out of the distribution process. Thus the more C-parties compete which are likely not to be included in government and votes are spread widely, the greater the probability that a C-voter is losing in the ensuing scramble for resources. Voting G thus reduces the risk of finding oneself excluded from the distribution process altogether. The reduced variability of the payoff makes G-politics more attractive if voters are risk averse.

If the opportunity costs of C-politics are properly considered, and account is taken of the reduction in payoff because of imperfect discrimination, the shrinkage in revenue, the added uncertainty in the distribution of taxes and benefits and the non-material costs, it becomes increasingly dubious whether C-voting is welfare maximizing even for clients. Indeed, this view is shared implicitly by most commentators. It is recognized in modernization theory, where clientelism is considered a passing phase which will be superseded by G-voting: as businessmen and laborers each come 'to appreciate their broader, long run interest as a sector of society', their interests are increasingly met by general legislation (Scott 1979, 113). It is also implicit in the position that clientelism benefits in the main a small group of individuals active in politics, or that it protects 'the interests of certain dominant classes' (Caciagli and Belloni 1981, 46). Thus the explanation that well informed rational voters support clientelism in order to maximize their personal welfare is not plausible.

If it is not in the material interest of the benefit-maximizing voter to support clientelism, explanations which associate clientelism and corruption with excessive materialism collapse.[12] Excessive materialism cannot explain why people support a political style that diminishes their material welfare.

Nigeria exemplifies the ruinous case of a political system that has traditionally been dominated by several competing C-parties based on ethnic allegiance - the Igbo, Yoruba, and Hausa-Fulani peoples. If the argument expounded so far holds, one would expect voters to support Igbo, Yoruba, and Hausa-Fulani G-parties promising general legislation to redress, for example, the poverty of the north, or to ensure equal opportunity for the west, but not C-parties which impoverish even most of the winners in the political game! But the optimal outcome from the point of view of the voters of all groups is probably a national G-party promising to distribute benefits according to some principle of equality. It is likely to be optimal because it reduces the risk of paying the bulk of taxes and receiving very few benefits. This risk is substantial if future possible realignments are taken into account. Thus voting G would eliminate the main fear of Nigerian voters 'of being left out of the sharing altogether by having backed the wrong party' (Joseph 1987, 150).

7.3 Market Approach to Voting Behavior and Market Failures

What induces people to promote a type of politics that reduces their welfare? The most obvious answer is that they do not have a choice. The choice may be absent because political entrepreneurship is deficient or because of barriers to entry into politics. Even if a choice is available, however, voters may still support clientelism because of imperfect information, prisoner's dilemmas, value orientations and socio-economic factors which prevent individuals from following the most promising course of action.

7.3.1 Supply Side Failures

As Schumpeter has pointed out, the volitions of the voter 'do not as a rule assert themselves directly. Even if strong and definite they remain latent, often for decades, until they are called to life by some political leader who turns them into political factors' (1976, 270).

Etzioni-Halevi's elitist explanation of clientelism may serve as a starting point for why the G-vote remains untapped. She rejects the idea that clientelism is caused by the preferences of voters: 'what counts is not so much the tendencies found in the rank-and-file public' but rather changes in norms and values of the elites'. Changes in norms and values of the elite are in turn a function of previous states of the elite culture, 'of growing self-restraints introduced at the level of the elites and the political-administrative establishments they head'. Socio-cultural developments at the level of the public itself may have marginally contributed to these changes but were not their major initiating or driving force (1979, 8).

The thesis that clientelism expands and declines independently of public opinion is hardly borne out even by her own evidence. She argues, for example, that clientelist practices in Britain declined when 'the political elite turned unequivocally against electoral manipulation' (47). However, she continues that at that time, too,

> there were various organizations that strove to turn public opinion against electoral corruption. Trade unions, chapels, friendly societies, all instilled into their members the virtues of democratic participation. In line with this general climate of opinion among politicians and leaders of various organizations, newspapers now strongly opposed electoral corruption (1979, 47).

Thus her own evidence seems to show that the elite changed attitudes under the influence of trade unions, chapels, and friendly societies.

Nevertheless, Etzioni-Halevi continues: 'As the elites changed their attitudes toward electoral corruption, so too, did the public, which gradually became socialized to the new style of political culture' (1979, 47). She reaches this conclusion by a rather drastic redefinition of the elite, which now not only includes 'the ruling elite' 'that holds the key positions in the governmental structures (2)', but also humble preachers, trade unionists and leading lights of friendly societies - in other words anybody in advance of public opinion. The assertion that the elite forms public opinion then is little more than a tautology.

Time and time again Etzioni-Halevi shows that contrary to her thesis public opinion did influence elite behavior, or at least that such an influence cannot be ruled out: In the US 'the merit system was further expanded as political appointments were adversely affected by public opinion' (137). In Australia, 'the period in which manipulation of material inducements to individuals declined was also the time at which working-class organizations began to take an active part in politics' (88, 105). One must therefore conclude that she has by no means established the 'clear chain of influence which runs from the structures and traditions of the governmental institutions in general, to those of the public administration in particular' (121).

Even if a change in political structure does not come about through changes in norms and values of the elite influencing the behavior of the populace at large, the approach still sheds useful light on the causes of clientelism. It opens up the possibility that even if voters would like to vote G, they are unable to do so because of the absence of a G-option, an absence which may well be related to the norms and values of the elite.[13] If political entrepreneurs are likely to originate from an elite whose members lack the personal traits that make successful reformers, elite culture will impede the emergence of alternatives to clientelism.[14]

The stress on political entrepreneurship links up with the familiar view that a bourgeoisie plays an important role in the development of democratic institutions. This group has an interest in stable and secure property rights and is powerful because of the financial resources it controls. Its interests, therefore, coincide with the promotion of political reforms. Thus the formation of a bourgeoisie is likely to provide an impetus for the development of G-parties.

At this stage a further interpretation can be put to rest. Chubb thinks that the reason why parties offering generalized benefits have difficulty emerging is the absence of an incentive 'for any individual member to assume the costs of participation necessary to achieve the goals of the group, because he will in any case participate in any collective benefits attained' (Chubb 1982, 211).[15] However, the cost of organizing opposition are borne by the political entrepreneurs and not the ordinary voters. The cost to the voters consists of casting their vote, something they need to do whether they vote C or G. Thus the cost to the voters cannot explain the lack of opposition. The cost to political entrepreneurship then leads directly to the problem of barriers to entry into the political 'marketplace'.

The persistence of C-voting might originate in barriers to entry into the market for politics, or in the high cost of organizing a G-party. The most obvious way to increase costs of organizing opposition is to control the courts and the legal system and to harass such parties, to ban them, to arrest and imprison their leaders, to tamper with the information flow in the media, and to control and fraudulently use the electoral machinery.[16]

Even in the absence of such practices, where competitive and fair elections are held regularly and voting is anonymous, opposition to clientelism may still be difficult and costly. A major weapon of clientelist governments is to withhold government resources from opponents, or to offer inducements to abstain from opposing the government. Our Ghanaian cocoa farmer from the last chapter illustrates the first kind of pressure. His economic existence depends on his titles, permits, and licenses. These would in all likelihood be threatened if he opposed the regime (Bates 1981, 117). Alternatively, cooptation is employed to exact conformity. Independent candidates, whether in Britain in the 18th century or in contemporary societies, are lured 'into voting for the government by the award of contracts, pensions, and patronage posts' (Scott 1972, 102).

The cost of organization may be affected by influencing related institutions which traditionally have facilitated the organization of political parties, such as trade unions, cooperatives, employer associations or even church organizations (Krischke 1990). By coopting and clientelising such institutions, the government significantly increases the difficulty of organizing political parties opposed to it.

The persistence of clientelism therefore may be due to the lack of political entrepreneurship and the high costs of political opposition.

7.3.2 Demand Side Failures

Nevertheless, people have been observed to promote clientelist politics even where alternative political styles have been available. In this case, we are left with the puzzle of why voters support a political system that is opposed to their interests. The Sicilian case illustrates the point. Chubb observes that the key 'to understanding the patron-client bond is that it depends not on a continuous stream of benefits, but rather on sustaining the expectation of rewards in the maximum number of people with the minimum payoff in concrete benefits' (1982, 5, 98, 247).This conforms to the thesis that the average client does not benefit from clientelism. So why do clients continue supporting it? Chubb believes that 'hope has clearly played a critical role in sustaining support for the machine even among those who have never directly experienced its benefits' (94).This answer simply leads to the next question: why do voters fail to learn? If we stay within the economic approach to voting behavior, two explanations offer themselves: imperfect information and a prisoner's dilemma.

The most obvious market failure arises if information is imperfect. Thus people may be uninformed about the costs and benefits of clientelism. As Scott suggested, supporters of American machines seldom appreciated the substantial long term costs of machine politics to the community as a whole (1972, 149). On this high level of abstraction the claims sound plausible enough. But are we really to believe that an individual who just cheated the tax office or a government buying agent, who exploited his connections to get his dim son into a school where he has no right to be, does not see the connection between his own actions and the inefficiency of the government agencies involved? The argument is certainly open to question.

Alternatively, individuals might not appreciate the distributional consequences, particularly if the manipulation of media is widespread (Caciagli and Belloni 1981, 47). However, conspicuous consumption among politicians is often rampant and widely resented.[17] In fact, arguments about lacking information have worn increasingly thin as experience about the effects of clientelism has accumulated. As Cruise O'Brien put it, the people 'may not have the means to understand just *how* they are being swindled, but it must be said that they do (at least among the Wolof) realize that they *are* swindled' (1975, 195).

There may be information deficiencies on a different level. People might realize that the political system leaves something to be desired, but not believe that G-politics is a superior alternative. Bailey, for one, does not think 'that the majority, as yet, have any conception of the meaning of "responsible" government; their horizons are too narrow for this' (1963, 32).

Last, the voter may not recognize that G-politics is available. This may take the form of a signaling problem where it is difficult for a C-party to convince a voter that it really will execute G-politics after it is elected. Considering that even the most corrupt politician denounces corruption before elections and promises to increase government efficiency, the voter might well have difficulties in sorting out the signals.[18]

Imperfect information or ignorance arguments are widely held despite the singular lack of supporting evidence. Moreover, they may successfully explain the emergence of clientelism, but as an account for its persistence they become more implausible as time goes by and the consequences of clientelism become increasingly manifest. Perhaps more important than ignorance, therefore, is a prisoner's dilemma.

A prisoner's dilemma might occur in the following way. Assume that two parties contest an election, one C- and one G- party, and it is possible to discriminate between clients and non-clients. The best possible outcome for everybody will be the elimination of C-politics, but the worst possible outcome for a voter is to support a G-party but for a C-party to win.

A payoff matrix may illustrate the point. If an individual votes G and the majority also votes G, the payoff will be 1. If the individual votes C and the G-party wins, the payoff is the same. If he supports the losing G-party, the benefits will be much reduced, say to 0. If the winning C-party is supported the benefit will be 0.5.

Payoff Matrix		G-party wins	C-party wins
Individual votes	G	1	0
	C	1	0.5

Which party will an individual support? The best outcome is achieved if everyone abstains from predatory behavior and votes G. However, the worst one is not to belong to the clientelist network and to have the party representing that network win. Thus the risk-averse voter is likely to vote C.

Such a dilemma is precisely that of an average villager: the best possible outcome of an election is a change in the political system, but the worst result is having thrown in one's lot with reformers, and to see the old patronage system remain unchanged. It is not surprising, therefore, that such voters will continue to support their patrons.[19]

The introduction of cheating by voters reverses the outcome if the patron is unable to distinguish between clients and non-clients. Not only can the voters often avoid sanctions[20] for disloyalty, they can always claim to have supported the winning C-party. The best option is then to vote G, and claim after the election to have supported C if C wins.

People might still vote for their patrons if loyalties discourage cheating. However, we have discussed the argument of the Maussian tradition that a system of exchange creates debts of gratitude and permanent relations, and found that even in fairly traditional surroundings people are unlikely to consistently support politicians who deliver inferior gains. Indeed, empirical evidence shows that politicians know this and act accordingly. It is no accident 'that in weeks preceding national or local elections squatters were given at least verbal assurances of legalization' (Ozbudun 1981, 261).[21] Thus loyalty is unlikely to prevent at least some cheating.

Cheating may be difficult, however, particularly in a tightly knit community. As an Indian politician put it: 'Even the secret ballot isn't really much protection because the money lender or zemindar soon finds out how people voted, because often they themselves can't keep quiet about it' (Bailey 1963, 194). If it is true that cheating is difficult, the prisoner's dilemma remains.

The persistence of clientelism may also be due partly to the disruption to many people's lives that accompanies political change. As clientelist politics unfolds, an increasingly wide range of people depend on particularistic favors: businesspeople whose existence is underwritten by the state;[22] bureaucrats in the extremely overstaffed civil service; managers and employees in inefficient parastatals; or illegal squatters in Latin America (Cornelius 1977, 34). Thus the number of people who are threatened by a transition to G-politics can be large, particularly where, as in some African states, the government employs half of those in formal employment.[23] All of these individuals[24] have a *prima facie* interest in the *status quo*. Change will be resisted even more because it takes lengthy periods of time for the private sector to recover, during which there are few prospects for former clients to retrieve their losses.

Uncertainty and risk aversion aggravate the problem. If voters are risk averse and there is a probability of losing in the ensuing redistribution process, they may prefer the *status quo* even if a change leads to an expected gain in welfare. For example, a bureaucrat may well vote for the existing system if the alternative will lead to his retrenchment, even if it is probable that more promising jobs will be available in the private sector. Similarly, an entrepreneur or worker in a factory may prefer the certainty of government contracts to the vagaries of a thriving private sector.

One would therefore expect that a large sector of society will resist a change to G-politics. Still, it remains true that the majority of the populace is likely to be disadvantaged by clientelism.[25] The existence of vested interests therefore does not explain why the average voter continues to support C-politics.

7.4 Culturalist and Structural Explanations of Voting Patterns

So far we have accounted for C-voting by market failures: on the supply side, by a possible lack of entrepreneurship and barriers to entry; on the voter's part, by imperfect information, prisoner's dilemmas, and risk and uncertainty. We now turn to value orientations and socio-economic conditions which will shed light on clientelist voting practices. As it turns out, both value orientations and structural factors influence the severity of the information problem and the prisoner's dilemma.

7.4.1 Culturalist Explanations

Culturalists assume, as we have seen earlier,[26] that actors acquire value orientations in the process of socialization, and that these orientations influence behavior and adapt only slowly to changes of circumstances.[27] Such assumptions open the possibility of dysfunctional behavior, in our case of political actions ostensibly against one's self-interest.

Some culturalists see in the client's behavior a form of 'residual ruralism', where the first generation 'of slum dwellers imports into the slum traditional rural attitudes of social deference and political passivity' (Huntington 1968, 281; Huntington and Nelson 1976, 58; Nelson 1979, 180). Thus rural migrants replicate traditional patron-client relationships after migrating to town (Lemarchand 1981, 20). Moreover, it is thought that such attitudes can persist for a long time. Thus 'clientelism ought not to be viewed as a passing phenomenon characteristic of tradition, back-wardness, or marginality and subject to replacement by more impersonal styles of interaction. Rather it might be viewed as a viable and deeply institutionalized perception of role interaction, one which surely can survive many structural and ecological changes' (Schmidt 1977, 317). Accordingly, it is this residual ruralism which encourages people to make political decisions that are against their self-interest.

Another line of culturalist thought concentrates on attitudes which hinder cooperation outside the family, and thus obstruct political organization of large groups and classes. One of the earlier theories - particularly influential in the analysis of peasant societies - proposed that clients generally do not take the long term into account and see themselves as competing for a given amount of resources (Huntington and Nelson 1976, 132; Scott, 1968 120). This 'constant-pie orientation' (Scott 1968, 119) combined with a short term view deters people from aiming at increasing the benefits for the class as a whole in the medium or long term

(Huntington and Nelson 1976, 132).[28] Constant-pie orientation and short-termism, then, provide a motivation to prefer particularistic to generalized benefits.

Another orientation which is thought to encourage clientelism is the high degree of mistrust which permeates many traditional societies.[29] Moral laws and principles do not, in general, apply to people outside the narrow bounds of communal life (Wilson 1991, 221). Rather, the moral universe is bounded by custom and habitual proximity, and people outside the family, and even more so complete strangers, are viewed with suspicion. This not only justifies the exploitation of those outside this narrow bound, but equally villagers 'cannot conceive that anyone should consistently and continually do favors for people who are not his relatives, much less for the general public, unless he makes something out of it' (Bailey 1963, 63). Mistrust is not limited to tradition-bound rural areas. Huntington, for example, observes that in 'Latin America, a high level of mutual distrust and antagonism exists in many urban slums' (1968, 280).

Political organization along class or broad group lines, however, demands some degree of extended cooperation with nonfamily members, which in turn requires a certain level of generalized social trust (Scott 1968, 122). The absence of trust then 'makes difficult any sort of organized cooperation to articulate demands and engage in political action' (Huntington 1968, 280). Clientelism then becomes linked to 'the moral solidarity and isolation of the family, and to the reciprocal hostility and distrust that exist between families unrelated by kinship or marriage ... [M]en do not associate, even within the community, on the basis of any universal principle of fair dealing. Nepotism is an obligation not a moral fault; and honor is opposed to the canon of honesty' (Campbell 1977, 261).[30] Consequently, people might be trapped in a 'culture of poverty' where they are unwilling to cooperate, mistrust political parties and unions, and limit their interests to the purely local: the 'voters themselves feel no direct interest in the common weal' (Bailey 1963, 35).

Culturalists not only provide a theory of dysfunctional behavior, they also attempt to explain the predatory behavior of the voter. If cultural discontinuity disrupts value orientations and thereby subverts traditional authority without putting anything in its place, individuals may view the new political structures purely instrumentally as a means to extract maximum benefits. They cease to conform with authority altogether, or their conformity becomes entirely ritualistic or else self-serving by bending norms and rules for private advantage (Eckstein 1988, 797). Hence the self-serving behavior of the voter may be a consequence of cultural disruption.

Some culturalist ideas have traveled better than others. Most commentators today would accept that peasants do take the long view and invest when economic opportunities arise.[31] They therefore cannot be tied to constant-pie orientations and the short view to the degree assumed by some culturalists.[32] The residual ruralism argument is also of dubious validity. It can equally well be argued that people who escaped the clutches of rural landowners are not well disposed to enter the same kind of dependence after migrating to town. There is no evidence for either view.

The distrust argument is more interesting.[33] Culturalists assume that people act against their self-interest permanently because they adhere to particular habits and customs, like the peasants or the migrants who persist with actions even if they reduce their welfare. A market approach, on the other hand, starts with the assumption that people learn and alter their behavior much more readily. The mistrust argument is compatible with the economists' approach because it does not violate the hypothesis that people do as well as they can. Mistrust is simply the familiar dilemma in a different guise. Although it would be optimal if everyone could trust each other, being the only trusting persons around is not a desirable option. Thus it may be rational to be mistrustful, and mistrust becomes self-perpetuating even if people recognize the quandary they are in.

The voting behavior which has been discussed is simply a case of this more basic dilemma. If everyone could be trusted to abandon clientelist politics, it would be the sensible course of action to vote for generalized benefit oneself. Since the ability to make agreements, and justified trust that such agreements will be adhered to, are central for overcoming prisoner's dilemmas, mistrust becomes the reason for their persistence.

The high level of distrust adds to the difficulty of organizing villagers, and thus to the cost of organization. It is difficult to establish a political party promising generalized benefits where society has been 'divided within itself for centuries', where people unite not on the basis of mutual trust but only when forced by necessity (Graziano 1973, 11). In the same way, the lack of trust hampers civic organizations such as unions which facilitate political organization indirectly.

Where does the culturalist argument leave us? First, it provides one rationale for the materialist bias of the voters by suggesting a mechanism for how self-serving behavior may evolve: rapid social, economic, or political change may induce people to adopt the materialistic self-serving behavior we have observed. Second, it shows that prisoner's dilemmas will be particularly severe in societies pervaded by distrust, and that organizing collective action will prove difficult.

7.4.2 Socio-economic Explanations

Socio-economic explanations, like culturalist explanations, attempt to explain certain types of behavior. They differ in that whereas culturalists analyze the effects of unchanging value orientations, the locus of socio-economic analyses is to show how behavior is shaped by the socio-economic environment. At the heart of many socio-economic explanations of clientelism is poverty and the social structure, which inhibit the development of horizontal ties among the populace.

How do socio-economic approaches explain this absence of horizontal ties and their failure to develop? One possibility is the predominance of vertical ties in society generally. Thus clientelism in Latin America has been thought to stem from the relatively great influence of vertical ties, unbroken by class conflict, that 'link upper and lower statuses and establish superior-subordinate relationships' (Chalmers 1977, 403).These vertical social hierarchies not only fail to 'represent clearly defined and specific interests' (404), but at the same time inhibit their emergence.

The Marxist approach focuses on economic factors. These are responsible for the absence of horizontal ties as well as for the absence of class-consciousness, a prerequisite of class action. Even more specifically, clientelism has been thought to stem ultimately from the system of land tenure:

> In central Italy, land ownership was very unequal; society was polarized between a small number of large landowners and a large number of tenants and labourers; the peasants were, as a result, brought together into a collective class consciousness. In the Italian Deep South, on the other hand, landowning was fragmented, and there were few large estates; consequently, there was no one against whom the peasants could organize (MacDonald, from Huntington and Nelson 1976, 101).

Graziano's economic explanation is more general: he attributes clientelism in southern Italy to the incomplete capitalistic penetration of the southern economy (1973, 4). Market relations which are 'anonymous, general, and abstract' are believed to depersonalize all human relations, and by depersonalizing them they destroy the 'particularistic ties of personal-concrete dependence' (6). Instead, these particularistic ties flourish where people 'feel no moral bond outside the family', and view the clientele networks as the specific remedy for a disjointed society' (11).

All of these explanations take for granted that the absence of horizontal ties is a self-evident factor in promoting clientelist politics.[34] This is not so, however. The absence of horizontal ties in itself does not entice individuals to act against their material interests. As Nelson has pointed out, 'class consciousness is probably not necessary for class actions' (Nelson 1979, 162). Nevertheless, there are reasons to believe that horizontal ties matter. First, the absence of horizontal ties might be reinforcing distrust. Generalized trust is unlikely to be fostered where each individual family or kin-group is isolated and fends for itself. Second, the absence of horizontal ties may exacerbate the information problem. If individuals and families remain 'a disaggregated social mass' they will not develop 'an awareness of any collective interests' (Caciagli and Belloni 1977, 50). Nor are they able to see that something can be done to promote them, since even perceiving the possibility of action may presuppose 'structures for collective organization' (Chubb 1981, 81, 85). Thus horizontal ties engender the information flows and broad loyalties on which collective action by large groups and classes rests.

The case that horizontal ties or 'civic culture' are a means to overcome dilemmas of collective action is forcefully made by Putnam. He believes that social trust in complex modern settings is partly a result of norms of reciprocity (1992, 171). Effective norms of generalized reciprocity are in turn 'likely to be associated with dense networks of social exchange' (172). The denser 'the networks in a community, the more likely that its citizens will be able to cooperate for mutual benefit' (172). Those integrated in these networks acquire a reputation for honesty and reliability, an important asset for any participant (168). On the other hand, social sanctions are effective because they diminish reputations, and reputations constitute a valuable asset. Where networks of civic engagement cut across social cleavages wider cooperation is nourished (175), and 'personal trust becomes social trust' (171). On the other hand, the absence of horizontal ties, or the isolation of the family, are part of the foundation on which clientelism rests.

Apart from the absence of horizontal ties, clientelism is often attributed to poverty: 'Machines characteristically rely upon the votes of the poor and naturally prosper best when the poor are many and the middle class few' (Scott 1972, 117). Poverty, it is thought, reinforces a materialist bias, the mistrust of non-family members, constant-pie orientations and the short view, and it sustains ignorance.

Poverty might sustain a materialist bias because the poor's concern with survival leaves little room for non-material considerations. One common approach is to rely on Maslow's hierarchy of needs, or a variant thereof, and assume that until lower level material needs are satisfied, people will not focus upon the next level on the scale.[35] However, as has been discussed already, materialism alone does not bring on clientelist voting.

Moreover, poverty allegedly 'shortens a man's time horizon and maximizes the effectiveness of short-run material inducements' (Scott 1972, 117–118). Furthermore it may exacerbate the 'belief in the inevitability of scarcity or the permanence of conflict over distribution shares' (1968, 120). Poverty, then, is responsible for the short term view and the constant-pie orientation of the voters, and ultimately explains why on their own accord 'very poor people do not take part in politics ... They remain interested in the welfare of themselves and their families and will not spare time or energy to work for the collectivity' (Bailey 1963, 88). In short, the value orientations which allegedly characterize peasant societies originate in poverty.

Poverty might have such consequences because of the 'intellectually and emotionally' 'stultifying and narrowing' effects of 'extreme material poverty' (Kitching 1983, 50, 53), leading to an 'incapacity' of the populace which thus becomes incompatible with 'meaningfully democratic societies' (48). The presupposition of such an incapacity sustains the traditional view that a threshold of material welfare has to be transcended before democratic governance will succeed. The argument suffers from neither specifying how serious poverty has to be in order to bring forth these stultifying effects, nor indicating the minimum degree of knowledge necessary for the working of a 'meaningfully' democratic society.

The experience of Palermo shows that the poor are not always the only principal base of mass support for political machines (Chubb 1982, 6–7). In fact, the middle classes are as important a source of machine strength as are the poor (7). Poverty alone, therefore, cannot explain clientelism.

Perhaps it is less poverty alone which induces people to vote C, but poverty combined with variability of income. As has been pointed out before, if people are poor and their income varies in an unpredictable way for reasons not connected to clientelism, patronage may guarantee subsistence insurance. If that is the case, patronage politics may indeed be attractive.

7.5   Policy Reform and the Decline of Clientelism

What is the significance of this analysis of the causes of clientelism for the success or failure of policy reform? Inward-looking anti-market policies, it has been argued, can be a result of clientelism. Moreover, in a democracy where competitive elections are held regularly, clientelism reflects the voting behavior of the populace. Thus inward-looking development becomes a function of voting behavior.

The argument suggests that inward-looking development policies are unlikely to be permanently abandoned unless voting behavior changes and clientelism recedes. Thus policy reforms are likely to be unsuccessful unless they are underwritten by a behavioral change. An example may illustrate the point: as long as traditional Ecuadorian politics continues to be dominated by electoral campaigns that mobilize support around clientelistic ties to personalistic leaders who make extravagant promises of benefits to flow from government (Grindle and Thoumi 1993, 128), it is difficult to see that structural reforms will be permanent and successful.

Clientelist analysis supports the conventional wisdom that reforms tend to fail because of a deficient capacity of the administrative apparatus,[36] a low degree of insulation of the state from demands by societal forces, and factionalism and thus a fragmented political system. The latter two factors combine to produce the 'bidding wars' among rival political elites which undermine reform programs (Haggard and Kaufman 1992, 271).[37] The thesis put forward does not take these factors as ultimate data, however: in many cases they are shown to be an emanation of the structure of the political system and the behavior of the voters.

Why do governments adopt policy reforms? One would expect that politicians who depend for much of their support on patronage are unlikely to adopt or implement structural changes that shift the allocation of resources to impersonal market mechanisms (Nelson 1990, 24). Thus a shift to 'market friendlier' policies occurred generally only in the wake of severe economic crises,[38] and after the politically more acceptable alternatives to structural reform had been exhausted (Remmer 1993, 404).

This was certainly the case of Senegal,[39] where in August 1983, in the depths 'of drought, Senegal raised consumer prices, froze civil service salaries and hiring, lowered producer prices for groundnuts, and imposed an emergency tax on the public payroll to relieve the drought-stricken countryside. No leader would ever want to take on such a broad array of interests voluntarily. Senegal's president Abdou Diouf, however, had his back to the wall' (Waterbury 1989, 39).[40]

The financial strains of an economic crisis promote policy reform in other ways. During an economic crisis benefits to clients are small. For instance, in the 1980s in Ghana even senior government officials 'reported that they were going hungry' (Herbst 1993, 153). Thus it has been said that structural reforms, such as in Ghana, were possible because the economic collapse meant that clients did not receive much from the state in any case (31). The same mechanism is responsible for the disappearance of the prisoner's dilemma. The economic crisis may thus lead to an upsurge in support for alternative political styles. In addition, economic crises may goad political competition: information flows are facilitated as a discredited elite loses its grip on the media, and constraints on organizing opposition become less effective.

However, will such a crisis be sufficient to alter voting behavior permanently? Crises, and not only economic ones, certainly have shaken voters out of their self-serving habits temporarily. For example Neapolitan politics had been dominated by the machine of the Christian Democrats for decades. However, in local elections in June 1975 'the Communist Party defeated the incumbent Christian Democrats ... and went on to form, for the first time in Naples' history, a left-wing city government together with the Socialists' (Chubb 1981, 91). What caused this shift? Although there was a general trend to the left during the elections in 1975, 'Observers on both sides of the political fence agree that the "moment of truth" arrived in August-September 1973, when Naples was struck by a sudden outbreak of cholera and, for a few agonizing weeks, the threat of a major epidemic loomed over the city' (Chubb 1981, 99).

In Ghana, the vivid memories of the economic collapse of 1982–83 had a similar traumatic effect.

> Well-being, dignity, integrity, and self-image were shattered. The vivid, searing memories of these two years and the legitimacy of the new military regime helped to get Ghana through the early years of the economic reform effort. Something had to be done. Ghanaians remembered how very bad it was, and they did not want to go through it again. Many understood the counterfactual of inaction; they had lived it (Callaghy 1990, 274).

It is too early to know whether this change in political behavior is permanent. Opposition has increased over time, particularly from the urban population that bore the great bulk of the adjustment costs (278). Even the relatively high growth rates of the 1980s dampened opposition only marginally (286). The current popularity of Nkrumah, one of the fathers of machine politics in Africa, points in the direction that clientelist voting may be far from overcome.

Thus policy reforms may be popular temporarily, but as the economy improves in the wake of economic reform clientage ties become more lucrative again and the old habits may re-establish themselves. A permanent departure from inward-looking anti-market policies requires the removal of the causes of clientelism. This implies easy access to political competition, and a reduction of the information problem and of prisoner's dilemmas. These in turn are related to attitudes such as the level of trust, and to socio-economic variables like the nature of social structure, poverty and variability of income.

The analysis thus supports the predictions of modernization theory that improved education, the decline of poverty, the development of civic society and a widening of loyalties tend to weaken clientelism. These factors add to the information flow about the nature of political systems, and reduce the need for subsistence insurance and prisoner's dilemmas become less virulent as generalized mistrust recedes. On the other hand, the tendency of clientelism to entrench itself impedes political change. The vertical structuring of clientele networks opposes the formation of horizontal loyalties, control of information flows deflects criticism and leads to systematic information deficiencies, barriers to entry in the market of politics prevent opposition groups from emerging, and vested interests become more pronounced as time goes by. It is too facile therefore to assume a mechanistic transcendence of clientelist politics.

Grindle criticized the neo-classical political economy approach because it is unable to predict reforms short of resorting to cataclysms and benevolent dictators (1991, 60): 'I argue that the perspective is reductionist in a way that impedes efforts to conceptualize or explain what is most sought after by many of its adherents - change and improvement in the nature of development policy in a society'. For this to happen, a model of policy-making would be one 'in which politics is assumed to be neither inherently negative nor inherently positive for the selection and pursuit of public policy'. Unfortunately, the new political economy perspective is not helpful because it sees politics exclusively 'as a spanner in the economic works' (45). Does the argument developed here escape this criticism?

On one level it is true that politics is seen as a spanner in the works: in a clientelist system politicians have no incentives to institute reforms. On another level, however, politics is not 'reductionist' in the sense that Grindle uses the term: it is 'neither inherently negative nor inherently positive for the selection and pursuit of public policy'. The clientelist explanation does allow for successful policy reforms if they are accompanied by structural changes. Thus politics as such is 'neither inherently negative nor inherently positive for the selection and pursuit of public policy'. Moreover, the analysis specifies conditions under which a change in the political system is likely to occur.

Just as importantly, the approach is neutral in its assessment of democracy and authoritarianism. Remmer attacks the pessimistic assessment of Latin America's political future which is based on three main assumptions: that the level of support of elected governments varies directly with their capacity to deliver short term material benefits to voters; that democratic governments pursue policies to maximize political support; and that these policies jeopardize long term economic performance (Remmer 1993, 394). She believes that this pessimism in not borne out by the evidence: 'Contrary to both the political business cycle literature and the conventional wisdom about Latin democracy, competitive elections in the region have enhanced, not undermined, political leaders' capacity to address major problems of macroeconomic management' (393). She then generalizes that 'competitive elections should perhaps be seen less as threats to economic stability than as catalysts for policy reform and responsible macroeconomic management' (404).[41] There is little to disagree with. If it is indeed true that the clientelist assumptions about the nature of the political structure are inapplicable, democracy may well be compatible with successful policy reforms.

Nor are authoritarian regimes necessarily successful. If their legitimacy is widely questioned, they rely on patronage to remain in power, the bureaucracy is weak, state autonomy is low and factionalism is rampant, stabilization programs are equally likely to fail. Thus in a 'weak authoritarian regime' like the Philippines under Marcos, stabilization programs are as difficult to implement as in a clientelist democracy (Haggard 1990, 216–218).

7.6   Conclusion

If it is true that policy failures are at least partly caused by clientelism, transcending patronage politics may become a prerequisite to overcoming these failures. An understanding of the causes of clientelism is thus fundamental for assessing the likelihood of success or failure of policy reforms.

One of the puzzling features of political life in many countries is the widespread support for politicians who promise particularistic gains, since the style of politics is likely to lead to a decrease in welfare for the average voter. Voters would undoubtedly be better off supporting candidates who dole out benefits according to general rules.

In many cases the answer is obvious: the voter does not have a choice because force and fraud are employed against opposition candidates, or opposition parties are prevented from emerging through more subtle means of persuasion like the cooptation of individuals and corporate groups. Such constraints explain some but not all cases of clientelism. They do not explain its popularity in African countries when competitive elections were held, nor the attraction of machine politics in India, where competitive elections occur regularly, nor the survival of clientelism in southern Italy, where parties standing for alternative political styles did in fact compete.

Voters may pursue actions detrimental to their welfare because they are misinformed or are caught in a dilemma. Imperfect information may well explain the emergence of clientelism. As the evidence of its detrimental effects accumulates and the education of the average voter improves, ignorance arguments ring increasingly hollow. Nevertheless, it remains possible that voters may have difficulty envisaging the working of different political styles, particularly in a divided society.

Patronage voting might more plausibly stem from a prisoner's dilemma: individuals are best off if a different voting pattern is adopted, but the worst case is not to belong to a patron-client network in a situation where patronage politics prevails. Such a dilemma is greatly favored by the low degree of horizontal cooperation and the high level of mistrust that prevail in many societies where clientelism dominates.

It is widely believed that increased cooperation along group and class lines help to overcome prisoner's dilemmas of this kind. Members of a group engage in continuous or repeated interaction out of hope of reciprocation or fear of retaliation in later interactions. Moreover, cooperation may transform individual value systems so as to include feelings of solidarity, altruism, fairness and the like (Elster 1985, 132).

Putnam's Italian evidence reinforces this conclusion. He showed that civic culture was a better indicator of successful democratic regional institutions and future economic development than any other, including economic, factors. From the argument put forward here that is hardly surprising: if it is true that civic culture is one of the causes of clientelism, and clientelism is negatively related to economic growth, this is the correlation one would expect.

The modernization view that clientelism is a transitory phenomenon has been partly supported. An increased standard of living eliminates the need for subsistence insurance. A higher level of education attenuates the severity of the information problem and improves the level of political entrepreneurship. On the other hand, these improvements might not be sufficient to overcome the effects of imperfect information and prisoner's dilemmas, barriers to entry to non-clientelist politicians, and vested interests supporting the *status quo*.

As long as clientelism remains rampant, it is likely to be accompanied by anti-market policies. This means that successful stabilization efforts require the transformation of the political system: success hinges on the demise of the causes that generate political clientelism. Moreover, economic crises lead to permanent changes in policies only if the emergency serves as a catalyst for structural change.

Notes:

1. Viz. the re-election of Papandreu.
2. Similar views can be found, for example, in Bailey (1963, 135) and Caciagli and Belloni (1981, 37).
3. Often the answer is taken as self-evident. Caciagli and Belloni claim that the Christian Democratic Party of Catania is 'sustained by the support it is able to purchase from its clients in exchange for its distribution of benefits to them ... Their [the *apparatichi*] survival as patrons, as well as the survival of the party apparatus, depends upon the votes and consensus of the clients' (1981, 37). It is entirely unclear why clients continue their support if 'their interests are subordinate to the interests of the dominant classes' (54).
4. Another example along the same line comes from Israel, where party activists were frequently approached to solve employment or housing problems, and 'functionaries continued to generate support by helping people to solve their financial problems' (Etzioni-Halevi 1979, 93–94).
5. In an Italian city, for example, 'there are literally thousands of ways in which a vigilant police officer can either perform a favour or make life miserable for a shopkeeper or street vendor' (Chubb 1981, 78). In the Philippines, political leaders not well disposed towards a transport business would generally have the power to have the constabulary harass or fine the owner, or even have the load confiscated as well (Wolters 1984, 150).
6. The problem is by no means restricted to Europe. In Senegal, the Kayor aristocracy lived, apart from slave-trading, 'by what might best be called a protection racket, whereby the subjects paid "taxes" for the service of not being enslaved, having their villages burned or their harvests taken' (Cruise O'Brien 1975, 26).
7. The position has to be qualified: for people who are illiterate it is indeed difficult to deal with a bureaucracy, and for them intermediation can be a substantive benefit.

8. See also Scott (1972, 103); Ozbudun (1981, 261).
9. I.e. public goods.
10. Rothchild and Foley, for example, argue that African governments are made up of inclusive coalitions representing most segments of society (1988). Similarly, it has been observed that government officials do not lightly refuse a request by an opposition leader, partly 'to secure some form of reinsurance against the day when the Government changes' (Campbell 1977, 258).
11. See also Etzioni-Halevi (1979, 102–103).
12. Thus Brownsberger attributes political behavior in Nigeria to the materialism of the inhabitants, which in turn is partly a result of demonstration effects of colonial society. The 'dazzling status of the white man (and the successor black elite) burned into the populace a desire to appear and act as did their dominators ... and this led the most successful to corrupt desires' (1983, 227).
13. The argument here is analogous to the familiar problem that the lack of economic development may be caused by the lack of entrepreneurship in a particular population.
14. Demand and supply constraints may become indistinguishable if the same widely held norms and values prevent the supply of political entrepreneurs and the demand for them.
15. Along the lines of Olson (1965).
16. Bates (1981, 106); Cornelius (1977, 340); Lemarchand (1981, 20). Joseph describes the elections in Nigeria in 1983: 'If the rules of the system, and those appointed to interpret them, cannot disinterestedly determine the nature of the electoral arena, but themselves become spoils to be fought over and shifted to favor one person or group rather than another, then the critical step in the transition from a Hobbesian state-of-nature to a constituted political society cannot occur. And that is one difference between military and civilian governments in Nigeria. The former, for all their failings, are able to give the country a political order ... while the latter eventually carry the war-of-all-against-all into the legislative chambers, the executive offices of government, the temporary headquarters and sub-offices of the electoral bureaucracy and, most fatally, into the courtrooms and the nation's judiciary' (157).
17. For the case of Nigeria see for example Diamond (1988).
18. In Senegal, 'the most devious Senegalese politicians are among the most vehement in their denunciations of the prevalence of corruption' (Cruise O'Brien 1975, 193). Another example is that of the opposition to the Marcos administration in the Philippines (Wolters 1984, 142). It is exceedingly naive to take such proclamations at face value (Klitgaard 1988, 2).
19. The dilemma is unaffected if we introduce more than one C-party. The payoff from voting G and C remains the same if all C-parties have equal probabilities of being represented in government.

20.   Sanctions against disloyal supporters are widespread. In Israel, people 'who were helped by the party machine were not free to change their allegiance at will. It has even been claimed that those rebels who tried to do so (and they were not too numerous) were dismissed from their jobs or even evicted from their apartments' (Etzioni-Halevi 1979, 93).

21.   Or we find building equipment making its appearance shortly before elections. Perhaps one the most blatant cases is the distribution of one shoe before the election and one afterwards (Chubb 1981, 93).

22.   Including in the Philippines, for example, illegal logging operators and those who depend on them, or those employed in running illegal lotteries (Wolters 1984, 38).

23.   For Senegal see Cruise O'Brien (1975, 131).

24.   The number of such individuals is boosted by all those who rely on that income, such as the members of extended families.

25.   It is sometimes forgotten that satisfying interest groups alone does not win elections. For example, we find Radelet asserting that in the Gambia a policy was 'politically rational' which channeled resources from rural producers to the main interest groups (urban residents, businesspeople, politicians, bureaucrats and key rural leaders) (1992, 1090). But that policy was not necessarily rational, because Radelet fails to explain why the ruling party managed to win the votes of the majority of the rural producers.

26.   See chapter 4.

27.   This is of course very much the modernization perspective, where basic value orientations adjust with a considerable lag (Scott 1968, 127).

28.   'When most members join a group to achieve a variety of short-run personal advantages, it becomes impossible for the group as a whole to pursue long-run objectives and still retain its membership. Under these circumstances, groups tend to be short-lived and fragile and seek only immediate, limited objectives' (Scott 1968, 120).

29.   Such as the Javanese (Scott 1968, 121; Banfield 1958).

30.   See Landé (1977, xxxii) and Bailey (1963, 65, 140).

31.   A view heavily influenced by Schultz (1964), but the most ground-breaking empirical work making exactly this point was done by Bauer in Ghana (1956).

32.   Scott's view of the 'moral economy view' of peasant agriculture, of which the constant pie orientation is one element, was strongly criticized by Popkin (1979).

33.   There is a strong association of clientelism with 'absence of faith in each other's probity' (Bailey 1963, 33). 'It is no accident that societies such as the Mediterranean region ... often are also described as societies characterized by strong feelings and expressions of distrust, envy and vindictiveness' (Landé 1977, xxxii). Similarly, Bailey writes of India that 'the peasant sense of moral obligation does not go beyond family, village, and caste' (1963, 140). Beyond the boundary of the community

peasants 'expect to be cheated or bullied, as they would themselves deal with a stranger' (65).

34. E.g. Scott (1972, 104); Caciagli and Belloni (1981, 50).
35. For a test of this perspective see Anderson (1990).
36. E.g. Evans (1992).
37. For an extensive treatment see Haggard and Webb (1993); also Nelson (1990, 17–29); Callaghy (1990, 262–266).
38. As in Bolivia (1985), Brazil (1989), Argentina (1989), Peru (1990) and Venezuela (1988).
39. See also Radelet's account of the Gambia (1992).
40. More specifically, Waterbury argued that the perception of a fiscal crisis is a necessary condition for the reform of government-owned enterprises, which is generally one of the central components of policy reform (1992, 183, 189). Evidence in support of his thesis is adduced from Egypt (201), India (205), Turkey (211), and Mexico (213).
41. The main burden of Remmer's argument is carried by the fact that a number of Latin American governments engaged in orthodox stabilization policies shortly after they were elected: typically they reduced inflation through slow growth of the money supply, devalued their currencies, and reduced budget deficits. These policies, according to her, provide strong indications that elections are causally related to stabilization programs (403).

8   Conclusion

This monograph has attempted to show how political structures can influence economic growth. A framework has been developed to illustrate how a particular kind of political clientelism is likely to go hand in hand with political corruption, impaired government legitimacy, a high degree of politicization and a low level of state autonomy. It has been maintained that these factors tend to influence policy-making. Indeed, their tendency to induce failed inward-looking development strategies is seen as a major contributing factor to the impoverishment of many Third World countries. The forces generated by clientelism go at least some way towards explaining a particular historical phenomenon: why in the wake of World War II many countries adopted and pursued manifestly welfare-reducing policies of the inward-looking type.

In the main the topic was approached through a one-way causation: a particular political system impairs economic growth. It constitutes a type of analysis that Staniland called *politicism*, where political rationality prevails over economic rationality, and political power is seen as 'fundamental to the shaping of the economic system' (1989, 7). However, the reasoning was not exclusively in that vein. There is some feedback from economic to political conditions. As modernization theorists pointed out long ago, 'Economic development, producing increased income, greater economic security, and widespread higher education largely determines the form of "class struggle" by permitting those in the lower strata to develop longer time perspectives and more complex and gradualist views of politics' (Lipset 1960, 45). In the terminology of this monograph, the political style that prevails will be strongly influenced by economic performance.

There is little doubt that clientelism has detrimental effects on economic growth by influencing the types of economic policies politicians are prone to adopt. Policy actions aim mainly at increasing the scope for patronage: by increasing the size of the public administration; by producing and distributing those goods and services that are most conducive to patronage allocation; by expanding the public sector beyond its optimal size; by nationalizing industry or by takeovers of firms by the ruling elite; and by imposing regulations on the private sector that serve political and not economic ends.[1]

Such policies lead to substantial misallocation of resources both in the private and in the public sector, including the neglect of public goods such as infrastructure, excessive transaction costs and wasteful rent-seeking activities. Moreover, as the pressure to expand government activities mounts and the revenue base deteriorates, government budget deficits escalate. Financing large budget deficits generally involves excessive borrowing from abroad and prompts spiraling inflation and exchange rate volatility, and thus upsets macroeconomic stability. The misallocation of resources and macroeconomic instability are likely to seriously impede the process of capital accumulation and economic development.

Patronage politics is unlikely to tolerate an allocation process based on unfettered market forces. Thus import substitution strategies may merely reflect patronage politics: the protection of industries and particular firms is a means to increase the scope for patronage and to generate rent for the owners and workers of sheltered firms. Protection against foreign competition is generally supplemented by a process of licensing which also eliminates internal competition and thus assures the accrual of monopoly rent. It is believed, therefore, that the adoption of anti-market inward-looking development strategies in many countries has been heavily influenced by such a political structure.

Clientelism is one of the major causes of corruption. Because the politicians' political power depends on the amount of particularistic benefits they pass on to their supporters, they will be tempted to allocate benefits - including goods and services, licenses, credit, and jobs in the public administration - in a way that violates bureaucratic rules. Administrative corruption, therefore, is the consequence of the political structure.

If corruption is an emanation of the political system, and thus is tolerated if not actively abetted by the government, analyses of this phenomenon which limit their focus to the administrative system are unlikely to advance very far. In particular those analyses of the principal-agent type are singularly inappropriate where the principal acts in the public interest and the corrupt agent undermines the welfare maximizing-measures devised by the principal.[2] Moreover, conventional narrowly based anti-corruption programs that attempt to alter the behavior of administrators are liable to fail. Partial successes are of course possible, but tend to be short lived.[3] In such an environment, anti-corruption strategies need to be much broader based. In effect, they have to address the problem of reducing the degree of clientelism in politics.

Corruption in a clientelist setting has few redeeming features. It is difficult to believe that it improves welfare by undermining policies which are socially detrimental. On the contrary, clientelism and corruption are more likely to have engendered those deleterious policies which corruption is supposed to alleviate. The position that corruption has beneficial consequences apart from subverting the implementation of sub-optimal policies is equally misguided, mainly because it suffers from simplistic assumptions. The case that corruption improves bureaucratic efficiency and the allocation of contracts and licenses collapses as soon as it is accepted that information is not perfect, wages do no reflect opportunity costs, and politicians are not exclusively concerned with maximizing their income.

Clientelism is sufficient to explain the absence of economic growth in many countries. This is particularly true where, as on the African continent, it causes not only misallocation of resources and macro-economic instability, but also great instability of property rights. Where a firm's profits are the result of property and quasi-property rights granted by the government, and frequent political changes lead to periodic redistribution of these privileges, the economic environment becomes extremely insecure. The low level of investment and the high level of capital flight are then mainly a consequence of the political instability, which breeds economic instability.

The prime responsibility for the economic disasters which have overtaken many Third World countries has been squarely assigned in this monograph to domestic factors. This does not preclude that other sources may have contributed to economic crises, only that domestic causes have to take much of the blame. Of course it could be argued that the internal political processes are simply a reflection of external dependency: on foreign governments, on foreign firms, on international agencies. However, international organizations have generally actively opposed anti-market policies, and transnational corporations have no interest in an environment of endemic insecurity.[4] Clientelism is a home-grown phenomenon. Nevertheless, there is little doubt that external financial support has prolonged the life of some clientelist regimes.

Clientelism is associated with both democracy and autocracy. Thus democratic clientelist regimes and the faction-ridden 'weak' clientelist authoritarian governments are likely to have similarly deficient growth performances. The crucial factor that explains different development paths then is not whether regimes are democratic or autocratic, but the nature of their democracy or autocracy. Consequently, to search for a significant difference in the rates of growth between authoritarian and democratic regimes is misplaced without controlling for the nature of these governments. The empirical evidence bears out the main contention: no relationship has been discovered between regime type and growth.

For the same reasons, it is of dubious value to search for systematic influences of democracy and authoritarianism on macroeconomic stability. Where clientelism is entrenched, macroeconomic stability is likely to be shattered every so often, and stabilization packages return at regular intervals without having permanent effects. Again, there is little reason to believe that authoritarian and democratic regimes differ much in this respect.

Generalizations about the size of government and economic growth are equally misplaced.[5] The optimal size of the government sector will vary with its relative efficiency, a point well known already to Adam Smith.[6] The more efficient the government, the greater the optimal size because even relatively minor market failures justify intervention. In the clientelist case, where the government sector is singularly inefficient, the optimal size of government is small. Thus without considering the political structure and administrative capacity, generalizations about the optimal size of government are fruitless.

Equally futile are speculations about a systematic variation of the level of corruption between democratic and authoritarian regimes. Indeed, there is a view which holds that attempts at limiting corruption 'are more likely to succeed the further the country is along the democratization path' (LeVine 1993, 271).[7] However, a democratic clientelist regime is not likely to limit the level of corruption.

The central thesis of this monograph - that a particular type of clientelism in conjunction with particular institutional factors tends to induce politicians to adopt welfare-reducing inward-looking development policies - does not lead to a general condemnation of such policies, however. In a clientelist environment they failed not because they aimed at import substitution, but because they served as a thinly disguised program to increase the wealth and political power of patrons and clients, independent of their economic consequences.

Nor ought the argument be construed as condemning government intervention as such. Failed inward-looking development is generally closely associated with a substantial degree of government intervention. That does not preclude, however, that intervention may succeed in different circumstances. The inquiry does suggest, however, that in a clientelist environment structural reform involving a shift towards an outward-looking strategy and less intervention leads to welfare improvements.

Neither does the position imply that outward-looking strategies are incompatible with all kinds of clientelism. The association of *traditional* clientelism and export promotion in the early phases of Latin American development are recognized, but they do not refute the case that has been made. Similarly, where state autonomy has not been eroded by clientelism, outward-looking development may well prevail.

Nor does an analysis focusing on clientelism conflict with the proposition that 'the single most important factor in generating sustained developmental momentum has been the presence in each of a particular type of state, a "developmental state"' (Leftwich 1995, 401). What the analysis does show is that clientelism precludes the existence of a developmental state. A developmental state is characterized by a commitment to economic development by the political and bureaucratic elite, a high degree of state autonomy and thus a weak and subordinated civil society, and a powerful, competent and insulated economic bureaucracy. These factors in turn allow for effective intervention (416) and a high degree of legitimacy based on an excellent economic performance despite extensive repression (418–419). In a clientelist world, on the other hand, considerations of maintaining political power take precedence over commitments to economic growth, the bureaucracy is incompetent and ineffective, economic growth is slow and legitimacy weak. Thus a clientelist state is the antithesis of the developmental state.

What are the chances of successful economic reforms where clientelism prevails? The necessary reforms, even where the conditions are propitious, are a matter of much broader scope than orthodox reform policies which focus on the government budget, the exchange rate, parastatals and infrastructure provision. As long as the reform program is limited to such a limited economic sphere it is unlikely to succeed. This analysis brings to the fore the importance for economic reform of a of host of social and political factors capable of reducing the prevalence of clientelist politics: the breaking down of barriers to entry into politics; the reduction of rent generated by state intervention in economic life; a withdrawal of the state from controlling society, allowing a sphere where civic culture can thrive; education beyond the provision of human capital; the dissemination of information about the nature of prisoner's dilemmas and the problems associated with clientelism; and avoidance of the conventional shift of blame to imperialism, capitalism, or the low moral stature of the upper classes generally or the politicians particularly.

In the case of the pathological clientelism where private property is extremely insecure because political change leads to a large scale rearrangement of property and quasi-property rights, there is little hope for successful reform. The foundation for successful policy adjustment is a thriving private sector, which is stymied by insecure property rights. The emergence of secure property rights may well presuppose a relatively high degree of security of tenure by the ruling elite as a class and greatly reduced intra-class competition. These factors then become ultimately prerequisites for successful reform.

In a democratic setting clientelism and its consequences, including the nature of property rights, are closely associated with voting behavior. Indeed, the attitudes towards politics of the populace at large are sometimes the *cause* of clientelism. Western social scientists, obsessively afraid of 'blaming the victim', tend to shrink from the conclusion that average Africans, for example, must share a responsibility for the disasters which have afflicted them. However, acceptance of the need of political change by the populace is often a cornerstone of successful reform.

Democratic government can fail badly. Hence in this monograph a jaundiced view has been taken of the fashionable position that democracy is a panacea for providing clean government, economic stability and growth. Indeed, one possible explanation for the breakdown of democracy in many Third World countries is economic collapse in the wake of clientelist politics, as unbridled clientelism induces economic failures and undermines the legitimacy of the state. Even though the experience of the past is not necessarily a guide to the future, there must be some doubt that, at least in Africa, the fate of a 'second round' of democratic experiments would differ very much from that of the first.

Notes:

1. As Ravenhill put it, 'Africa's political crisis is rooted in a system of clientelist politics where economic efficiency is willingly sacrificed in order to generate resources to satisfy political constituencies' (1986, 27).
2. E.g. Klitgaard (1991, xii, 74).
3. Klitgaard uses an example from the Philippines, where a tax commissioner markedly reduced the level of corruption in the tax office under the notoriously corrupt Marcos administration. That gain was, as one would expect, temporary (1991, 60–61).
4. And thus they have no interest to influence their home governments to promote such a policy stance in the Third World.
5. E.g. Williams and Daniel (1991).
6. When he assigns a larger scope for intervention in the case of the relatively efficient governments of Holland and Venice.
7. See also Noonan (1984).

Bibliography

Abercrombie, N., and B.S. Turner. 1978. The Dominant Ideology Thesis. In *Classes, Power, and Conflict*, ed. A. Giddens and D. Held. London: Macmillan.

Adelman, I, and C. T. Morris. 1967. *Society, Politics, and Economic Development.* Baltimore: John Hopkins University Press.

Ake, C. 1981. *The Political Economy of Africa.* London: Longman.

Alam, M.S. 1989. Anatomy of Corruption. *American Journal of Economics and Sociology* 48:441–45.

————. 1990. Some Economic Costs of Corruption. *The Journal of Development Studies* 27:89–97.

Alavi, H. 1973. The State in Postcolonial Societies: Pakistan and Bangladesh. In *Imperialism and Revolution in South Asia*, ed. K. Gough and H. Sharma, 145–74. New York: Monthly Review Press.

Almond, G.A. and S. Verba. 1963. *The Civic Culture.* Princeton University Press.

Anderson, L.E. 1990. Post-Materialism from a Peasant Perspective: Political Motivation in Costa Rica and Nicaragua. *Comparative Political Studies* 23:80–113.

Andreski, S. 1979. Kleptocracy as a System of Government in Africa. In *Bureaucratic Corruption in Sub-saharan Africa: Towards a Search for Causes and Consequences,* ed. M.U. Ekpo. Washington, D.C.: University Press of America.

Andvig, J.C., and K.O. Moene. 1990. How Corruption may Corrupt. *Journal of Economic Behaviour and Organisation* 13:63–76.

Appelbaum, E., and E. Katz. 1987. Seeking Rents by Setting Rents. *Economic Journal* 97:685–699.

Attalides, M. 1977. Forms of Peasant Incorporation in Cyprus during the Last Century. In *Patrons and Clients in Mediterranean Societies,* ed. E. Gellner and J. Waterbury, 137–57. London: Duckworth.

Azarya, V., and N. Chazan. 1987. Disengagement from the State in Africa: Reflections on the Experience of Ghana and Guinea. *Comparative Studies in Society and History* 29:106–131.

Bailey, F.G. *1963. Politics and Social Change: Orissa in 1959.* London: University of California Press.

Balandier, G. 1970. *Political Anthropology.* London: Allen Lane.

Balogun, M.J. 1983. *Public Administration in Nigeria. A Developmental Approach.* London: Macmillan.

Banfield, E.C. 1958. *The Moral Basis of a Backward Society.* London: Macmillan.

———. 1975. Corruption as a Feature of Governmental Organizations. *Journal of Law and Economics* 18:587–605.

Banfield, E.C., and J.Q. Wilson. 1963. *City Politics.* Cambridge, Mass.: Harvard University Press.

Barrows, W.L. 1974. Comparative Grassroots Politics in Africa. *World Politics* 26:283–297.

Barry, B. 1985. Does Democracy Cause Inflation? Political Ideas of Some Economists. In *The Politics of Inflation and Economic Stagnation,* ed. L.N. Lindberg and C.H. Maier, 280–317. Washington, D.C.: Brookings Institution.

Bates, R.H. 1981. *Markets and States in Tropical Africa. The Political Basis of Agricultural Policies.* Berkeley: University of California Press.

———. 1983. *Essays on the Political Economy of Rural Africa.* Cambridge University Press.

Bates R.H., and A.O. Krueger. 1993. Generalizations from the Country Studies. In *Political and Economic Interactions in Economic Policy Reform,* ed. R.H. Bates and A.O. Krueger, 444–72. Oxford: Basil Blackwell.

Bauer, P.T. 1956. *West African Trade.* Cambridge University Press.

Bauer, P.T., and B.S. Yamey. 1957. *The Economics of Under-developed Countries.* Cambridge: James Nisbet.

Bayley, D.H. 1966. The Effects of Corruption in a Developing Nation. *Western Political Quarterly* 19:719–732.

Baylies, C.L., and M. Szeftel. 1982. The Rise of a Zambian Capitalist Class in the 1970s. *Journal of Modern African Studies* 8:187–213 .

Becker, G.S. 1968. Crime and Punishment: An Economic Approach. *Journal of Political Economy* 76:169–217.

Beckman, B. 1982. Whose State? State and Capitalist Development in Nigeria. *Review of African Political Economy* 23:37–51.

Beenstock, M. 1979. Corruption and Development. *World Development* 7:15–24.

Bellin, E. 1994. The Politics of Profit in Tunisia: Utility of the Rentier Paradigm? *World Development* 22:427–436.

Ben-Dor, G. 1974. Corruption, Institutionalization, and Political Development. *Comparative Political Studies* 7:63–83 .

Berman, B.J. 1974. Clientelism and Neocolonialism - Center-Periphery Relations and Political Development in African States. *Studies in Comparative International Development* 9:3–25.

Bhagwati, J. 1966. *The Economics of Underdeveloped Countries*. London: World University Library.

———. 1982. Directly Unproductive Profit-seeking Activities. *Journal of Political Economy* 90:988–1002.

Bienen, H. 1971. Political Parties and Political Machines in Africa. In *The State of Nations: Constraints of Development in Independent Africa*, ed. M.F. Lofchie, 195–213. Berkeley: University of California Press.

Blau, P. 1964. *Exchange and Power in Social Life*. New York: Wiley.

Bloch, M. 1962. *Feudal Society*. London: Routledge and Kegan Paul.

Boissevin, J. 1977. Factions, Parties, and Politics in a Maltese Village. In *Friends, Followers, and Factions*, ed. S. Schmidt, J. Scott, L. Guasti and C. Landé, 279–86. Berkeley: University of California Press.

Bollen, K. 1979. Political Democracy and the Timing of Development. *American Sociological Review* 44:572–587.

Bottomore, T.B. 1964. *Elites and Societies*. London: Watts.

Braibanti, R. 1962. Reflections on Bureaucratic Corruption. *Public Administration* 40:365–371.

Brownsberger, W.N. 1983. Development and Governmental Corruption; Materialism and Political Fragmentation in Nigeria. *Journal of Modern African Studies* 21:215–233.

Caciagli, M., and F.P. Belloni. 1981. The "New" Clientelism in Southern Italy: The Christian Democratic Party in Catania. In *Political Clientelism, Patronage and Development*, ed. S.N. Eisenstadt and R. Lemarchand, 35–56. London: Sage.

Cadot, O. 1987. Corruption as a Gamble. *Journal of Public Economics* 33:223–244

Caiden, G.E. 1988. Toward a General Theory of Official Corruption. *Asian Journal of Public Administration* 18:3–26.

———. 1993. Commentary. *Corruption and Reform* 7:265–269.

Caiden, G.E. and N.J. Caiden. 1977. Administrative Corruption. *Public Administration Review* 37:301–309.

Callaghy, T.M. 1979. The Difficulties of Implementing Socialist Strategies of Development in Africa: The "First Wave". In *Socialism in Sub-Saharan Africa: A New Assessment*, ed. C.G. Rosberg and T.M Callaghy, 112–30. Berkeley: University of California Press.

———. 1984. *The State-Society Struggle: Zaire in Comparative Perspective*. New York: Columbia University Press.

———. 1986. The Political Economy of African Debt: The Case of Zaire. In *Africa in Economic Crisis*, ed. J. Ravenhill. London: Macmillan.

———. 1987. The State as Lame Leviathan: The Patrimonial Administrative State in Africa. In *The African State in Transition*, ed. Z. Ergas, 87–116. London: Macmillan.

——. 1990. Lost Between the State and the Market: The Politics of Economic Adjustment in Ghana, Zambia, and Nigeria. In *Economic Crisis and Policy Choice: The Politics of Adjustment in the Third World, ed.* J.M. Nelson. Princeton University Press.

Cammack, P., D. Pool, and W. Tordoff. 1988. *Third World Politics. A Comparative Introduction.* London: Macmillan.

Campbell, B. 1978. Ivory Coast. In *West African States: Failure and Promise,* ed. J. Dunn. Cambridge University Press.

Campbell, J.K. 1977. Honour, Family and Patronage: A Study of Institutions and Moral Values in a Greek Mountain Community. In *Friends, Followers, and Factions,* ed. S. Schmidt, J. Scott, L. Guasti and C. Landé, 250–63. Berkeley: University of California Press.

Chalmers, D.A. 1977. The Politicized State in Latin America. In *Authoritarianism and Corporatism in Latin America,* ed. J.M. Malloy, 23–46. Pittsburgh: University of Pittsburgh Press.

Chibnall S., and P. Saunders. 1977. Worlds Apart: Notes on the Social Reality of Corruption. *British Journal of Sociology* 28:138–154.

Chirot, D. 1977. *Social Change in the Twentieth Century.* New York: Harcourt, Brace, Jovanovich.

Chubb, J. 1981. The Social Bases of an Urban Political Machine: The Christian Democratic Party in Palermo. In *Political Clientelism, Patronage and Development,* ed. S.N. Eisenstadt and R. Lemarchand, 57–90. London: Sage.

——. 1981. Naples Under the Left: The Limits of Social Change. In *Political Clientelism, Patronage and Development,* ed. S.N. Eisenstadt and R. Lemarchand, 91–124. London: Sage.

——. 1982. *Patronage, Power, and Poverty in Southern Italy.* Cambridge University Press.

Clapham, C. 1982. Clientelism and the State. In *Private Patronage and Public Power,* ed. C. Clapham, 1–35 London: Frances Pinter.

——. 1985. *Third World Politics. An Introduction.* London: Croom Helm.

——. 1986. The Horn of Africa. In *Politics & Government in African States, 1960-1985.* P. Guignan and R.H. Jackson, 253–282. London: Croom Helm.

Clarke, M. 1983. Introduction. In *Corruption: Causes, Consequences and Control.* London: Frances Pinter.

Cohen, R. 1972. Class in Africa: Analytical Problems and Perspectives. *Socialist Register* 1972:231–255.

Cohen, Y. 1985. The impact of Bureaucratic-Authoritarian Rule on Economic Growth. *Comparative Political Studies* 18:123–136.

Cornelius, W.A. 1975. *Politics and the Migrant Poor in Mexico City.* Stanford University Press.

——. 1977. Leaders, Followers, and Official Patrons in Urban Mexico. In *Friends, Followers, and Factions,* ed. S. Schmidt, J. Scott, L. Guasti and C. Landé, 337–53. Berkeley: University of California Press.

Crook, R.C. 1989. Patrimonialism, Administrative Effectiveness and Economic Development in Côte-D'Ivoire. *African Affairs* 88:205–228.

Cruise O'Brien, D. 1975. *Saints and Politicians: Essays in the Organisation of a Senegalese Peasant Society.* Cambridge University Press.

Currie, K., and L. Ray. 1984. State and Class in Kenya - Notes on the Cohesion of the Ruling Class. *Journal of Modern African Studies* 22:559–593.

Decalo, S. 1976. *Coups and Army Rule in Africa. Studies in Military Style.* London: Yale University Press.

DeSchweinitz, K. 1964. *Industrialization and Democracy.* Glencoe, Ill: The Free Press.

Diamond, L. 1987. Class formation in the Swollen African State. *Journal of Modern African Studies* 25:567–596.

———. 1988. *Class, Ethnicity and Democracy in Nigeria: The Failure of the First Republic.* London: Syracuse University Press.

———. 1993. Nigeria's Perennial Struggle Against Corruption: Prospects for the Third Republic. *Corruption and Reform* 7:215–225.

DiFranceisco, W., and Z. Gitelman. 1989. Soviet Political Culture and Modes of Covert Influence. In *Political Corruption. A Handbook,* ed. A.J. Heidenheimer, M. Johnston and V.T. LeVine, 467–488. London: Transaction Publishers.

Dobel, J.P. 1978. The Corruption of a State. *American Political Science Review* 72:958–973.

P. Duignan. 1986. Introduction In *Politics & Government in African States, 1960–85,* ed. P. Duignan and R.H. Jackson, 1–29. London: Croom Helm.

Eckstein, H. 1988. A Cultural Theory of Political Change. *American Political Science Review* 82:789–804.

Ekholm Friedman, K. 1992. Afro-Marxism and its Disastrous Effects on the Economy: The Congelese Case. In *Economic Crisis in Africa. Perspectives and Policy Responses,* ed. M. Blomstrom and M. Lundahl. London: Routledge.

Elster, J. 1986. *An Introduction to Karl Marx.* Cambridge University Press.

Etzioni-Halevi, E. 1979. *Political Manipulation and Administrative Power. A Comparative Study.* London: Routledge & Kegan Paul.

———. 1989. Exchanging Material Benefits for Political Support: A Comparative Analysis. In *Political Corruption. A Handbook,* ed. A.J. Heidenheimer, M. Johnston and V.T. LeVine, 287–304. London: Transaction Publishers.

Evans, P. 1992. The State as Problem and Solution: Predation, Embedded Autonomy, and Structural Change. In *The Politics of Economic Adjustment. International Constraints, Distributive Conflicts, and the State,* ed. S. Haggard and R.R. Kaufman. Princeton University Press.

Fanon, F. 1966. *The Wretched of the Earth.* New York: Grove Press.

Fieldhouse, D.K. 1986. *Black Africa. 1945-1980. Economic Decolonisation and Arrested Development.* London: Macmillan.

Findlay, R. 1991. The New Political Economy: Its Explanatory Power for LDC's. In *Politics and Policy Making in Developing Countries. Perspectives on the New Political Economy,* ed. G.M. Meier. San Francisco: ICS Press.

Findlay R., and J.A. Wilson. 1987. The Political Economy of Leviathan. In *Economic Policy in Theory and Practice,* ed. A. Razin and E. Sadka. New York: Macmillan.

Flynn, P. 1974. Class, Clientelism and Coercion: Some Mechanisms of Internal Control. *Journal of Commonwealth and Comparative Politics* 12:133–56.

Foltz, W.J. 1977. Social Structure and Political Behaviour of Senegalese Elites. In *Friends, Followers, and Factions*, ed. S. Schmidt, J. Scott, L. Guasti and C. Landé, 242–250. Berkeley: University of California Press.

Friedrich, C.J. 1963. *Man and His Government.* New York: McGraw-Hill.

———. 1966. Political Pathology. *Political Quarterly* 37:70–85.

Fukuyama, F. 1992. *The End of History and the Last Man.* London: Penguin.

Gardiner, J.A. 1993. Defining Corruption. *Corruption and Reform* 7:111–124

Gellner, E. 1977. Patrons and Clients. In *Patrons and Clients in Mediterranean Societies*, ed. E. Gellner and J. Waterbury, 1–6. London: Duckworth.

Gibbons, K.M. 1989. Variations in Attitudes Toward Corruption in Canada. In *Political Corruption. A Handbook*, ed. A.J. Heidenheimer, M. Johnston and V.T. LeVine, 763–780. London: Transaction Publishers.

Goodell, G., and J.P. Powelson, 1982. The Democratic Prerequisites of Development. In *Freedom in the World: Political Rights and Civil Liberties*, ed. R. Gastil. New York: Freedom House.

Goodman, M. 1974. Does Political Corruption Really Help Economic Development: Yucatan, Mexico. *Polity* 7:143–162.

Gould, D.J. 1980. *Bureaucratic Corruption and Underdevelopment in the Third World. The Case of Zaire.* New York: Pergamon.

Graziano, L. 1973. Patron-Client Relationships in Southern Italy. *European Journal of Political Research* 1:3–34.

Grindle, M.S. 1991. The New Political Economy: Positive Economics and Negative Politics. In *Politics and Policy Making in Developing Countries. Perspectives on the New Political Economy*, ed. G.M. Meier, 41–67. San Francisco: ICS Press.

Grindle, M.S., and F.E. Thoumi. 1993. Muddling Toward Adjustment: The Political Economy of Economic Policy Change in Ecuador. In Political and Economic Interactions in Economic Policy Reform, ed. R.H. Bates and A.O. Krueger, 123–178. Oxford: Basil Blackwell.

Guasti, L. 1977. Peru: Clientelism and Internal Control. In *Friends, Followers, and Factions*, ed. S. Schmidt, J. Scott, L. Guasti and C. Landé, 422–438. Berkeley: University of California Press.

Hager, L.M. 1973. Bureaucratic Corruption in India: Legal Control of Maladministration. *Comparative Political Studies* 6:197–219.

Haggard, S. 1990. *Pathways from the Periphery: The Politics of Growth in the Newly Industrializing Countries.* Ithaca, N.Y.: Cornell University Press.

———. 1990b. The Political Economy of the Philippine Debt Crisis. In *Economic Crisis and Policy Choice. The Politics of Adjustment in the Third World*, ed. J.M. Nelson, 215–55. Princeton University Press.

Haggard, S., and R.R. Kaufman, 1989. Economic Adjustment in New Democracies. In *Fragile Coalitions: The Politics of Economics Adjustment*, ed. J.M. Nelson. New Brunswick, N.J.: Transaction Books.

———. 1992. Economic Adjustment and the Prospects for Democracy. In *The Politics of Economic Adjustment,* ed. S. Haggard and R.R. Kaufman. Princeton University Press.

Haggard, S., and S.B. Webb, 1993. What do we know about the Political Economy of Economic Policy Reform? *World Bank Research Observer* 8:143–168.

Harsch, E. 1993. Accumulators and Democrats: Challenging State Corruption in Africa. *Journal of Modern African Studies* 31:31–48.

Heidenheimer, A.J. 1970. Introduction. In *Political Corruption. Readings in Comparative Analysis,* 2–28. New Brunswick, N.J.: Transaction Books.

Heilbroner, R. 1963. *The Great Ascent.* New York: Harper & Row.

Herbst, J. 1993. *The Politics of Reform in Ghana, 1982–1991.* Berkeley: University of California Press.

Himbara, D. 1993. Myths and Realities of Keynian Capitalism. *Journal of Modern African Studies* 31:93–107.

Hirschman, A.O. 1957. Economic Policy in Underdeveloped Countries. *Economic Development and Cultural Change* 5:362–370.

———. 1981. The Rise and Decline of Development Economics. In *Essays in Trespassing. Economics and Politics and Beyond.* Cambridge University Press.

Huntington, S.P. 1968. *Political Order in Changing Societies.* New Haven: Yale.

Huntington, S.P., and J.M. Nelson. 1976. *No Easy Choice. Political Participation in Developing Countries.* Cambridge, Mass: Harvard University Press.

Iliffe, J. 1983. *The Emergence of African Capitalism.* London: Macmillan.

Jackson, R.H., and C. Rosberg. 1982. *Personal Rule in Black Africa: Prince, Autocrat, Prophet, Tyrant.* Berkeley: University of California Press.

———. 1986. Why Africa's Weak States Persist: The Empirical and Juridical in Statehood. In *The State and Development in the Third World,* ed. A. Kohli, 259–282. Princeton University Press.

Johnson, O.E.G. 1975. An Economic Analysis of Corrupt Government, with Special Application to less Developed Countries. *Kyklos* 28:47–61.

Johnston, M. 1982. *Political Corruption and Public Policy in America.* Monterey, CA: Brooks-Cole.

———. 1989. Right and Wrong in American Politics: Popular Conceptions of Corruption. In *Political Corruption. A Handbook,* ed. A.J. Heidenheimer, M. Johnston and V.T. LeVine, 743–61. London: Transaction Publishers.

Joseph, R.A. 1984. Class, State, and Prebendal Politics in Nigeria. In *State and Class in Africa,* ed. N. Kasfir, 21–38. London: Frank Cass.

———. 1987. *Democracy and Prebendal Politics in Nigeria: The Rise and Fall of the Second Republic.* Cambridge University Press.

Jowitt, K. 1974. An Organizational Approach to the Study of Political Culture in Marxist-Leninist System. *American Political Science Review* 68:1171–91.

———. 1979. Scientific Socialism in Africa: Political Differentiation, Avoidance, and Unawareness. In *Socialism in Sub-Saharan Africa: A New Assessment,* ed. C.G. Rosberg and T.M Callaghy, 133–173. Berkeley: University of California Press.

Kaplinsky, R. 1980. Capitalist Accumulation in the Periphery - The Kenya Case Re-examined. *Review of African Political Economy* 17:83–105.

Kasfir, N. 1984. State, *Magendo,* and Class Formation in Uganda. In *State and Class in Africa,* ed. N. Kasfir, 84–103. London: Frank Cass.

———. 1987. Class, Political Domination and the African State. In *The African State in Transition,* ed. Z. Ergas, 45–60. London: Macmillan.

Katsenelenboigen, A. 1983. Corruption in the USSR: Some Methodological Notes. In *Corruption: Causes, Consequences, Control,* ed. M. Clarke, 220–38. London: Frances Pinter.

Kaufman, R.R. 1974. The Patron-Client Concept and Macropolitics. Prospects and Problems. *Comparative Studies in Society and History* 16:284–308.

Killick, T. 1978. *Development Economics in Action. A Study of Economic Policies in Ghana.* London: Heineman.

King, D.Y. 1981. Regime Type and Performance. Authoritarian Rule, Semi-Capitalist Development and Rural Inequality in Asia. *Comparative Political Studies* 13:477–504.

Kitching, G. 1983. *Rethinking Socialism. A Theory for a Better Practice.* London: Methuen.

———. 1985. Politics, Method and Evidence in the "Kenya Debate". In *Contradictions of Accumulation in Africa,* ed. H. Bernstein and B. Campbell. Beverley Hills: Sage Publications.

Klitgaard, R. 1988. *Controlling Corruption.* Berkeley: University of California Press.

———. 1991. *Adjusting to Reality. Beyond State Versus Market.* San Francisco: ICS Press.

Kpundeh, S.J. 1994. Limiting Administrative Corruption in Sierra Leone. *Journal of Modern African Studies* 32:139–157.

Kramer, J.M. 1989. Political Corruption in the U.S.S.R. In *Political Corruption. A Handbook,* ed. A.J. Heidenheimer, M. Johnston and V.T. LeVine, 449–66. London: Transaction Publishers.

Krischke, P.J. 1990. Social Movements and Political Participation: Contributions of Grassroots Democracy in Brazil. *Canadian Journal of Development Studies* 11:173–184.

———. 1991. Church Based Communities and Democratic Change in Brazilian Society. *Comparative Political Studies* 24:186–210.

Krueger, A.O. 1974. The Political Economy of the Rent-seeking Society. *American Economic Review* 64:291–303.

———. 1992. *Economic Policy Reforms in Developing Countries.* Oxford: Blackwell.

———. 1993. *Political Economy of Policy Reform in Developing Countries.* London: MIT Press

Kurer, O. 1991. *J.S. Mill. The Politics of Progress.* New York: Garland Press.

———. 1993. Clientelism, Corruption, and the Allocation of Resources. *Public Choice* 77:259–273.

Laitin, D.D. 1979. Somalia's Military Government and Scientific Socialism. In *Socialism in Sub-saharan Africa,* ed. C.G. Rosberg and T.M. Callaghy. Berkeley: University of California.

Lal, D. 1984. The Political Economy of the Predatory State. Paper Prepared for the Western Economic Association Meeting, Las Vegas, June 24–28.

———. 1988. *The Hindu Equilibrium. Volume I: Cultural Stability and Economic Stagnation. India c1500BC–AD1980.* Oxford: Clarendon Press.

Lampert, N. 1983. The Whistleblowers: Corruption and Citizens' Complaints in the USSR. In *Corruption: Causes, Consequences and Control,* ed. M. Clarke, 268–87. London: Frances Pinter.

Landé, C.J. 1977a. Introduction. In *Friends, Followers, and Factions,* ed. S. Schmidt, J. Scott, L. Guasti and C. Landé, xiii–xxxvii. Berkeley: University of California Press.

———. 1977b. Networks and Groups in Southeast Asia: Some Observations on the Group Theory of Politics. In *Friends, Followers, and Factions,* ed. S. Schmidt, J. Scott, L. Guasti and C. Landé, 75–99. Berkeley: University of California Press.

Langdon, S. 1980. *Multinational Corporations in the Political Economy of Kenya.* London: Macmillan.

———. 1987. Industry and Capitalism in Kenya. In *The African Bourgeoisie. Capitalist Development in Nigeria, Kenya, and the Ivory Cost,* ed. P.M. Lubeck, 343–82. Boulder, Col.: Lynne Rienner Publishers.

LaPalombara, J. 1963. Bureaucracy and Political Development: Notes, Queries and Dilemmas. In *Bureaucracy and Political Development.* Princeton University Press.

LaPalombara, J., and M. Weiner, 1966. Political Parties and Political Development. Items 29:1–7.

Leff, N. 1964. Economic Development Through Democratic Corruption. *The American Behavioral Scientist* 8:8–14.

———. *Economic Policy-Making and Development in Brazil, 1947–1964.* New York: John Wiley.

Leftwich, A. 1995. Bringing Politics Back In: Towards a Model of the Developmental State. *Journal of Development Studies* 31:400–427.

Legg, K. 1969. *Politics in Modern Greece* Stanford: Stanford University Press.

Leith, J.C., and M.F. Lofchie. 1993. The Political Economy of Structural Adjustment in Ghana. In *Political and Economic Interactions in Economic Policy Reform,* ed. R.H. Bates and A.O. Krueger, 225–93. Oxford: Basil Blackwell.

Lemarchand, R. 1977. Political Clientelism and Ethnicity in Tropical Africa: Competing Solidarities in Nation-Building. In *Friends, Followers, and Factions,* ed. S. Schmidt, J. Scott, L. Guasti and C. Landé, 100–22. Berkeley: University of California Press.

———. 1981. Comparative Political Clientelism. In *Political Clientelism, Patronage and Development,* ed. S.N. Eisenstadt and R. Lemarchand, 7–32. London: Sage.

———. 1988. The State, the Parallel Economy, and the Changing Structure of Patronage Systems. In *The Precarious Balance. State and Society in Africa,* ed. D. Rothchild and N. Chazan, 149–170. London: Westview Press.

Lemarchand, R., and K. Legg. 1972. Political Clientelism and Development: A Preliminary Analysis. *Comparative Politics* 4:149–78.

Leung, S.F. 1991. How to make the Fine fit the Corporate Crime? An Analysis of Static and Dynamic Optimal Punishment Theories. *Journal of Public Economics* 45:243–256.

LeVine, V.T. 1975. *Political Corruption. The Ghana Case.* Stanford: Hoover Institution Press.

———. Cameroon, Togo, and the States of Formerly French West Africa. In *Politics & Government in African States, 1960–1985,* ed. P. Guignan and R.H. Jackson, 78–119. London: Croom Helm.

———. Administrative Corruption and Democratization in Africa: Aspects of the Theoretic Agenda. *Corruption and Reform* 7:271-78.

Lewis, A.W. 1965. A Review of Economic Development (Richard T. Ely Lecture). *American Economic Review, Papers and Proceedings* 40:1–16

———. 1984. The State of Development Theory. *American Economic Review, Papers and Proceedings* 74:1–10.

Leys, C. 1965. What is the Problem about Corruption? *Journal of Modern African Studies* 3:215–30.

———. 1976. The 'Overdeveloped' Post Colonial State: A Re-evaluation. *Review of African Political Economy* 5:39–48.

———. 1978. Capital Accumulation, Class Formation and Dependency. *Socialist Register* 241–266.

Lien, D.D. 1990. Corruption and Allocation Efficiency. *Journal of Development Economics* 33:153–164.

Lipset, S. M. 1959. Some Social Requisites of Democracy: Economic Development and Political Legitimacy. *American Political Science Review* 53:69–105.

———. 1960. *Political Man.* New York: Doubleday.

Liu, A.P.L. 1989. The Political of Corruption in the People's Republic of China. In *Political Corruption. A Handbook,* ed. A.J. Heidenheimer, M. Johnston and V.T. LeVine, 489–511. London: Transaction Publishers.

Loizos, P. 1977. Politics and Patronage in a Cypriot Village, 1920–1970. In *Patrons and Clients in Mediterranean Societies,* ed. E. Gellner and J. Waterbury, 115–36. London: Duckworth.

Lowenstein, D.H. 1989. Legal Efforts to Define Political Bribery. In *Political Corruption. A Handbook,* ed. A.J. Heidenheimer, M. Johnston and V.T. LeVine, 29–38. London: Transaction Publishers.

Lui, F.T. 1985. An Equilibrium Queuing Model of Bribery. *Journal of Political Economy* 93:760–781 .

MacDonald, J.S. 1963–64. Agricultural Organisation, Migration and Labour Militancy in Rural Italy. *Economic History Review* 16:61–75.

MacGaffey, J. 1987. *Entrepreneurs and Parasites.* Cambridge University Press.

Malloy, J.M. Authoritarianism and Corporatism: The Case of Bolivia. In *Authoritarianism and Corporatism in Latin America,* ed. J.M. Malloy, 459–85. Pittsburgh: University of Pittsburgh Press.

Markovitz, I.L. 1977. Introduction. In *Power and Class in Africa. An Introduction to Change and Conflict in African Politics.* Englewood Cliffs: Prentice-Hall.

Marsh, R.M. 1979. Does Democracy Hinder Economic Development in Latecomer Developing Nations? *Comparative Social Research* 2:215–248.

Martin, G. 1976. Socialism, Economic Development and Planning in Mali. *Canadian Journal of African Studies* 10(7):23–47.

Marx, K. 1976. *Capital: Volume 1.* London: Penguin.

Mayer, A.C. 1977. The Significance of Quasi-Groups in the Study of Complex Societies. In *Friends, Followers, and Factions,* ed. S.W. Schmidt, L. Guasti, C.H. Landé, and J.C. Scott, 43–54. Berkeley: University of California Press.

McCord, W. 1965. *The Springtime of Freedom.* New York: Oxford University Press.

McMichael, P., J. Petras and R. Rhodes. Imperialism and the Contradictions of Development. *New Left Review* 85:83–104.

McMullan, M. 1961. A Theory of Corruption. *The Sociological Review* 2:181–201.

Meillassoux, C. 1970. A Class Analysis of the Bureaucratic Process in Mali. *Journal of Economic Development* 6:97–110.

Merriam, C.E. 1929. *Chicago: A More Intimate View of Urban Politics.* New York: Macmillan.

Merton, R.K. 1957. Some Functions of the Political Machine. In *Social Theory and Social Structure,* 72–82. New York: Free Press.

Miliband, R. 1970. The Capitalist State: Reply to Nicos Poulantzas. *New Left Review* 59:53–60.

Mill, J.S. 1835. Rationale of Representation. Collected Works of John Stuart Mill (CW), Toronto University Press, Vol. 18:15–46.

———. 1861. Considerations on Representative Government. CW, Vol. 19:371–577.

Mintz, S.W., and E.R. Wolf. 1977. An Analysis of Ritual Co-Parenthood (Compadrazgo). In *Friends, Followers, and Factions*, ed. S. Schmidt, J. Scott, L. Guasti and C. Landé, 1–14. Berkeley: University of California Press.

Moore, C.H. 1977. Clientelist Ideology and Political Change: Fictitious Networks in Egypt and Tunisia. In *Patrons and Clients in Mediterranean Societies,* ed. E. Gellner and J. Waterbury, 255–74. London: Duckworth.

Mosca, G. 1929. *The Ruling Class.* New York: McGraw-Hill.

Mouzelis, N. 1994. The State in Late Development: Historical and Comparative Perspectives. In *Rethinking Social Development,* ed. D. Booth, 126–151. Harlow: Longman.

Myrdal, G. 1968. *Asian Drama. An Inquiry into the Poverty of Nations.* Harmondsworth: Penguin.

Nelson, J. 1979. *Access to Power. Politics and the Urban Poor in Developing Countries.* Princeton University Press.

———. 1989. The Politics of Long-Haul Economic Reform. In *Fragile Coalitions. The Politics of Economic Adjustment.* New Brunswick, N.J.: Transaction Books.

———. 1990. Introduction: The Politics of Economic Adjustment in Developing Nations. *Economic Crisis and Policy Choice. The Politics of Adjustment in the Third World.* Princeton University Press.

Newman, B.A., and R.J. Thomson. 1989. Economic Growth and Social Development: A Longitudinal Analysis of Causal Priority. *World Development* 17:461–471.

Nicholas, R.W. 1977. Factions: A Comparative Analysis. In *Friends, Followers, and Factions*, ed. S. Schmidt, J. Scott, L. Guasti and C. Landé, 53–73. Berkeley: University of California Press.

Noonan, J.T., Jr. 1984. *Bribes.* New York: Macmillan.

North, D.C. 1981. *Structure and Change in Economic History.* New York: Norton.

Nye, J.S. 1967. Corruption and Political Development: A Cost Benefit Analysis. *American Political Science Review* 61:417–427.

Olson, M. 1965. *The Logic of Collective Action.* Cambridge, Mass.: Harvard University Press.

———. 1982. *The Rise and Decline of Nations* New Haven: Yale University Press.

Ouma, S.O.A. 1991. Corruption in Public Policy and its Impact on Development. *Public Administration and Development* 11:473–490.

Ozbudun, E. 1981. Turkey: The Politics of Political Clientelism. In *Political Clientelism, Patronage and Development,* ed. S.N. Eisenstadt and R. Lemarchand, 249–268. London: Sage.

Pashigian, B.P. 1975. On the Control of Crime and Bribery. *Journal of Legal Studies* 4:311–327.

Peck, L.L. 1990. *Court Patronage and Corruption in Early Stuart England.* London: Routledge.

Peters, J.G., and S. Welch, 1978. Political Corruption in America: A Search for Definitions and a Theory. *American Political Science Review* 72:974–984.

Pitt-Rivers, J. 1954. *The People of the Sierra.* London, Weidenfeld and Nicholson.

Popkin, S. 1979. *The Rational Peasant. The Political Economy of Rural Society in Vietnam.* Berkeley: University of California Press.

Poulantzas, N. 1969. The Problem of the Capitalist State. *New Left Review* 58:67–80.

———. 1973. *Political Power and Social Classes.* London: New Left Books.

Powell, J.D. 1970. Peasant Society and Clientelist Politics. *American Political Science Review* 64:411–425.

Price, R. 1975. *Society and Bureaucracy in Contemporary Ghana.* Berkeley: University of California.

Przeworski, A., and F. Limongi. 1993. Political Regimes and Economic Growth. *Journal of Economic Perspectives* 7:51–69.

Putnam, R.D. 1992. *Making Democracy Work. Civic Traditions in Modern Italy.* Princeton University Press.

Pye, L.W. 1966. *Aspects of Political Development.* Boston: Little, Brown.

Radelet, S. 1992. Reform without Revolt: The Political Economy of Economic Reform in the Gambia. *World Development* 20:1087–99.

Ranis, G., and S.A. Mahmood. 1992. *The Political Economy of Development Policy Change*. Oxford: Basil Blackwell.

Ravenhill, J. 1986. Africa's Continuing Crises: The Elusiveness of Development. In *Africa in Economic Crisis*, 1–43. London: Macmillan.

Remmer, K.L. 1978. Evaluating the Policy Impact of Military Regimes in Latin America. *Latin American Research Review* 13:39–54.

————. 1986. The Politics of Economic Stabilization. *Comparative Politics* 19:1–25.

————. 1990. Democracy and Economic Crisis: The Latin American Experience. *World Politics* 52:315–335.

————. 1993. The Political Economy of Elections in Latin America, 1980–1991. *American Political Science Review* 77:393–407.

Reynolds, L.G. 1983. The Spread of Economic Growth to the Third World: 1850–1980. *Journal of Economic Literature* 21:941–980.

————. 1985. *Economic Growth in the Third World. 1850-1980*. New Haven: Yale University Press.

Riley, S.P. 1983. The Land of the Waving Palms. In *Corruption: Causes, Consequences and Control*, ed. M. Clarke. London: Francis Pinter.

Rimmer, D. 1984. *The Economies of West Africa*. London: Weidenfeld and Nicholson.

Robbins, L. 1952. *The Theory of Economic Policy in English Classical Political Economy*. London: Macmillan.

Rogow A.A., and H.B. Lasswell. 1989. The Definition of Corruption. In *Political Corruption. Readings in Comparative Analysis*, ed. A.J. Heidenheimer, 54–55. New Brunswick, N.J.: Transaction Books.

Romero-Maura, J. 1977. Caciquismo as a Political System. In *Patrons and Clients in Mediterranean Societies*, ed. E. Gellner and J. Waterbury, 53–62. London: Duckworth.

Rose-Ackerman, S. 1975. The Economics of Corruption. *Journal of Public Economics* 4:187–203.

————. 1978. *Corruption. A Study in Political Economy*. New York: Academic Press.

Roth, G. 1968. Personal Rulership, Patrimonialism and Empire-building in the New States. *World Politics* 20:194–206.

Rothchild, D., and M. Foley, 1983. The Implications of Scarcity for Governance in Africa. *International Political Science Review* 4:311–326.

————. 1988. African States and the Politics of Inclusive Coalitions. In *The Precarious Balance. State and Society in Africa*, ed. D. Rothchild and N. Chazan. London: Westview Press.

Rottenberg, S. 1975. Comment. *Journal of Law and Economics* 18:611–615.

Ruccio, D.F., and L.H. Simon. 1988. Radical Theories of Development: Frank, the Modes of Production School, and Amin. In *The Political Economy of Development and Underdevelopment*, ed. C.K. Wilber. New York: Random House.

Sahlins. M.D. 1977. Poor Man, Rich Man, Big-man, Chief: Political Types in Melanesia and Polynesia. In *Friends, Followers, and Factions*, ed. S. Schmidt, J. Scott, L. Guasti and C. Landé, 220–31. Berkeley: University of California Press.

Sandbrook, R. 1972a. Patrons, Clients, and Factions: New Dimensions of Conflict Analysis in Africa. *Canadian Journal of Political Science* 5:104–119.

———. 1972b. Patrons, Clients, and Unions. *Journal of Commonwealth Political Studies* 9:3–27.

———. 1985. *The Politics of African Economic Stagnation.* Cambridge University Press.

Saul, J. S. 1979. *The State and Revolution in East Africa.* London: Monthly Review Press.

Sayari, S. 1977. Political Patronage in Turkey. In *Patrons and Clients in Mediterranean Societies*, ed. E. Gellner and J. Waterbury, 103–14. London: Duckworth.

Schatz, S.P. 1977. *Nigerian Capitalism.* Berkeley: University of California Press.

———. 1984. Pirate Capitalism and the Inert Economy of Nigeria. *Journal of Modern African Studies* 22:45–57.

Schmidt, S.W. 1977. The Transformation of Clientelism in Rural Columbia. In *Friends, Followers, and Factions*, ed. S. Schmidt, J. Scott, L. Guasti and C. Landé, 305–22. Berkeley: University of California Press.

Schultz, T.W. 1964. *Transforming Traditional Agriculture.* New Haven: Yale University Press.

Schumpeter, J.A. 1954. *History of Economic Analysis.* London: George Allen & Unwin.

———. 1976. *Capitalism, Socialism and Democracy.* London: George Allen & Unwin.

Scott, J.C. 1968. *Political Ideology in Malaysia. Reality and the Beliefs of an Elite.* London: Oxford University Press.

———. 1972. *Comparative Political Corruption.* Englewood Cliffs, N.J.: Prentice Hall.

———. 1977a. Patronage or Exploitation? In *Patrons and Clients in Mediterranean Societies*, ed. E. Gellner and J. Waterbury, 21–39. London: Duckworth.

———. 1977b. Patron-Client Politics and Political Change in Southeast Asia. In *Friends, Followers, and Factions*, ed. S. Schmidt, J. Scott, L. Guasti and C. Landé, 123–46. Berkeley: University of California Press.

———. 1979. Corruption, Machine Politics and Political Change. In *Bureaucratic Corruption in Sub-saharan Africa: Towards a Search for Causes and Consequences*, ed. M.U. Ekpo, 101–35. Washington, D.C.: University Press of America.

———. 1985. *Weapons of the Weak. Everyday Forms of Peasant Resistance.* New Haven: Yale University Press.

Scott, J.C., and B.J. Kerkvliet. 1977. How Traditional Rural Patrons Lose Legitimacy: A Theory with Special Reference to Southeast Asia. In *Friends, Followers, and Factions*, ed. S. Schmidt, J. Scott, L. Guasti and C. Landé, 439–457. Berkeley: University of California Press.

Sears, D.O., and C.L. Funk. 1990. Self-Interest in Amercians' Political Opinions. In *Beyond Self-Interest*, ed. J.J. Mansbridge, 147–170. Chicago: University of Chicago Press.

Sender J., and S. Smith, 1986. *The Development of Capitalism in Africa*. London: Methuen.

Shleifer, A., and R.W. Vishny. 1993. Corruption. *Quarterly Journal of Economics* 108:599–616.

Silverman, S. 1977. Patronage and Community-Nation Relationships in Central Italy. In *Friends, Followers, and Factions*, ed. S. Schmidt, J. Scott, L. Guasti and C. Landé, 293–304. Berkeley: University of California Press.

Sirowy, L., and A. Inkeles. 1990. Effects of Democracy on Economic Growth. *Studies in Comparative International Development* 25:126–157.

Skalnes, T. 1993. The State, Interest Groups and Structural Adjustment in Zimbabwe. *Journal of Development Studies* 29:401–428.

Sklar, R. 1965. Contradictions in the Nigerian Political System. *Journal of Modern African Studies* 3:201–213.

———. 1979. The Nature of Class Domination in Africa. *Journal of Modern African Studies* 17:531–552.

Skocpol, T. 1982. Bringing the State Back In. *Items* 36:1–8.

Smith, T. 1979. The Underdevelopment of the Development Literature: The Case of Dependency Theory. *World Politics* 32:247–288.

Smith, T.M. 1989. Corruption, Tradition, and Change in Indonesia. In *Political Corruption. A Handbook*, ed. A.J. Heidenheimer, M. Johnston and V.T. LeVine, 423–440. London: Transaction Publishers.

Somjee, A.H. 1974. Social Perspectives on Corruption in India. *Political Science Review* 13:180–186.

Sorauf, F.J. 1956. The Silent Revolution in Patronage. *American Political Science Review* 50:1046–1056.

Sorensen, G. 1991. *Democracy, Dictatorship and Development - Economic Development in Selected Regimes of the Third World*. London: Macmillan.

Springborg, R. 1979. Patrimonialism and Policy-making in Egypt: Nasser and Sadat and the Tenure Policy for Reclaimed Lands. *Middle Eastern Studies* 15:49–69.

Staniland, M. 1985. *What is Political Economy? A Study of Social Theory and Underdevelopment*. New Haven: Yale University Press.

Streeten, P. 1977. The Distinctive Features of a Basic Needs Approach to Development. *International Development Review* 3:8–16.

———. 1981. *First Things First*. London: Oxford University Press.

Swainson, N. 1977. The Rise of a National Bourgeoisie in Kenya. *Review of African Political Economy* 8:21–38.

——. 1978. State and Economy in Post-Colonial Kenya, 1963–1978. *Canadian Journal of African Studies* 12:357–381.

——. 1980. *The Development of Corporate Capitalism in Kenya, 1918–1977.* Berkeley: University of California Press.

Szeftel, M. 1982. Political Graft and the Spoils System in Zambia - the State as a Resource in itself. *Review of African Political Economy* 28:4–21.

Tamarkin, M. 1978. The Roots of Political Stability in Kenya. *African Affairs* 67:297–320.

Tignor, R.L. 1987. The Sudanese Private Sector: An Historical Overview. *Journal of Modern African Studies* 25:179–212.

Tilman, R.O. 1979. Emergency of Black Market Bureaucracy: Administration, Development and Corruption in the New States. In *Bureaucratic Corruption in Sub-saharan Africa: Towards a Search for Causes and Consequences,* ed. M.U. Ekpo, 341–53. Washington, D.C.: University Press of America.

Toye, J. 1991. Comment. In *Politics and Policy Making in Developing Countries. Perspectives on the New Political Economy,* ed. G.M. Meier, 111–119. San Francisco: ICS Press.

Trivedi, V. 1988. Corruption, Delivery Systems and Property Rights: A Comment. *World Development* 16:1389–1391

Tullock, G. 1981. The Welfare Cost of Tariffs, Monopolies, and Theft. In *Toward a Theory of the Rent-seeking Society,* ed. J.M. Buchanan, R.D. Tollison and G. Tullock, 39–50. College Station: Texas A&M University Press.

Van Klaveren, J.J. 1964. Comment. *Comparative Studies in Society and History* 6:195.

——. 1970. The Concept of Corruption. In *Political Corruption. Readings in Comparative Analysis,* ed. A.J. Heidenheimer, 38–41. New Brunswick, N.J.: Transaction Books.

Wade, R. 1982. The System of Administrative and Political Corruption: Canal Irrigation in South India. *Journal of Development Studies* 18:287–328.

——. 1985. The Market for Public Office: Why the Indian State is not better at Development. *World Development* 13:467–497.

——. 1989. Politics and Graft: Recruitment, Appointment, and Promotions to Public Office in India. In *Corruption, Development, and Inequality,* ed. P.M. Ward. London: Routledge.

——. 1990. *Governing the Market. Economic Theory and the Role of Government in East Asian Industrialization.* Princeton University Press.

Warren, B. Imperialism and Capitalist Industrialization. *New Left Review* 81:3–45.

——. 1980. *Imperialism: Pioneer of Capitalism.* London: Verso.

Waterbury, J. 1970. *The Commander of the Faithful.* New York: Columbia University Press.

——. 1983. *The Egypt of Nasser and Sadat.* Princeton University Press.

——. 1989. The Political Management of Economic Management and Reform. In *Fragile Coalitions: The Politics of Economics Adjustment, ed.* J.M. Nelson. New Brunswick, N.J.: Transaction Books.

——. 1992. The Heart of the Matter? Public Enterprise and the Adjustment Process. In *The Politics of Economic Adjustment,* ed. S. Haggard and R.R. Kaufman. Princeton University Press.

Weber, M. 1968. *The Theory of Social and Economic Organization.* Oxford: Oxford University Press.

Weede, E. 1983. The Impact of Democracy on Economic Growth: Some Evidence from Cross-National Analysis. *Kyklos* 36:21–39.

Weingrod, A. 1968. Patrons, Patronage and Political Parties. *Comparative Studies in Society and History* 10:376–400.

Wellisz, S., and R. Findlay. 1988. The State and the Invisible Hand. *World Bank Research Observer* 3:59–80.

Werlin, H.H. 1972. The Roots of Corruption: The Ghanaian Enquiry. *Journal of Modern African Studies* 10:247–266.

——. 1973. The Consequences of Corruption. *Political Science Quarterly* 88:171–185.

Werner, S.B. 1983. New Directions in the Study of Administrative Corruption. *Public Administration Review* 43:146–154.

——. The Development of Political Corruption in Israel. In *Political Corruption. A Handbook,* ed. A.J. Heidenheimer, M. Johnston and V.T. LeVine, 251–274. London: Transaction Publishers.

Wertheim, W.F. 1970. Sociological Aspects of Corruption on Southeast Asia. In *Political Corruption. Readings in Comparative Analysis,* ed. A.J. Heidenheimer, 195–211. New Brunswick, N.J.: Transaction Books.

Whitaker, C.S. 1965. *The Politics of Tradition.* Ann Arbor: University of Michigan.

Williams, M., and C. Daniel, 1991. Government Activity and Economic Performance in a Small Developing Economy. *Economia Internazionale* 44:269–81.

Wolf, E. 1956. Aspects of Group Relations in a Complex Society: Mexico. *American Anthropologist* 58:1065–78.

——. 1977. Kinship, Friendship and Patron-Client Relations in Complex Societies. In *Friends, Followers, and Factions,* ed. S. Schmidt, J. Scott, L. Guasti and C. Landé, 167–78. Berkeley: University of California Press.

Wolters, W. 1984. *Politics, Patronage and Class Conflict in Central Luzon.* Quezon City: New Day Publishers.

World Bank. 1990. World Development Report 1990: Poverty. Washington, D.C.: World Bank.

——. 1993. *The East Asian Miracle.* Oxford University Press.

Wraith, R., and E. Simpkins. 1963. *Corruption in Developing Countries.* New York: Norton.

Young, C. 1982a. *Ideology and Development in Africa.* New Haven: Yale University Press.

——. 1982b. Patterns of Social Conflicts: State, Class and Ethnicity. *Daedalus* 111(Spring):71–98.

Young C., and T. Turner. 1985. *The Rise and Decline of the Zairian State.* Madison: University of Wisconsin Press.

Young, K.T. Jr. 1961. New Politics in New States. *Foreign Affairs* 39(April).

Zolberg, A.R. 1966. *Creating Political Order. The Party-States of West Africa.* Chicago: Rand McNally.

Index